THE

London

MONSTER

THE

London

MONSTER

TERROR *ON THE* STREETS

IN 1790

Jan Bondeson

TEMPUS

First published 2000
This edition first published 2003 by arrangement with
Free Association Books

Tempus Publishing Limited
The Mill, Brimscombe Port,
Stroud, Gloucestershire, GL5 2QG

British Library Cataloguing in Publication Data.
A catalogue record for this book is available from the British Library.

ISBN 0 7524 2583 8

Typesetting and origination by Tempus Publishing Limited
Printed in Great Britain by Midway Colour Print, Wiltshire

CONTENTS

Terrific Fiend! Thou Monster fell!
Condemn'd in haunts profane to dwell,
Why quit thy solitary Home,
O'er wide Creation's paths to roam?
Pale Tyrant of the timid Heart...

Mrs Mary Robinson, 'Ode to Despair'

THE CAST

Catherine and Molly Alman   Two of Rhynwick Williams' alibi
 witnesses. But were they telling the truth?

John Julius Angerstein   A wealthy philanthropist and art collector,
 who took a great interest in the bottoms and thighs of
 wounded ladies.

Miss Barrs   The devious daughter of a fruiterer, who pretended
 to be a Monster victim.

Elizabeth and Frances Baughan   Respectable young ladies; both
 victims of the Monster.

Sir Francis Buller   Also known as Judge Thumb. He presided at
 the first Monster trial, at the Old Bailey.

John Coleman   The Monster-catcher. Also known as the
 Catamite, the Dastard, Miss Porter's Puppy and the Cowardly
 Fishmonger. A deeply flawed hero.

'Captain' Crowder   A robber and highwayman. Transported to
 Botany Bay.

The Hon. Mr Cuffe   Brother of Viscount Netterville. Once accused of being the Monster by Charley Jones, alias Fat Phillis, a dangerous transvestite.

Elizabeth Davis   A washerwoman who refused to smell a nosegay, and who had her bottom cut by the Monster as a consequence.

Mary Forster   A 'Greffe Street Vestal' according to Theophilus Swift. Another Monster victim.

Typhone Fournier   A Frenchman with a silly name.

'Sir' John Gallini   A lecherous dancing-master; the tutor of Rhynwick Williams.

Sarah Godfrey   A beautiful lady assaulted by the London Monster.

George Hanger   A crony of the Prince of Wales. Depicted as the Monster on a well-known caricature drawing.

Walter Hill   A rowdy Lieutenant in the Royal Navy, who once made a riot in the Tottenham Court Road, and was arrested as the Monster as a consequence.

Newman Knowlys   The barrister of Rhynwick Williams at the first trial.

Colonel Charles Lennox   Rake and duellist. He once nearly blew out the brains of the Duke of York. In another duel, he shot Theophilus Swift in the stomach. He later became Duke of Richmond, but was bitten by a young fox in Canada and died of hydrophobia shortly after.

John Macmanus   A Bow Street Runner.

William Mainwaring   A corrupt Judge, who was Chairman of the Middlesex Sessions; nevertheless, he took pains to elucidate the Monster mystery, and left valuable notes regarding the second trial.

Aimable Michelle, alias Amabel Mitchell   An artificial flower-maker, and the former employer of the scapegrace Rhynwick Williams.

Reine Michelle   Sister of the above. Another artificial flower-maker.

Mrs Miel   An old lady who received a knock on the head in St James's Street.

Moses Murrant   Another Bow Street Runner, who was once tricked by the Monster in Castle Street.

Mr Pearson, alias *Pearce*   Lived in Bond Street. Took an interest in ornamented chip-hats.

Sir Arthur Leary Pigot   The prosecuting attorney. A clever, experienced man.

William Pitt   The Prime Minister. Depicted as the Monster on a ribald drawing.

Anne Porter   The Beauty of the Bagnio. The charming young heroine of our tale, but a lady who may have had a colourful past.

Sarah Porter   Anne's sister, also a victim of the London Monster.

Thomas Porter   Father of Anne and Sarah. Keeper of Pero's Bagnio, a notorious den of vice in late eighteenth-century London, as alleged by Theophilus Swift.

Elizabeth Porter   Wife of the above. A strong, forceful woman, who once waved her fist in the Monster's face.

Mr Smith   A man of mystery, living in South Moulton Street.

Theophilus Swift   The bad guy. An Irish lawyer, adventurer, duellist and pamphleteer. The Monster's Champion, and the Bane of the Wounded Ladies. My favourite in the cast.

Deane Swift   Son of Theophilus, and helped him to investigate the Monster mystery. Later sent down from Trinity College, Dublin, for kicking his mathematics tutor.

Captain Philip Thicknesse   Also known as Lieutenant-Governor Gall-Stone. Accused of being the Monster on posters all over London.

William Tuffing   A wimpish ladies' hairdresser turned clothes salesman, who was nevertheless thought by some to be the London Monster.

Lady Wallace   A female playwright, of a violent temper, who once claimed to have been frightened by the Monster. She later tried to frame Amabel Mitchell as the Monster's accomplice.

Kitty Wheeler   A beautiful 'Tavern Vestal', as alleged by Mr Swift. Insulted by the Monster, and testified against him.

'Parsloe' Wheeler   Kitty's father. A tavern-keeper. Grappled with the Monster once, but had to release him. A rough character, and an alleged arsonist.

Rhynwick Williams   A foul-mouthed little man with a big nose, who was obsessed with sex. Another artificial flower-maker. A thoroughly despicable character. Was he the London Monster?

Thomas Williams Senior   Rhynwick's father. A respectable Welsh apothecary who settled in London.

Thomas Williams Junior   Rhynwick's respectable brother, another apothecary.

Joshua Williams   Another kinsman of Rhynwick Williams. Not the sharpest tool in the box.

Sir Sampson Wright   A Bow Street magistrate. Led the investigation of the Monster mystery.

Extras: Bow Street Runners and patrols; Night watchmen; Monster-hunters; Snobs; Swells; Pimps; Prostitutes; Bullies; Pickpockets; also the Augsburg Girl-Cutter, the Halifax Slasher, Jack the Snipper and the Monkey-Man of New Delhi.

I

The Coming

OF THE

MONSTER

From thorny wilds a Monster came,
that fill'd my soul with fear and shame;
The birds, forgetful of their mirth,
Droop'd at the sight, and fell to earth...

William Cowper, 'Self-love and Truth Incompatible'

One of the more enigmatic figures in the old Newgate Calendar is that of the London Monster. The strange crimes of this mysterious offender have earned him the title of a forerunner of Jack the Ripper.[1] Indeed, the alarm and terror caused by the Monster's wanton outrages against unprotected women was equal to the uproar after the Marr and Williamson murders on the Ratcliffe Highway in 1811, or the Ripper murders in 1888; and the general alarm amongst London's female population was without precedent. A certain John Williams was arrested for the Ratcliffe Highway murders, but later committed suicide under highly suspicious circumstances; later research has cast considerable doubt on whether he was really the murderer.[2] As we know, no arrest was made for the Ripper crimes, and in spite of a bevy of suspects being paraded by imaginative writers, the case is still unsolved and likely to remain so.[3] By a combination of chance and vigilante effort – the police of 1790 were incapable of tackling the London Monster – an arrest was finally made for these crimes: the young Welshman Rhynwick Williams was taken as the Monster and committed to Newgate Gaol after a sensational trial at the Old Bailey. He was eloquently described in Wilson and Caulfield's *Wonderful Characters*: 'His unnatural and unaccountable propensities in maliciously cutting and stabbing females whenever he found them unprotected, soon made him a terror to the metropolis: his behaviour was so revolting to the feelings, and carried with it such hellish appetite, and dreadful consequences, that the horror he spread, it is impossible to describe.'[4] Given the Monster's over-the-top 'stagy' appearance and language, and his abusive and violent behaviour, it must almost have seemed to Londoners as if Mr Punch had jumped down from his stage at Bartholomew Fair and headed towards the West End of town. There were no less than twelve caricature prints on this subject, some of them praiseworthy attempts to present a likeness of the perpetrator to the public, others lewd fantasies on the subject of sharp rapiers piercing exposed female buttocks.

Quite a few contemporaries believed that Rhynwick Williams was an innocent man, wrongly convicted for the Monster's heinous crimes. He was energetically defended by the eccentric Irish poet Theophilus Swift, a blood relation of the great Dean, who wrote a pamphlet depicting Williams as the victim of an elaborate conspiracy. The wealthy philanthropist John Julius Angerstein, one of the founders of Lloyd's, had offered a reward of £100 to the person capturing the London Monster, and Swift claimed that this immense sum had induced several of the key witnesses to perjure themselves. Theophilus Swift actually appeared as the barrister for Rhynwick Williams in a farcical second trial, a transcript of which reads like an episode of *Blackadder III*. The doubts concerning the guilt of Williams have persisted. In Knapp and Baldwin's *New Newgate Calendar*, it is remarked that Rhynwick Williams had a modestly solid alibi and that all were not convinced about his guilt, 'believing that the female witnesses (a circumstance which we have shown too frequently to have happened) mistook the man who wounded and ill-treated the prosecutrix.'[5] Some other writers have presumed that there never was a Monster, and that the panic in 1790 was merely some weird kind of mass hysteria: the London Monster was a bogeyman in the tradition of Sawney Beane, the Scottish cannibal, Spring-heeled Jack, the fire-breathing horror who mystified the Londoners, or Sweeney Todd, the Demon Barber of Fleet Street.[6] Rhynwick Williams was just a scapegoat, one of the men who habitually pestered and insulted women on the London streets, and he was unlucky enough to fall into the hands of the authorities to personify the Monster in a trial that could be likened to a ceremony of exorcism: after Williams had been committed to Newgate, the Monster attacks ceased.

My first acquaintance with the London Monster was made in 1996, when I was looking through some large, late eighteenth-century scrapbooks in the British Library. They had once been the property of Miss Sophia Sarah Banks, the sister of Sir Joseph Banks, the President of the Royal Society of London. Miss Banks collected handbills and broadsides relating to popular entertainments: ballooning, firework displays and theatrical productions. More pertinent for my book *The Feejee Mermaid* was a section on 'learned pigs' and other eighteenth-century performing animals. The most intriguing discovery that day, however, was Miss Banks' scrapbook on the London Monster.[7] She had taken much interest in the Monster-hunt, and built up an extensive collection of newspaper cuttings, prints and manuscript material. She herself took an active part in the vigilante efforts to catch the Monster. At first, I believed that Miss Banks' collection was the definitive account of the Monster-mania that consumed London in the spring and summer of 1790, but this turned out to be very far from the truth. Not only was there a wealth of information about the Monster in various other newspapers, not covered by Miss Banks, but no less than seven pamphlets had been written about the hunt for this elusive criminal, and the indictment and trials of

Rhynwick Williams. Three of these pamphlets were kept at the British Library; one had once been there but was a casualty of wartime action; three had never been held even by this famous library. Fortunately, it turned out that two very rare and valuable Monster pamphlets could be consulted at the Free Library of Philadelphia.[8] Another vital clue to the Monster mystery was unearthed at the Public Record Office in Kew, in a dusty volume of reports on criminals. The majority of my research on the London Monster was carried out in the venerable North Library at the old British Museum, next to the famous Round Reading Room that is now, alas, gone forever. The final chapters were added at the present-day abomination at St Pancras, the monstrous ugliness of which may well have inspired my work further.

2

A Melancholy Occurrence

IN

ST JAMES'S STREET

If in the Park, as usual, my walk I should pursue,
And civilly accost a Miss – 'My pretty, how do you do?'
So strange the times! Each Miss is sure my meaning to misconstrue,
And jumps and squeaks, and cries aloud – 'O Heavens!
    Here's the MONSTER!
You nasty thing,
You'll surely swing!'
And then she'll swear,
Would make you stare,
She saw me ready to – O rare!
To stab her thro' the pocket-hole – exactly like the MONSTER.

Mr Hook, 'The Monster',
from the *World* newspaper, 31 May 1790

If one wishes to go back in time 210 years, to study the daily life of the Londoners in 1790, and how it was disrupted by the terror and rage caused by the Monster's crimes, there is no better way than to consult the Burney newspaper collection at the British Library.[1] This collection was originally built up by the

Revd Charles Burney, brother of Fanny the novelist. The Burney Collection is today all microfilmed, and thus one does not get the agreeable smell and feel of the huge, bedraggled-looking tomes of old newspapers in the Colindale Newspaper Library. The year 1790 is reasonably well covered: long-defunct newspapers like the *Argus*, the *World*, the *Oracle*, and the *Diary* paint a vivid picture of the metropolis, soon to be threatened by the Monster in its midst, with many curious details. One should remember that these late eighteenth-century newspapers were notoriously unreliable, and that many reports were inserted by interested parties, or invented by unscrupulous journalists; yet this historical snapshot is untroubled by hindsight and political correctness, and independent of the various modern theories of historiography. After all, there are three elements to history: what actually happened, what people felt about it when it happened, and how people have related to these events afterwards.

The newspapers of 1790 devote a good deal of attention to the revolutionary activities in France, and there is much apprehension regarding the fate of the captive King Louis, Queen Marie Antoinette and their poor children. The future of the French republic is viewed with much concern, and there is a well-grounded fear that this kind of political extremism will not do Europe any good. The war between Sweden and Russia is another important foreign event, and the warring galleys and gun-sloops in the icy Baltic Sea are a recurring topic in the newspapers. The slave trade is also much debated: most writers seem to be convinced that this barbarian practice should be abolished, but a notice in the *World* mentions, without any further comment, that 'At the sale of a Gentleman's effects lately in Jamaica, a Negro blacksmith was sold for two hundred and sixty pounds; the highest prize ever known to have been given.'[2] The miraculous escape of Captain Bligh from the mutineers of the *Bounty* is a piece of hot news, and even surpasses the arrest of Lieutenant John Frith, who had thrown a large stone at King George III; this dastardly assailant is described as a man of genteel, but frantic, appearance.

There are many parallels between the 1790s and the present time. The most popular sport at that time was boxing, and the activities of the notorious bruisers William Ward, Richard Humphries and Daniel Mendoza were followed as avidly in the newspapers as those of today's footballers. The boxers used to publish polite challenges to each other in the letter columns of the newspapers, often with some barbs and teases attached to make the opponent more eager to accept the proposed fight. The Lottery is another recurrent theme, but it seems as if the late eighteenth-century players would have invested rather more heavily than the present-day suburban couples hoping for the big win: 'the melancholy effects of insuring in the Lottery, may be seen in our streets every day, and the bitter cries of the Poor are incessant.'[3] Many ruined servants stole the property of their masters to be able to keep gambling, and were turned out without a character, without clothes, and without bread: 'Can it then be wondered that the Cities of London and Westminster should swarm with thieves and vagabonds?' The late eighteenth-century morals were little better than those advertised by the tabloids today. In a much-publicised incident, a brewer's clerk bought another man's wife for a guinea, with her child into the bargain. The husband made his lady a most obsequious bow, wished her a good day, collected the payment and then made off and left her. 'Shame unto the morals and follies of the day!' the *Public Advertiser* censured these immoral proceedings.[4] The *World* newspaper published a somewhat callous epitaph on a young lady who had thrown herself out of a window after her mother had forbidden her to wear stiffened stays:[5]

> *Women, they tell us, have strange ways,*
> *So Harriett pin'd for stiffen'd stays;*
> *Till hopeless grown, and in the dumps,*
> *For want of Stays, she took to Jumps.*

These rather superficial similarities do not make the late eighteenth-century into today's world in fancy dress, however. The poverty of the lower classes of society was appalling, the ignorance of both high and low abysmal, and the barbarity of olden times lurked just beneath the polite veneer of the Age of Improvement. In 1780, London suffered full-scale riots, which had begun as an anti-Catholic manifestation led by the fanatical Lord George Gordon.[6] Things soon got out of hand, and the mob marched on the Houses of Parliament. They harried the Peers and Members arriving, and smashed their coaches. Sections of the mob burned and looted Roman Catholic chapels, schools and private houses; the police, the Lord Mayor and even the military were powerless to intercede. In the late evening, Charles Burney the newspaper collector looked out of his observatory window (his house had formerly belonged to Sir Isaac Newton) and saw the whole of Leicester Fields illuminated as brightly as in the daytime by the many fires that raged. What had begun as an anti-Catholic demonstration soon became a social protest: the rioters, 60,000-strong, attacked the houses of the wealthy and typical symbols of authority, like the prisons, banks and the magistrate's house in Bow Street. Armed with cutlasses, clubs and pole-axes, the mob stormed Newgate Prison and freed 300 prisoners; they then set the prison alight, and proceeded to treat the Bridewell, King's Bench and New Prisons in a similar manner. Not until the militia had been summoned, and supplementary troops called in, could the mob be confronted: after a violent onslaught on the Bank of England, there was a pitched battle, from which the rioters retired in confusion. Had many of them not been the worse for wear after pillaging the Holborn gin distilleries, the outcome might have been a yet more violent one.

London's population had risen from approximately 60,000 in the year 1500 to 400,000 in the mid-seventeenth century, and to nearly one million by the late 1700s. This gave the criminal underworld unique opportunities for vice and crime.[7] The crime rate was appallingly high, with armies of burglars, pickpockets, footpads and highwaymen at large in the metropolis and its vicinity. There were rookeries where the police hesitated to arrest any criminal, since his friends, and any other ruffian standing nearby, were sure to fall upon them with bludgeons, knives and axes, to free him by use of force. The many ale-houses, hotels and seamen's hostels in London gave the brothels a roaring trade, the increasing wealth of the upper and upper middle classes attracted the burglars, and the immense number of lanes, courts and narrow alleyways gave the street criminals unique possibilities for concealment and anonymity. In 1782, after the American war, London was hit by a veritable crime wave: both robberies and burglaries increased, and the pickpockets were more numerous than ever. The Londoners were fearful of going outdoors after dark, even in the well-lit main streets, due to the threat from the violent footpads infesting the city. Although the policing of London was notoriously lax and ineffective, the sheer number of crimes committed meant that the prisons were nevertheless crammed full of villains of every description.

The problem was what to do with all these criminals? The system of criminal law for this period, called the Bloody Code, had originally contained just a few crimes punishable by execution, such as treason, murder and rape, but throughout the eighteenth century more than 100 capital offences were added to the Code. The reason for this was that capital wealth of the moneyed classes was not adequately protected in the absence of a regular police force; in a vain attempt to deter criminals, an increasing number of property crimes were made subject to the death penalty. By the 1790s, there were more than 200 capital offences punishable by death. For example, it was a capital offence to steal a sheep, to pickpocket more than a shilling, to illegally cut down trees in an orchard, to break the border of a fish-pond as to allow the fish to escape, or to break a pane of glass on a winter's evening with intent to steal. But the objective of the criminal law was to frighten and deter the potential criminal, and at the same time as the number of capital statutes had been increasing, the number of executions had been decreasing in the mid-eighteenth century. An increasing proportion of the convicted felons had instead been deported to the American penal colonies. But after the War of Independence, this was no longer possible, and the prison hulks on the Thames and the penitentiaries for hard labour were woefully inadequate both as crime deterrents and as a measure to get rid of the villains. After the crime wave in the early and mid-1780s, an increasing number of prisoners were executed, sometimes for very insignificant crimes. It was not until the Botany Bay penal colony in Australia was founded in 1786, and the first fleet of prisoners were sent there the year after, that the overpopulated prison system was able to recover.

Thus there was a rising scale of punishment in the 1780s and 1790s. Minor property offenders were whipped and/or imprisoned in houses of correction for six to nine months. More serious thieves, housebreakers and pickpockets were usually transported to the penal colonies. Finally, murderers, highway robbers, arsonists and hardened burglars and robbers were hanged. Late eighteenth-century justice was overwhelmingly concerned with property, and pickpockets could be hanged for stealing trifling amounts. In December 1789, fourteen-year-old Thomas Morgan and twelve-year-old James Smith were convicted of stealing seven silk hand-kerchiefs from a shop, and sentenced to death.[8] On the other hand, many rapists walked free because their victims were disbelieved. In general, women were considered less trustworthy witnesses, and a lower-class woman had particularly little chance of winning a case against a gentleman of some social distinction.[9]

Visitors to London, and many of the less fastidious Londoners themselves, regarded the public executions as a major attraction. When, in 1789, the housebreaker William Skitch was executed, *The Times* reporter on the spot was shocked to see that the rope slipped off the gallows, and that Skitch's body fell heavily to the ground. Even the crowd was moved by his predicament, but Skitch just stood up and said to the executioner and his assistant, who were getting another rope ready: 'Good people, be not hurried; I can wait a little.' Another writer in the same newspaper found it a melancholy contrast that, from 1775 until 1787, just six people had been executed in Amsterdam and Utrecht, while during the same period of time, 624 prisoners convicted at the Old Bailey had been hanged at Tyburn or Newgate.[10] In 1790, a humanitarian writer in the *Gentleman's Magazine* blasted the laws of England as cruel, unjust and useless. The number of fellow mortals strung up in the gallows was sufficient proof that they were cruel; the fact that the same punishment was inflicted on the parricide and on a starving wretch who took three shillings on the highway proof that they were unjust; and the frequency and multiplicity of serious crime in London offered ample proof that they were useless as a deterrent.[11]

Long prison sentences were rare, and reserved for 'special cases', like a woman of good family who had murdered her child, and who was protected from the gallows and transportation by family influence. A considerable percentage of London's prisoners were debtors, some of whom were incarcerated for protracted periods of time until their debts were settled. The pillory was irregularly used for crimes thought particularly heinous. To be pilloried for a sexual offence could literally be a death sentence in itself. When, in early 1790, two homosexual valets (caught 'in the act') were put in the pillory, an enormous mob had gathered to see them punished. The mob did not arrive empty-handed, but set about the two criminals as soon as the pillory was secured: a punning newspaper reporter was delighted to find that the valet named *Bacon* was pelted heavily with *eggs*. Potatoes, stones and brickbats were showered over the two blood-spattered wretches in the pillory; the police took cover from the torrent of missiles, and the two valets could barely be extricated from the pillory alive.[12]

In London of 1790, several debating societies met to discuss the burning questions of the day. They had many female members, and some catered almost exclusively for the fair sex; with this in mind, one is somewhat surprised that one of the questions for late 1789 was whether the view that women had no soul was justified.[13] It is unlikely that this proposition found much favour among the female audience. But by this time, women were regarded as defective men: they were weak, imbecile creatures fit only for gossip and embroidery, and with little interest in, or understanding of, public concerns. In one of the newspaper comments prompted by the debate about the souls of women, a disgruntled misogynist wrote that women who attended debating societies would be better employed at needle and thread. A question in another debating society was whether 'the tender sensibility of the female heart lessened or increased the happiness of the fair sex.' The 1780s and early 1790s were the height of the culture of sensibility.[14] While courage and cleverness were seen as male attributes, kindness, attentiveness and delicacy belonged to the female sex. It was widely believed that a woman's weaker, finer nerves made her more delicate, timid and tender-hearted, and liable to vapours and hysterical paroxysms when under strong emotion. Indeed, these attributes were considered quintessentially feminine, and it became fashionable among the ladies to weep, faint and go off in hysterics at the slightest provocation to show off their refined, delicate nerves. The ideal woman in contemporary fiction was a pale, helpless, timorous creature, with a nervous system strung as high as a violin. A banging door, a violent gust of wind, a peal of thunder, or the appearance of a toad or a mouse, was enough to send her off into hysterics. The contrast between the predatory male gallant, strong, fierce and sexual, and the innocent, passive young heroine, who suffers endless crises of nerves, was particularly marked in the Gothic novels of Mrs Radcliffe and her various imitators, that were enormously popular in the 1790s, not least among female readers.[15]

The sexual world of London of 1790 was male-dominated. The chastity of a young woman before marriage was considered of paramount importance. Her life after marriage was dull and respectable: she gave birth, took care of the household and obeyed her husband in everything. The young men had a more interesting time. Sexuality was on public view everywhere in the metropolis: there were erotic novels, lewd songs and pornographic prints.[16] It was regarded matter-of-factly rather than with the typical Victorian idealisation of romantic love. The most prominent feature in the female dress of the time was the low décolletage. The newspapers had advertisements for brothels, aphrodisiacs and cures for venereal disease, and Jack Harris's *The Whoremonger's Guide to London* was a famous directory of prostitutes, detailing addresses, physical characteristics and 'specialties'. Sexual exploitation of maidservants was very common; the image of the chambermaid as sexual fodder for the young master has become a cliché, but it has its basis in reality. Even very young girl servants were raped or seduced by libertines who were either aroused by paedophilia or fearful of venereal disease. Actresses, dancers and serving-girls in the taverns were considered as sexually 'easy'; some of them played along with the morals of the time and preferred to be the well-kept mistresses of a string of reasonably attractive men to being exploited as a domestic servant, or becoming the 'respectable' wife of some boring prig. There were brothels in every part of town. Mrs Hayes' Seraglio in Pall Mall was famous for its live-show with naked dancers of both sexes, and at Mother Wisebourne's house off the Strand, the girls were said to cost £250 a night. It has been calculated that London at this time had 10,000 prostitutes, who were openly plying their trade in the streets, markets and theatres. The district between Charing Cross and Drury Lane, and well into Soho, was the favourite haunt of these prostitutes. The Covent Garden area was particularly notorious. In addition to the regular brothels, it had many ale-houses where prostitutes were available, and a number of Bagnios, brothels disguised as bath-houses, some of which were veritable dens of vice and catered for all sexual tastes. When the constables made a raid in Covent Garden, and arrested twenty-two prostitutes, two turned out to be men dressed as women.[17]

If the sexuality of London of 1790 was earthy and abandoned, the popular amusements were of a corresponding vigour and brutality. The upper-class rakes spent their time at the racecourses and gaming-parlours, bet on pugilists and caroused around the streets of London, fighting, drinking and whoring. One newspaper report states that it was a popular pastime of the 'bloods' to blacken the faces of elderly, respectable people passing through the West End, by the use of a long brush and a bucket full of a mixture of eggs and lampblack.[18] The common man of 1790 did not much care for a reading from the works of Shakespeare, or indeed anything that even hinted of intellectual activity, as long as there was hope of going down to the pub to have a jug of ale while watching a badger with its tail nailed to the floor being harried by three fierce fox terriers. There were several rat-pits, where bets were made on how many rats a dog could kill in a certain number of minutes.[19] After a couple of sacks of squirming rats had been poured into the pit, an evil-looking cur was introduced in their midst, to begin his gory work of destruction. When sewer rats were used, the lady visitors used perfumed handkerchiefs to withstand the pungent smell of the rodents. It is recorded that the champion dog Billy could kill 100 rats in five minutes. The fellow champion Jacko once piled up 1,000 corpses in one hour and forty minutes, but there were allegations that the rats had been drugged with laudanum beforehand. Henry Mayhew once spoke to a costermonger who sometimes took the dog's place, leaping down into the pit and killing the rats with his teeth: his face was badly scarred from the bites from the infuriated rodents. In March 1790, after a bet had been agreed, a man drank five quarts of ale, and then masticated and swallowed the earthen mug; he died two days later.[20] In January 1790, after another bet had been agreed upon in a public house near Windsor, a man ate a living cat, tearing it to pieces with his teeth and leaving only the bones, 'as the memorials of the exercise of a brutal appetite, and the degradation of human nature'.[21] A few weeks later, the newspapers reported that the Windsor cat-eater had once more showed the brutality of his disposition: suddenly, and without reason, he had hacked off his own right hand with a bill-hook.[22] The reason given for this depraved action was that he was 'disinclined to work', and hoped that the overseers of the parish would provide for him in his present maimed condition. This sinister outbreak of brutality in early 1790, heralding the coming of the Monster, even spread to the animal kingdom: 'A Poney seized a sheep, and bit and kicked it till it died. The Poney then separated the head from the neck, and devoured near two quarters of the sheep.'[23]

A less sinister event in early 1790 was the Queen's birthday on 19 January. To celebrate the day, flags were up everywhere, church bells were rung and guns were fired. The illuminations on the main streets were more numerous than on any previous Royal birth-night: the theatres in Drury Lane were splendidly lit up, and the gunsmith's shop at Ludgate's Hill had a brilliantly illuminated front, with a transparency of the Queen.[24] The *World* newspaper published an exhaustive feature about the dresses of the ladies. The Queen and Princesses were soberly dressed and could not compete with such extravagant fashionables as the Countesses of Westmoreland and Warwick, and Lady Elizabeth Waldegrave, who were glittering with diamonds and dressed according to the latest fashions. A huge crowd, some in the ballroom and some in the galleries, as befitting their respective social stations, had admired the dazzling crowd of courtiers and nobles. The Prince of Wales made a brief appearance at the ball, wearing a Mazarine coat emblazoned with silver, before going out to his normal rakehelly nocturnal pursuits. The Princess Mary, Her Majesty's fourth daughter, made her first public appearance in the ballroom that night.

Among the crowd assembled in the galleries, mainly consisting of those who were not quite considered as gentlefolk, were twenty-one-year-old Miss Anne Porter and her nineteen-year-old sister Sarah. Their father, Mr Thomas Porter, did not belong to the nobility or gentry, nor was he of an old and respected family; he was a contented, relatively well-to-do member of the lower middle classes who kept a combined hotel, tavern and cold-bath establishment, called Pero's Bagnio, at No.63, St James's Street. This Bagnio was one of long standing, and had existed already in 1699; it had been named after an early owner, a Frenchman named Peyrault.[25] Unlike the rowdy Bagnios of Covent Garden, this was a reasonably respectable establishment, and if it served as a concealed brothel, this was kept well-hidden. The area of St James's was at this time not as fashionable as it had been in Restoration days, but at least the vicinity of St James's Palace remained a well-to-do area, and Pero's Bagnio was likely to have attracted a good deal of custom from the gentleman's clubs nearby.[26] Thomas Porter was prosperous enough to give his six children a good education. Nor was he unwilling to give his four daughters, of whom Anne and Sarah were the two eldest, some experience of fashionable life. The Porter girls were all pretty and vivacious, and this was not the first time they had visited a ball. They liked to dance, and were regular visitors to various dancing-parties and assembly-rooms, chaperoned of course to keep them out of mischief, but it was not just in the ribald novels of the time that a chaperone might be careless in her duty, or persuaded to let her young charge wander off by a golden handshake from the girl's wealthy admirer.

The pleasure-loving Anne and Sarah would have liked to stay at the ball as long as possible, but the Queen retired early, already at eleven o'clock, and the others followed her. Reluctantly, the two Misses Porter left the ballroom gallery. Their father had arranged to come and escort them home at twelve, but they were tired and did not want to stand about for an entire hour waiting for him. After consulting their chaperone, a stockily built, middle-aged lady named Mrs Miel, Anne and Sarah decided to walk the short distance home to Pero's Bagnio in nearby St James's Street, without waiting for any male companion to protect them.[27] Neither of them was fully at ease with the situation, however, and they set out on their short walk with some trepidation, for this was the time when the London Monster was known to prowl the dark streets of the metropolis.

To begin with, the Misses Porter and their companion made swift progress. It was a quarter past eleven, but due to the festivities of the day, the streets were still brightly lit and there were still quite a few people about. When they had come about half-way up St James's Street, and could see the Bagnio just a few houses away, Anne and Sarah believed themselves secure. Some men carrying a sedan chair approached them and called out 'By your leave!' and the ladies moved aside. This cry apparently alerted a man who had been lurking nearby. He went up to Sarah Porter and stared her hard in the face. As the sedan bearers walked away, he cried out:

'Oh ho! Is that you!' and struck her a violent blow on the back of the head. Sarah pitched forward with the force of the blow, but managed to keep her footing. She ran towards Pero's Bagnio as fast as she could. To alert her sister and Mrs Miel, she cried out, 'For God's sake, Nancy, make haste! Can't you see that – that *wretch* behind!' They all made a dash for the front door of the Bagnio: the terrified Sarah in front, Mrs Miel panting to keep up, and Anne bringing up the rear. Anne Porter had not quite heard what her sister had said, except that they should all make haste, and was not aware of the danger she was in.

The man did not, at first, pursue them, but as Sarah Porter was banging on the door of the Bagnio to get in, he suddenly ran up behind them and struck Anne Porter on the hip. It did not hurt much, and she only felt 'a strange sensation'. Turning round to see who or what had struck her, she saw a man in an odd posture with his legs stretched out. The man walked on to the next house, without any hurry, and then once more returned, to gloat at the sight of the terrified girls. He stared Anne full in the face and grinned at her. He stood close behind them when fourteen-year-old John Porter, brother of the Misses, finally opened the front door; in a wild stampede, the ladies rushed past him into the house. Their mysterious assailant remained standing outside looking at them, and made no attempt to run away. John Porter looked at him and asked Sarah whether this gentleman was in their company, making to invite him inside. Sarah replied, 'No; shut the door against the fellow', little knowing what had happened to her sister. Anne now complained about a sharp pain in her hip, and nearly fainted when she saw and felt that her dress was completely soaked with blood on one side. Blood dripped down from the garment and formed a growing pool on the floor. The Monster had struck again!

The entire Porter family came rushing along, full of concern for poor Anne. When Mr Porter saw that his daughter had been dangerously wounded, he sent a couple of servants after the man, but the Monster had absconded in time. A local practitioner, Surgeon Tomkins of Park Place, was promptly sent for. As he dressed the wound, which was situated on the outside and back of Anne's thigh and buttock, he found it to be upwards of six inches long and more than three inches deep in the middle. Apparently, the incision had been made with a particularly sharp instrument. A few days after his daughters had been assaulted, Mr Thomas Porter went to the Bow Street public office to lodge a complaint about this outrage. Sarah came with him, and described her assailant as a tall man, at least six feet in height, thinly built with light brown hair and a large nose. He appeared to be about thirty years old.[28] It is not clear whether this was just Sarah's own observations, or a composite view of the observations made of the Monster that fateful evening; it is likely that John Porter, Mrs Miel and Anne Porter herself had also seen him. Later, Sarah told Mr Richard Bond, one of the Bow Street magistrates, that she herself was quite unable to describe the man who attacked her, and when Anne was asked to describe the Monster for a newspaper account, all she could volunteer was that he had a very pale and fair complexion.[29]

The London police organisation in 1790 merits a brief discourse, since it is of importance to the story of the Monster and his strange crimes.[30] At this time, the metropolis was divided into parishes, each one responsible for their policing arrangements. If a parish chose to keep any police force at all, this was usually in the form of tradesmen serving as constables for a year each; they were on duty every fifteenth day, armed with staves and lanterns. Many tradesmen resented serving as part-time policemen and hired substitutes; this would have been beneficial had these substitutes been vigorous men, but in reality, they were often feeble old workhouse inmates. In addition, each parish had its force of night watchmen. Westminster had 300 of them, spread out among its nine parishes.[31] Led by an elderly Night Beadle, each of these watchmen had a beat to patrol; they also manned the watch-houses, where prisoners could be confined until removed by a constable. They were armed with a staff, a lantern and a rattle; the latter implement was to be used to give the alarm if anything untoward occurred on their beat. The watchmen called out the time at regular intervals, sometimes adding the comforting reassurance that all was well. But in reality, this was very far from true. The watchman's salary was a meagre one and the working hours singularly unattractive: the watchmen had to be recruited among the elderly, the destitute and the wretches who inhabited the workhouses. In the newspapers, it was said that their rattles served as a rallying-call to the criminals; there were also unkind comparisons between the cracking sound of the rattles, the cracking joints of the elderly watchmen, and their old weather-cracked voices calling out the time. The inefficiency of these watchmen was well known to the authorities, but very little was done about it. It was not infrequent that they abandoned their beats to sit in a drunken stupor in their watch-house. The more vicious of these old men took bribes from prostitutes and burglars to leave their activities alone. There were even instances of watchmen being in league with burglars: the watchman arrested some house-owner on a trumped-up charge, and when the victim came home after a miserable night at the watch-house, he found his house empty of valuables, which the burglar had been able to remove in complete safety! It is a tell-tale fact that the parish of St James's and Marylebone, which recruited its watchmen from the war invalids and old soldiers from the Chelsea Hospital, was well known for the great efficiency of their night watchman patrols; these tough old invalids were thus a force far superior to the corrupt and decrepit watchmen usually employed in the metropolis.

In 1785, there was a great debate on whether there should be a police reform: a new Bill suggested that London should be subdivided into nine divisions, each of which should have its own public office and magistrate, and a force of twenty-five fit and able men, properly armed and with far wider powers than the parish constables. These professional policemen were to be able to arrest any person in possession of articles presumed to be stolen, and to enter licensed premises without a warrant. The Gordon riots had demonstrated the meaning of mob rule to the London authorities, and one of the aims of the new system was to have a reliable anti-riot police force in the capital. But the old-fashioned Surrey and Middlesex justices defended the old system, and were supported by the Sheriffs of London. In particular, the influential Judge William Mainwaring MP, a chairman of the Middlesex Quarter Sessions, condemned the Bill as inexpedient and unnecessary.[32] From a combination of professional jealousy and a sincere belief that a professional police force would undermine the long-established voluntary system, the Bill was rejected. The sad result was that in 1790, the police force patrolling the streets of London was little different, in terms of organisation and efficiency, from that of 1690. The only major difference was the existence of the Bow Street public office, the centre of the London detective police. Founded by Sir Thomas de Veil in 1740, it became justly famous during the time of Henry Fielding and his brother John, both Bow Street magistrates. Sir John Fielding was succeeded by Mr Sampson Wright in 1782.[33] At Bow Street, a set of unbiased, honourable magistrates directed various criminal investigations. Their police detectives – the Bow Street Runners – had no distinctive uniform, but they often wore a red waistcoat, and carried a truncheon with a metal crest to show their authority. There were not very many Runners, just six or eight at a time, but they were tough and resilient thief-takers, often with extensive networks of informants who kept them abreast of the actions of the criminal underworld. Under them were the Bow Street patrols: ordinary policemen, who formed a much-needed core police force to combat riots and civil unrest.

When visiting the Bow Street public office, Thomas Porter was astonished to find out from Sir Sampson Wright, the magistrate on duty, that four other ladies had been attacked by a mystery assailant on the evening of the Queen's birthday.[34] A certain Miss Toussaint, who had, just like Anne Porter, been in the gallery at St James's Palace, was returning home together with her mother, her sister and two other ladies. As they were proceeding towards their home in Sackville Street, a man came up to them and began a highly indecorous conversation. His words were so extremely foul and improper that all the ladies ran away, helter-skelter, like a covey of quail flushed by a dog. The man pursued them, and was seen to strike at Miss Toussaint several times. When they reached their home, the ladies were aghast to observe that Miss Toussaint's dress was badly slashed with some sharp instrument. She herself was unhurt, thanks to her strong whalebone stays. At half past eleven the same evening, Mrs Harlow, a lady bookseller, was walking up St James's Street with a gentleman friend. Just outside Brooks' Club, she received a blow from a man who stood against a chair. When she came home, she noticed that all her clothes had been cut through, but without injury to her person. The same evening, Mrs Burney, the wife of Captain Burney, also had her clothes cut by an unknown person. The fourth of these outrages took place outside the house of a fashionable lady, the Hon. Mrs Walpole, in Dover Street. A young lady named Miss Felton had been cut through the pocket-hole of her dress with such force that the dress was completely shredded, and an apple in her pocket divided. There was a rumour at the time that Mrs Walpole had herself been cut, and that she had been saved from the Monster's rapier by this apple in her pocket. There was even a poem in her honour in one of the major newspapers:[35]

To Mrs R. Walpole,
On her escape from the Stab of the MONSTER, by an Apple in her pocket:

> *The Apple was, in days of yore,*
> *An Agent to the Devil,*
> *When EVE was tempted to explore*
> *The sense of Good and Evil.*
>
> *But present Chronicles can give*
> *An instance quite uncommon,*
> *How that which ruin'd mother EVE,*
> *Hath sav'd a modern woman.*

3

A MONSTER

ON THE

PROWL

My nose is really somewhat short – but what's the use of that?
The MONSTER, too, is monstrous thin, and I am monstrous fat:
But not a word the Lady hears, determin'd to misconstrue,
And up to Bow-street I'm convey'd, to try if I'm the MONSTER.
Of such a snare,
Ye Beaux beware!
Or chuse a Maid
Who will not swear
She saw me ready to – O rare!
To stab her thro' the pocket-hole – exactly like the MONSTER.

Mr Hook, 'The Monster'
(A song presented to the Proprietors of Vauxhall)

Mr Porter's report of the Monster's assault on his daughters is likely to have aroused some trepidation among the Bow Street magistrates, since it was now apparent that something quite serious was afoot. Since May 1788, there had been an alarming series of attacks on women in the streets of central London, many of them following the same pattern as those on the Queen's birthday. A certain Mrs Maria Smyth, the pretty young wife of Dr Smyth, of Stephen Street, Rathbone Place, had the dubious honour of being the Monster's first recorded victim.[1] Early on a Sunday evening, in the middle of May 1788, she was walking in Fleet Street when she was approached by a thin, vulgar-looking man with very ugly legs and feet. He was rather below the middle size, with a villainous, narrow face adorned by a cocked hat slapped on one side. In a remarkable voice, 'in which there seemed to be a *tremulous eagerness*', he started a highly shocking and indecent conversation, to which Mrs Smyth made no answer. He kept stalking her, at times making use of the same foul language, until she arrived at her destination, a house in Johnson's Court, just off Fleet Street. She asked him to go about his business, and not to follow her, but the man just stood there grinning at her, and made no reply. She then knocked hard on the door, but the man suddenly jumped up on the step beside her, and just as the door was opened, he struck her a violent blow beneath her left breast, which he immediately repeated on her left thigh. He did not run away, but just stood there looking at her with perfect composure, until the swooning Mrs Smyth had been helped inside. The wound fortunately proved to be a slight one, and the blood flow was easily stopped by the application of some balsam. The weapon used was presumed to have been a sharp instrument like a lancet or a penknife; there were marks from a similar cutting implement on her stays from the blow on her chest. Maria Smyth was a fragile, nervous woman, and in 1790 she claimed that the Monster's savage attack, and the ensuing wound, bruise and terror, had made her severely ill; she had been confined to her bed for many months, and her life had been despaired of no less than seven times.

In the summer of 1788, Mrs Franklin, a recently married young lady, had been grossly insulted by a thin, big-nosed little man, who had made use of the most indecent language. She was the daughter of a tavern-keeper in St James's Street, a rough character known as 'Parsloe' Wheeler. Parsloe's other daughter, Miss Kitty Wheeler, described as 'a fine, lively, spirited, beautiful young lady', had once, in early 1789, been at the Ranelagh pleasure garden in Chelsea, the night after the Spanish ambassador's gala. Her father had left her to get their carriage to go home. Suddenly, a small man with a long nose and face, regular features and curly hair, came up to her uninvited and made use of the most gross and indecent language. She was of course very frightened by this rude and threatening character, and called out to some gentlemen near her for protection. The Monster rapidly made himself scarce on their approach. A few days later, he made another attempt, when Kitty Wheeler was walking in St James's Park with her sister, but Miss Wheeler's instincts of self-preservation again proved sharper than those of the Monster's other victims. She very wisely called out to her father that the same man who had insulted her at the Ranelagh was again following her. The canny Parsloe advised his daughters to walk on before, while he kept an eye on them; if the fellow came up and insulted them, he would interfere. In Bennet Street, the Monster again spoke to the girls, in the same indecent manner as before. Parsloe Wheeler then tackled him from behind and brought him down! The stalker was shaken like a rat by the irate tavern-keeper, but the noise of the fight alerted a rough crowd. Since Parsloe was not particularly well-liked, they got the wrong end of the stick and sided with the Monster. The tavern-keeper was not willing to let go of his prey, but the mob was becoming more and more dangerous, and Kitty Wheeler persuaded her father to let the man go, fearing that her courageous parent might be seriously injured by the crowd. She had little thanks for this action, however, since she afterwards several times observed the Monster standing in front of their house, where he made use of his usual impertinent expressions to her and her sisters.[2]

In May 1789, Mrs Sarah Godfrey, a beautiful lady of fashion living in Charlotte Street, was accosted by a middle-sized man dressed in black, with the appearance of a gentleman, aged about thirty, and wearing a cocked hat and his hair well-dressed. Without speaking, he followed her from Bond Street into Leicester Square, and then into Piccadilly, walking sometimes before her, sometimes behind her and sometimes by her side. When she stepped into the doorway of an upholsterer's shop in Piccadilly, the man came up to her and made her a very indecent proposal. She did not reply, but merely went into the shop. As she came out, her persistent but foul-mouthed admirer was waiting outside. He did not speak to her again, but stalked her on her walk back to Charlotte Street, sometimes walking behind her, sometimes just in front of her. Just as Sarah Godfrey had stepped on the first step to walk in through her front door, the man came up to her very rapidly, and stabbed her in the upper part of the thigh with a very sharp instrument. He then walked away with much composure, as if nothing at all had happened. Mrs Godfrey had fallen, and lay bleeding in the street; before she had recovered her senses, the Monster was gone.[3]

Four months later, a young lady named Miss Mary Forster was returning from a visit to the Haymarket theatre, when she was accosted by a slender, thin man, about five feet six or seven inches tall, with regular features and a long nose. He seemed agitated and had 'something of an eagerness of countenance'. He first offered to call her a coach, and then to see her safe home himself, but she was distrustful of his intentions and declined. She even contemplated calling for assistance from two labouring men who were standing nearby, but determined to walk home without creating any alarm. Her strange admirer followed close behind her, and at times advanced to stare her directly in the face in an impertinent manner. Miss Forster declined all his attempts at opening a conversation. When they had reached Dean Street, near St Anne's Church in Soho, the man suddenly 'uttered very indecent, scandalous language, such as shocked and amazed her; and, after a horrid oath, he struck her upon the hip'. At first, Miss Forster was not even aware that she had been wounded, but she called out to the two labourers nearby, and they chased after the man, who ran away down King Street. The Monster was too quick for them, however, and they could not overtake him. Mary Forster now complained of a pain in the hip, and was unable to proceed home. She was helped by two gentlemen, but as soon as she came home, she fell down in fits. Her clothes were drenched through with blood, and the effusion of blood from her deep wound was no less than a quart. Interestingly, Miss Forster was able to give a very good description of the Monster, which agreed well with those of Mrs Franklin and Kitty Wheeler; it was appeared likely that these three ladies, at least, had been attacked by the same man.

Mary Forster also volunteered the information that she had seen this unprepossessing character several times before, lounging about in the theatres and public assembly rooms. In particular, she had had a most perilous encounter with him when she visited the Covent Garden theatre shortly after she had been wounded. As she sat in her box with another lady, she saw a man she thought resembled the Monster enter one of the other boxes. When the Monster perceived that he was being observed, he went out with an enraged look at Miss Forster, and shut the door with great violence. Miss Forster sensibly alerted some gentlemen, who ran after the Monster and secured him in the lobby; there was a scuffle 'which produced some disturbance'. The gentlemen did not want to miss the play, however, and they appealed to the box-keepers of the theatre to arrest him! The box-keepers very properly refused, since there was no warrant to detain him. No one had the sense to send a man to Bow Street to fetch one of the Runners. The Monster put on his best behaviour, and managed to persuade the gentlemen to let him go free, after he had given his address. Miss Forster, believing herself free from the Monster's persecution after she had seen him being collared in the lobby, was horrified when he leapt out in front of her as she left the theatre. He did not attack, but scowled terribly at her as he passed her by – so close that he could almost touch her dress.[4]

The London Monster's next victim was Miss Ann Frost, residing in Jermyn Street, and described as 'a tall genteel girl, with a pair of fine black eyes, an elegant person, brisk, lively, and agreeable'. On 9 November 1789 (Lord Mayor's day), she was returning from some gathering late at night, when a man came up to her. Those readers now acquainted with the Monster's habits will not be surprised that his language was 'very shocking and indecent'. She tried to get rid of him, but he followed her to her home in Jermyn Street, where he struck her on the hip just as she knocked at the door. Fortunately, she was not hurt, although her clothes were cut through. Ann Frost described the Monster in a similar way to Mrs Franklin, Miss Wheeler and Mary Forster: a thin, middle-sized individual with regular features and a long nose. She added that she would know his peculiar voice if she ever heard it again.

At about the same time, a certain Miss Ann Morley was assaulted in Whitehall on a Sunday evening. She was walking with another young lady when a man dressed in black, at least six feet tall, pale and sallow and with a vicious ill-look, left a woman with whom he had been talking and followed them along. He went first on one side of them and then on the other, and then violently pressed between them and struck Miss Morley on the hip. She called out, 'Good God!' He then struck her again and remained standing near her staring in her face. Miss Morley screamed, 'Good God, that man has struck me twice!' and he then struck her a third time for good measure and composedly made off. Just a few days later, a man of a similar description – very tall, dressed in black and with long ruffles – attacked Miss Eleanor Dodson near Charing Cross, and cut her in the hip with a sharp instrument believed to have been the blade of a penknife, or a long lancet.[5]

Next lambs to the slaughter were two sisters, Miss Elizabeth and Miss Frances Baughan, described as 'two very agreeable, genteel young ladies, blue eyes, fair complexion; one is of the middle size, the other smaller and very pretty, sensible, candid, and open: they were both dressed in blue silk'. On the evening of 7 December 1789, at about a quarter past seven, they were passing along Bridge Street, Westminster, when they noticed a short man following them close by. He was grumbling to himself in an odd manner. Suddenly, he came up to them and said, 'Blast you, is that you!' into Frances Baughan's ear. The sisters made no answer at all to this uncouth greeting, and tried to avoid him, but he persistently stalked them through the streets, all the time addressing them in very obscene and insulting language. When they came into Parliament Street, they both began to run, but the Monster ran after them and struck at them several times. The terrified girls stopped for a while, and the Monster stood looking at them very composedly, before walking off without any haste. The Misses Baughan found that their dresses had been badly slashed, and that they had both been slightly wounded by the ruffian's rapier. Their description of the Monster agreed well with that given by Miss Wheeler, Mrs Franklin and Ann Frost. Interestingly, Frances Baughan said that both she and her sister had seen the Monster several times before, the first time about two years earlier, and that it was his habit to come up to them in the street and insult them. Once, in Green Park, this strange character had behaved so obnoxiously that the enraged Frances Baughan had slapped his face.[6]

In the meantime, the Monster had apparently somewhat changed his *modus operandi*, but he continued to wreak havoc in the metropolis. From January 1790 onwards, his outrages became increasingly prevalent. One day in late January, Mrs Allan, the daughter-in-law of a plumber in Piccadilly, was taking a walk with her mother and sister, when she observed a man with a small parcel in his hand following them at a safe distance. In the court leading from Piccadilly into Vine Street, the man pushed hard against Mrs Allan, and nearly sent her sprawling. She first thought it had been an accident, but when she came home, she found that her gown and the rest of her clothes were very badly cut. A certain Mrs Drummond had an even more disagreeable experience. She was visiting the theatre, where she observed a short man with a narrow face and a prominent nose bustling about her in a disagreeable manner. When she came out from the playhouse, she was surprised and mortified to find that her gown and petticoat were totally in shreds. Her handkerchief, and even her hair, had been cut and hacked by the Monster.[7]

In late January, a maidservant of Mrs Gordon was standing outside her mistress's house, when a man suddenly and unprovokedly grasped her from behind and violently kicked her buttocks with his knee several times 'damning her all the while'. When she recovered from her terror and surprise, she found that she was 'dreadfully wounded' by some very sharp instrument that must have been fastened to the Monster's knee.[8] In the middle of March, a similar attack was made upon Mrs Charlotte Payne, the lady's maid of the Countess of Howe. Mrs Payne was a middle-aged, conventional lady, plain in appearance and unexceptional in dress. When, on one Sunday evening, she was walking along Brook Street on her way to Lord Howe's house, she was both surprised and dismayed when a well-dressed man in dark clothes, and a cocked hat with a cockade, came up to her and offered to see her home. Although he looked like the perfect gentleman, the prim lady's maid did not even honour this immodest proposal with an answer. The man took no notice of her disapproving looks, but continued to walk with her along Bond Street and Grafton Street, 'making love to her all the way with a rather uncommon energy'(!), although she requested him to leave her. At Lord Howe's door, she begged her persistent admirer to go away, but as she was going in, the man grabbed her from behind and violently kicked her up the steps with his knee, 'making use of the most horrid language and imprecations all the time'. One of his expressions was: 'Damn you, you bitch, I would enjoy a particular pleasure in murdering you, and in shedding your blood!' Fortunately for Mrs Payne, the door was opened by another servant of Lord Howe's, and with a final, resounding kick in the backside, the Monster sent her cannoning into this individual. It took some time for Mrs Payne to recover, and when the other servants went off in pursuit of the mysterious assailant, he was nowhere to be found. Some of Mrs Payne's wounds were quite deep, and they may have become infected. Several newspapers reported that she had died from her wounds, but this report was later contradicted: Charlotte Payne was still alive, but continued 'in a state of extreme danger'.[9] Not long after the attack on Mrs Payne, a certain Mrs Blaney was stabbed in the thigh outside her door in Bury Street by a man who she described as about thirty-five years old, tall, stout, and gentlemanly looking, with a very dark complexion.

The Monster had thought of another, no less dastardly tactic in his campaign to strike terror into London's female population. About the same time as the attack on Mrs Payne, a servant-girl was approached by a man in Holborn. He asked her to smell a large nosegay in his hand, and she complied. A moment later, she noticed a sharp pain in her nose, which, needless to say, she hastily withdrew from the ruffian's nosegay. The Monster, who had stabbed her in the nose with a sharp instrument concealed in the nosegay, walked away with much composure. One evening in April, just before dusk, another servant-girl, who was going about on her mistress's business, had the misfortune to be overtaken by four men in the Strand. One of them had a nosegay, and requested her to smell it, but she declined, since the flowers looked artificial. The man kept pestering her, however, and to get clear of the men, she accepted to smell the nosegay. As it was held to her face, she immediately felt herself wounded just under the eye, by a very sharp instrument. The men all set up a loud laugh, and immediately made off, leaving the terrified girl standing in the street, her face bleeding copiously.[10]

By early April, the Londoners had begun to despair about the ability of the Bow Street police to catch the Monster. Although Mr Porter had lodged a complaint at Bow Street after his daughters had been assaulted, he had also requested that the business should be investigated in some privacy, and the Monster's activities on 18 January had not been widely reported in the newspapers. The attacks on Mrs Payne and Mrs Blaney were widely publicised, however, and more than one newspaper writer compared these crimes with other attacks on women during the previous two years. In the *Morning Chronicle* of 3 April, the attack on Mrs Blaney was considered as another outrage by 'the miscreant whom we have noticed more than once for similar instances of brutality'. Several letters, some anonymous and others signed, were sent to the daily newspapers, complaining about the Monster's nefarious activities. Some deplored the lack of police activity and called for vigilante action; others actually accused the Runners of being in league with the Monster. Mr Andrew Franklin, husband of the Mrs Franklin who had been stalked and insulted by the Monster, was among the first to raise the alarm.[11] One anonymous letter came from a man who claimed that he himself had once been brought before the Bow Street magistrates, accused of being the Monster. He now boldly declared that he knew the Monster's identity, and that this criminal was a gentleman of some rank in life in the Temple. This gentleman was well-known to the Bow Street magistrates, but they still did not arrest him. Six days later, Sir Sampson Wright and Mr Nicholas Bond replied that, in consequence of an anonymous letter being sent to them, the gentleman in question had been taken to Bow Street. Anne Porter and several other wounded ladies had seen him, and all unanimously declared that he had not the slightest resemblance to the man who had wounded them.[12]

Dr William Smyth, the husband of Mrs Smyth, the very first lady who had been cut by the Monster, in May 1788, was aghast to observe the parallels between the attack on his wife, 'during which she very nearly lost her life', and these novel outrages. He sent a letter to the *Morning Chronicle* asking for the address of Mrs Blaney and other recently wounded ladies. Mrs Smyth and Mrs Blaney met and compared their experiences: the conclusion was that they had almost certainly been wounded by different men. Later, as a result of the Doctor's detective work, twelve other wounded ladies made themselves known to him. Dr Smyth was amazed that the Monster had been able to evade detection for so long, and joined in the call for vigilante action against this fiend in human shape.[13]

On 14 April, Mrs Maria Smyth was attending a public auction. Her consternation can be imagined when she suddenly saw the man who had assaulted her sitting nearby! She was a fragile, nervous lady, but managed to resist the impulse to jump up and cry 'Help! The Monster!' Instead, she kept her calm and informed her husband, who was sitting nearby, and the Doctor also acted quite rationally. After the auction, he followed the man to his home in Great Queen Street: he turned out to be Mr William Tuffing, a former ladies' hairdresser, who now worked as a clothes salesman. Dr Smyth acted very prudently (some Monster-hunters said too prudently). He first sent for Anne Porter and tried to organise a clandestine operation in which Mrs Smyth and Anne Porter were supposed to enter Tuffing's shop and point him out as the Monster. Doctor Smyth then changed his mind and instead decided to inform Mr Justice Addington, of Bow Street. The Doctor planned to perform a full-scale confrontation when William Tuffing was brought to Bow Street. He personally went round to London in his coach, to visit many of the wounded ladies, of whom Mrs Blaney, Mrs Newman, Miss Toussaint, Miss Felton, Mrs Godfrey, and the Misses Baughan promised to turn up. On her own initiative, Anne Porter went to Tuffing's shop beforehand, however. This was just at the time when a large reward had been posted for the arrest of the Monster, which may well have prompted her action. She declared that he was not the man who had cut her, although he had a strong resemblance of him.[14] William Tuffing denied the charge, and declared that he had never seen Mrs Smyth before in his life. The wimpish little man wept and moaned, lamenting his hard fate and that of his family. He was not strong, and could not bear life in prison, even for a couple of days.

At the confrontation, held at the Bow Street public office on 19 April, a considerable crowd of people, among them the Duke of Gloucester and several others of distinction, had assembled to see the suspected Monster face his victims. However, none of the wounded ladies, except Mrs Smyth, could identify Tuffing as the man who had cut or frightened them. Seeing them testify, a susceptible newspaper reporter wrote that these ladies had been 'wounded by some MONSTER (for such the perpetrator of such horrid deed must be, as there was not one but laid strong claims to beauty)'.[15] Mrs Smyth's husband the Doctor repeatedly urged his wife (as he had often done before) to be cautious and consider the consequences of her actions, but she remained adamant that Tuffing was the man. The *Oracle* newspaper reporter rather doubted Mrs Smyth's identification, since she was a very nervous lady, and the crime had been committed two years earlier. William Tuffing had never been convicted for any crime; he had a very good character and was a married man with a young family. It arose some suspicion that Mrs Smyth did not give any reason why she had fixed on William Tuffing; also that she volunteered the information that, three or four months earlier, she had seen Tuffing at another public auction, but had not mentioned her suspicion to Dr Smyth or any other person. After many character witnesses had appeared on Tuffing's behalf, and all the other wounded ladies had declared themselves convinced that Tuffing was innocent, Mrs Smyth 'then *thought* only, that he was like the person'.[16] Poor William Tuffing again turned on the water-works, wringing his hands and lamenting the fact that his family would become destitute if he were to be held in prison for much longer. Dramatically, just as this time, a Bow Street Runner brought the news that while Tuffing had been examined, a maidservant had just been cut by the Monster.[17] Mr Justice Addington committed William Tuffing for trial, but admitted him to find securities for his appearance, so that he could still support his family. There is no record of Tuffing ever being tried: fortunately for him, his plight was ended by the sensational events of early June.

4

THE
ANGERSTEIN
Reward

And when before the Justices, what justice 'tis to see
Of MONSTERS there, already charg'd — two hundred good as me!
For every Miss, thro' all the town, this scheme can aptly construe
'Tis 'touch and take': so if you touch, she takes you for the MONSTER.
'Gainst such a league,
Adieu INTRIGUE!
For here, ye fair!
I truly swear,
You'll find me ready to — O rare!
But not to stab — the pocket-hole, for I am not the MONSTER.

Mr Hook, 'The Monster'
(A song presented to the Proprietors of Vauxhall)

By early April 1790, the Monster business had caught the
interest of the wealthy Lloyd's insurance broker John Julius
Angerstein. This gentleman had been born in Russia in 1734.
According to the traditional accounts of his life, he was the son of
the German Dr Henry Angerstein, and the Doctor certainly brought
him up as his son, although one source states that he was actually

the natural son of the English merchant Andrew Poulett Thomson and Empress Anne of Russia.[1] John Julius Angerstein had come to London in 1749 as an office boy. He worked at the Lloyd's coffee-house, as it was then called, from 1756 onwards, became one of its leading brokers, and was instrumental in establishing Lloyd's as a great insurance house. Mr Angerstein was intrigued by the Monster's long catalogue of crimes against the fair sex, and did much to collate the annals of the havoc he had wrought among the female population of London. In addition to the cases known by the Bow Street magistrates, or discovered by Dr Smyth, there were quite a few others: as the newspapers were full of the Monster's activities, many ladies went forward to report their encounters with this brutal character. Angerstein personally went round to each and every one of the wounded ladies, to get their eyewitness accounts of the Monster attacks. He was aghast to find that there had been, from May 1788 until April 1790, no less than thirty attacks on unaccompanied women in the metropolis. Angerstein took copious notes of the various accounts of the Monster and his *modus operandi*; he also noted the dress and appearance of the ladies, and the details concerning their wounds. He was by no means unsusceptible to feminine charms, and an uncharitable individual would suspect that his frequent visits to the wounded beauties were not prompted by philanthropy alone. Miss Toussaint, whose clothes had been cut by the Monster on 18 January, was described as 'young, about or rather below the middle size, with dark hair, fine large black eyes, her face rather full and plump, a good agreeable countenance, lively, pleasant, and very pretty'. Sarah Porter was not quite Angerstein's type: she was only 'mild, genteel, and rather handsome', but her sister Anne met with his full approval: she was 'young, below the middle size, with fine black eyes, good skin, fine teeth, lively, sensible, delicate, and very pretty.'[2]

John Julius Angerstein wrote that if it was an act of the utmost cowardice for a man of superior strength to attack and beat up a weak and defenceless person of his own sex, then what to make of the Monster's offences? To attack unsuspecting women with a weapon of uncommon sharpness, that seemed to have been manu-factured for this inhuman purpose, was a crime 'rendered still more atrocious by the insult that generally accompanies the outrage, and by the savage delight he enjoys in the terror, pain, and distress of the lovely victim!' No woman was safe from this dastardly villain. Although the Monster had, in 1788 and 1789, mainly confined his attacks to elegant, good-looking women, his lust for blood had increased, and at the present time, age, deformities, or even indi-gence, were no protection against his diabolical attacks.

At a meeting in Lloyd's coffee-house on 15 April 1790, Angerstein opened a subscription to raise a reward for the person who apprehended 'that INHUMAN MONSTER, whoever he may be, who has of late so frequently wounded several young women'. Angerstein himself donated five guineas, and nineteen other gentlemen immediately did the same; two more impecu-nious gentlemen donated two pounds two shillings each, one of them anonymously. The next day, the newspapers were full of this sensational news. The Bow Street public office made it known that anyone who apprehended the Monster, or gave information to Sir Sampson Wright at this office that led to his arrest, would have a claim to £50, delivered by Mr Angerstein upon the man's commit-tal to prison, and the further sum of £50 upon his conviction. The advertisements also gave a description of the Monster:

> He appears to be about 30 years of age, of middle size, a little pock marked, of a pale complexion, large nose, light brown hair tied in a queue, cut short and frizzed low at the sides, is sometimes dressed in black, and sometimes in a shabby blue coat, sometimes wears straw-coloured breeches, with half-boots laced up before, sometimes wears a cocked hat, and at other times a round hat, with a very high top, and generally carries a Wangee cane in his hand.

A large poster with details of the reward and the description of the Monster was printed at Mr Angerstein's expense, and stuck up on the walls all over London.[3]

Fifty pounds was a princely sum at that time, and after the Angerstein reward had been advertised on 16 April, the Monster-hunt was on. Numerous amateur detectives were on the lookout for anything suspicious, and the Bow Street police received a torrent of information. Some person had had blood on his clothes, another had stayed out late a certain evening, a third has acted suspiciously, and so forth. All these informants were of course eager to get their hands on the reward. Even worse, the more impetuous Monster-hunters themselves made citizen's arrests of various suspicious characters. One Monster-hunter arrested his employer after beating and pummelling him; another took his brother-in-law into custody and brought him to Bow Street. One lunatic arrested a butcher, at gunpoint, after finding a bloody knife in his pocket. The number of individuals brought before the magistrates soon exceeded twenty, and there was absolutely no evidence against any of them: Anne Porter and the other wounded ladies could not identify them, and it was apparent that many of these arrests had been dictated by greed and mischief alone.[4]

Even the official police force was led astray by Mr Angerstein's generosity. On the evening of Monday 19 April, a party of Runners belonging to the Poland Street public office arrested a gentleman of some distinction outside Devonshire House, accused him of being the Monster, and took him to the watch-house, where he was confined all night. The morning after, the gentleman was taken to Justice Read's office by the exultant Runners, who hoped that he would be committed to prison and that the reward would become theirs. Several wounded ladies were sent for, but none of them could swear to him; furthermore, the judge commented that the man, although definitely a suspicious character, did not at all answer the description of the Monster issued on posters all over London. The gentleman was of course discharged, and *The Times* newspaper was full of censure against the impetuous Runners, who themselves deserved to be prosecuted for this wrongful arrest. Although the gentleman, whose name was not mentioned, had 'certainly on a former occasion appeared in a suspicious light before the public', this was no reason to drag him off to prison with no evidence at all.[5] In the same article, the wisdom of Mr Angerstein and the other generous gentlemen of Lloyd's coffee-house was questioned: the immense reward they had posted would evidently open a wide field for imposition and perjury. Very rightly, *The Times* journalist found it mysterious that although Miss Anne Porter had sworn that Tuffing was not the Monster, she did not come forward with a description of the man who had cut her; was she keeping this information to herself in the hope of pointing out the right man herself and claiming the reward? Angerstein continued his efforts, however: in a new advertisement dated 29 April, and headed 'One Hundred Pounds Reward', all servants were urged to take notice if some person had stayed at home for no apparent cause, hiding from the Monster-hunters scouring the streets, or if they observed any sharp weapon about the house. All washerwomen should take notice if some man came to them with blood on his clothes, and all cutlers were desired to watch out if some man came to them and wanted to have some weapon of attack made very sharp. At this time, it was an extraordinary step to entice servants to report on their masters; that such a stratagem, resembling those of the French revolutionaries, was at all contemplated, is further proof of the intensity of feeling arisen by the Monster's crimes.

In the meantime, the Monster had continued his one-man vendetta against London's female inhabitants with gusto. In mid-April, Mrs Susannah Thompson, described by Mr Angerstein as a 'plain woman, with every proper appearance of a tradesman's wife', went out to call on an acquaintance in Princess Street. A man, whom she could not afterwards describe, came up to her, and after having made her a couple of very improper and impertinent proposals, struck her violently on the hip. She found her clothes cut through, and the skin underneath slightly wounded. Mrs Harlow the bookseller, who had been one of the Monster's five victims on 18 January, was again attacked in April. While she was walking in the Pall Mall, a very tall man with a genteel appearance was follow-

Public-Office, Bow-Street, Thursday, 29th April, 1790.

One Hundred Pounds
R E W A R D.

SEVERAL LADIES having of late been inhumanly cut and maimed by a PERSON anfwering the following Defcription: Whoever will apprehend him or give fuch Information to Sir *SAMPSON WRIGHT*, at the above Office, as may be the Means of his being apprehended, fhall *immediately upon his Commitment to Prifon*, receive FIFTY POUNDS from Mr. ANGERSTEIN, of Pall-Mall; and the farther Sum of FIFTY POUNDS *upon his Conviction*.

N. B. HE appears to be about 30 Years of Age, of a middle Size, rather thin made, a little Pock-marked, of a pale Complexion, large Nofe, light brown Hair, tied in a Queue, cut fhort and frizzed low at the Sides; is fometimes *dreffed* in *black*, and fometimes in a fhabby *blue* Coat, fometimes wears *Straw coloured* Breeches, with half Boots, *laced up before*; fometimes wears a *cocked* Hat, and at other Times a *round* Hat, with a very high Top, and generally carries a *Wangee* Cane in his Hand.

ALL Servants are recommended to take Notice if any Man has ftaid at home without apparent Caufe, within thefe few Days, during Day light. All Wafherwomen and Servants fhould take Notice of any Blood on a Man's Handkerchief or Linen, as the *Wretch* generally fetches Blood when he ftrikes. All Servants fhould examine if any Man carries fharp Weapons about him, and if there is any Blood thereon, particularly Tucks; and Maid Servants are to be told that a Tuck is generally at the Head of a Stick, which comes out by a fudden Jerk. All *CUTLERS* are defired to watch if any Man anfwering the above Defcription is defirous of having his Weapon of attack very fharp.

Printed by J. MOORE, No. 134, Drury-Lane.

Mr Angerstein's first Monster poster, dated 29 April 1790.

ing her very closely. Suddenly, he pushed her violently against the house wall, and nearly threw her off her feet. When she came home, she again found that all her clothes had been badly cut, and that she herself was slightly wounded.[6]

Just after eight o'clock on the morning of 19 April, the servant-girl Rebecca Lohr, unflatteringly described as being 'about twenty years of age, middle sized, very plain, long nose, thin face, and a pale complexion', went out for some rolls. Opposite the oil shop in the Strand, next to Charing Cross, a man came up to her and took her hand, but she had read about the London Monster and snatched her hand away from him. The man then struck, or rather clawed, her on the arm, from the elbow down to the hand, with some very sharp instrument that appeared to be fastened to his hand. He then clawed her other arm in exactly the same manner, before making off with celerity. Poor Rebecca Lohr staggered into a baker's shop, where she bled very much; the efflux of blood from her (apparently quite deep) wounds was not quenched until after midday. She was so terrified by this unprovoked assault that she could not give any description of the Monster, except that he was wearing blue and white stockings.[7]

Next lamb to the slaughter was Jane Hurd, 'a stout well-grown young woman', servant to Mrs Jefferson, a lady of quality living in Edgware Road. At half past eight on the evening of 26 April, her mistress sent Jane out for some radishes. Just as she returned from this errand, and was standing at Mrs Jefferson's door, a man came up, laid hold of her arm, and said, 'Now, who shall treat with a glass of gin first, you or I?' She replied, 'Go along you nasty fellow!' and pushed him off. He then damned her, with a horrid oath, and struck her a violent blow on the breast. Jane Hurd screamed, and the Monster ran off. Mrs Jefferson helped her into the house, where it was found that the ruffian had delivered his slash with enough force to cut through the strong whalebone of her stays, and also divide an iron wire, giving her a wound nearly two inches long. She described the Monster as stout and middle-sized, with a full face and a large nose, and wearing a greatcoat.[8] A few days later, the Monster offered a young woman in Salisbury Square a nosegay to smell 'in which was concealed a knife, and took that opportunity to wound her in the face with it'.[9]

In late April, there were several other mysterious assaults on women, all of which were, in the gathering hysteria, blamed on the London Monster. In late April, a servant-girl in Greville Street, and another one in Holborn, had their clothes cut by mysterious assailants; one of these was described as a very tall man dressed in black. In the Strand, a girl was frightened by a man shouting 'Buh!' in her face; another maidservant, in Silver Street, received a punch in the face through a doorway, for no apparent reason, and was knocked out cold. On 30 April, a tall, foreign-looking Monster dressed in a brown greatcoat and a round hat pushed a woman in a crowded marketplace as she tried to avoid his company; he then forcibly struck another woman who was in his way. A man followed him as he made his escape, but this individual was 'timid of making any alarm' and the Monster escaped.[10]

Mr Angerstein's efforts nearly paid off on 4 May. When Doctor Bush, a young and vigorous medical practitioner, was returning from the house of a patient, he observed a man pursuing a well-dressed woman on the pavement opposite. The Doctor knew about the Monster from Angerstein's posters, and did not hesitate to intervene. As he hastily walked towards the poor woman, who appeared nearly overcome with fright and fatigue, the man followed her into the porch and made an attempt to stab her. The Doctor flourished his stout cane and directed a blow towards the man's head, but the Monster nimbly dodged the blow, put some bright shining object back into his waistcoat pocket, and made off with alacrity. Doctor Bush attended to the woman, who told him that she served as cook to Mr J. Sullivan. The Monster had followed her from St James's Street into Arlington Street, accosting her with uncommonly obscene and horrid language. When two gentleman's servants came along, the intrepid Doctor ordered one of them to remain with the lady, and the other one to accompany him in pursuit of the Monster. They ran after the man, who had obviously believed himself secure, and caught up with him just at the corner of St James's Street and Piccadilly. Just as he was to seize the Monster, a stout fellow collared the Doctor and accused *him* of being the London Monster! A large and threatening mob soon gathered, and just as usual, they got hold of the wrong end of the stick. The Doctor's attempts to persuade them at least to take both him and the man he had chased into custody were vain, and it looked as if he would be roughly treated. Just in time, the woman came along, and she called out to the mob that Doctor Bush was not the Monster, but her protector. Doctor Bush suspected that the muscular ruffian who had seized him was in fact the Monster's accomplice. He offered to stand forth as a witness against this elusive Monster, who had once more eluded capture.[11]

When the Monster struck again, on 5 May, his choice of victim was surprising. Mrs Elizabeth Davis was the wife of a labouring man, and by no means attractive. She was described by Mr Angerstein, whose eulogies to the wounded beauties have previously been quoted, by the highly uncomplimentary words that she was 'about forty years old, short, thick, and perfectly plain: her dress too corresponded with her person and business, which is that of a washerwoman (some degrees below a laundress), being a thread-bare cloak, which had been red, and the rest of her clothing in the same style'. At about ten o'clock in the evening, Elizabeth Davis was returning home after a long day's work washing dirty clothes. In Chancery Lane, a man came up to her and inquired where she was going. At first she tried to ignore him, but the persistent fellow repeated his question several times, and, at length, she replied that she was going home. As they passed along Holborn, the man pulled out a large nosegay and said, 'Are not these pretty flowers?' 'Yes, Sir,' Elizabeth Davis replied meekly, although she thought the flowers did not look quite *natural*. The Monster flourished his nosegay in an enticing manner and asked, 'Will you smell at it?' but (wisely, as we know!) she refused. The man repeated his request with some urgency, and shoved the nosegay into her face with the words, 'If these flowers were not pretty, for the time of year!' but she pushed it away, saying that they looked *artificial* to her. Without saying anything further, the Monster furiously seized her by the throat, pulled from his coat a short stick, and struck her across the left thigh with it. Poor Elizabeth Davis cried out 'Murder!' With his left hand, he struck her on the breast, and then made off with some urgency.[12]

Elizabeth Davis was very much alarmed, none less so when she came home and observed that her thigh had been badly slashed. She stood hallooing and banging on the door of her lodgings for some time before Mrs Gamson, her landlady, could be induced to open it at this late hour; when the suspicious landlady had finally undone all her locks, Elizabeth Davis almost fell into the room. She fainted, and medical attendants were sent for. Mr Davis suspected that the Monster had been at work, and a representative of the Bow Street Runners was also summoned. When the Runner asked Elizabeth Davis to describe the man who had wounded her, she was much surprised, and even a little flattered, that she had been the subject of the Monster's attentions: he only cut the nobility, she said, and she was but a washer-woman! She described the Monster as tall and gentlemanly-looking: he wore a greatcoat, an elegant striped waistcoat, and a high cocked hat with a cockade. He wore 'his hair frized at the sides in a bush, plaited behind and turned up' and had a large nosegay in his hand.

The same evening, an individual exactly fitting this description was detected by one of the night watchmen, and followed through the streets of London. This watchman was not particularly clever, however, and bumbled along after the Monster without any thought whether the criminal observed him or not. When the Monster knocked on the door of a house near Castle Street, Lincoln's Inn Fields, the watchman presumed this was his home address, and went to Bow Street to give information. The following day, the watchman, Elizabeth Davis and Runner Moses Murrant of Bow Street went to Castle Street to ferret the Monster out from his hiding place. Every person in the house was viewed by Elizabeth Davis, but she declared that none of them had even the slightest resemblance to the Monster who had wounded her. The watchman was non-plussed, but Runner Murrant was able to elucidate, from a maidservant, that someone had indeed been knocking at the door at that time in the evening, but when the girl had gone downstairs to answer the knock, the street was empty. Runner Murrant and Sir Sampson Wright sagely deduced that the Monster must have noticed that he was being followed, and 'made use of the above stratagem to avoid being apprehended'. They concluded that they were dealing with a criminal of superior intelligence and cunning, who had 'twice escaped in a most wonderful way; but surely, from the enormity of his offences, he cannot long elude that punishment he justly merits, and we hope very soon to announce his being in custody'. This dismal story tells us much about the detecting ability of the 1790 police organisation in London; even more remarkably, it was actually published in the newspapers as an *encouraging* sign of police activity in the Monster-hunt.[13]

On 5 May, the same Wednesday night Elizabeth Davis had been assaulted, a servant maid named Jane Read was sent out by her mistress to go fetch some brandy at a public house in Glanville Street. On her way home, she was accosted by a man who asked her where she lived, and then followed her to her master's door. Here, he drew from under his coat a terrible-looking instrument, which looked like a large knife or dagger; immediately on seeing it, Jane Read shrieked aloud and fainted. Mrs McKenzie, her mistress, heard a loud double knock on the door, and went to answer it; she found the girl in a fit, her hand clenched on the knocker of the door.[14] The histrionic girl, who had not received even a scratch from this supposed attack, 'remained in fits all that night, and the following day'!

On the evening of Friday 7 May, Lieutenant Walter Hill RN left his landlady's house to go out and make merry in the ale-houses. He was soon gloriously drunk, and stayed out well past midnight. When he finally reeled back towards his lodgings, something or somebody at the door of a certain Mr Grimes in Tottenham Court Road must have caught his fancy, since he stood banging on this door for quite some time, whooping and hallooing. Rowdy nocturnal behaviour was not unknown in this neighbourhood, then as well as now, but Lieutenant Hill had gone too far. Mr Grimes went down to confront him, and an angry altercation followed, which was finally resolved by the arrival of two stout night watchmen, who took Lieutenant Hill with them. These watchmen were not blundering fools like the one who had bungled the pursuit of the Monster after he had cut Elizabeth Davis a few days earlier. There had been an instruction that they were to be exceptionally careful in the region of Tottenham Court Road, where two women had recently been cut, and the capture of Lieutenant Hill was by some heralded as the end of the Monster's reign of terror.

On Saturday morning, the drunken Lieutenant probably sobered up considerably when he heard that he was suspected of being the London Monster.[15] On Monday 10 May, he was brought before the magistrates at the Litchfield rotation office. The session was to be a farcical one, even by Monster standards. First, Jane Read, the young woman who claimed to have been threatened by the Monster a few days before, was brought in. When she saw Walter Hill, she gave a shriek and nearly collapsed; her friends had to revive her with smelling salts. The magistrates, trying to preserve whatever dignity still remained in these proceedings, sternly asked her why she had nearly fainted when she saw the prisoner. 'Because he looked so like the Monster who nearly stabbed me!' was the reply. They then asked if she would swear that Lieutenant Hill was the London Monster? No, she certainly would not, since he was not the man! The magistrates were perplexed. 'I said he was *like* the Monster, not that he *was* the Monster,' Jane Read added. Shortly after this moronic statement, she was removed, but to the dismay of anyone hoping to uphold the dignity of the law, a rowdy, garrulous old fish-woman took her place. Like Jane Read, she was more frightened than hurt, but she immediately embarked on a long, meandering tale about how she had met a man with a *strange countenance* in Windmill Street, who spoke to her, and she was so frightened by his *countenance* that she turned back and ran away. On being questioned, she freely admitted that the prisoner's *countenance* did not bear the least similitude to the *countenance* of the man with the *strange countenance*. The magistrate dismissed her, swearing a horrid oath as he did so.

The *World* newspaper's reporter seems to have despaired of the common sense of the female creation after these two witnesses had been examined.[16] He described the proceedings as a complete farce, and warned against these volatile, capricious creatures being allowed to corrupt justice with their unreliable testimony. It was a shocking thing that any histrionic, feather-brained woman had been given the power to denounce someone as the Monster; clearly, these women acted merely out of impulse, and had no concern whatsoever about the consequences of their actions. Anne and Sarah Porter, who also gave testimony at these proceedings, were also in for criticism: 'Two Ladies thought he was like the man, (tho' they afterwards did not think he was the man)'. They described the man who had wounded them as having a brown coat. Lieutenant Hill's lodgings were searched, and the drunken sailor had the misfortune to own a brown coat as well as a blue one. This was considered very damning evidence, and Lieutenant Hill was committed for re-examination to Clerkenwell Prison. The *World*'s misogynous journalist generally painted a dark picture of the proceedings: according to him, it was a common danger for any innocent man to be taken as the Monster and clapped into prison. In fairness to the ladies examined, it should be noted that the other daily papers mentioned little about these things; the *Morning Herald* even stated that the Misses Porter and several other ladies had firmly declared that the prisoner was not the wretch who had wounded them.[17]

On 11 May, Lieutenant Hill was again examined at the Litchfield Street public office. Jane Read was kept in shorter reins this time, and had less scope for her histrionics: she had to declare that although Walter Hill was like the man who had frightened her, she could definitely not swear to his identity. Although Mrs Granger, the lady who owned the house in front of which the Lieutenant had made a riot, objected, Walter Hill was discharged.[18]

Until early May, John Julius Angerstein and his supporters had firmly believed that there was only one Monster. As he was collecting descriptions of other, earlier Monster assaults, quite a few ladies came forward, but it must have struck him as odd that the descriptions of the culprit varied so greatly. Mrs Chippingdale, the lady's maid of Viscountess Malden, had been approached in St James's

Place by a pale, thin, middle-sized man, who made her the most filthy proposals, and then stabbed her in the thigh after she had tried to ignore him. A servant maid, attacked at about the same time, was certain that her assailant had been a tall, stout officer, dressed in his uniform. Miss Eleanor Dodson, who had been wounded in November 1789, was certain that the Monster was very tall, six feet at least, and that he had been elegantly dressed in a suit of black clothes, with extremely long ruffles.[19]

In a new poster, issued on Friday 7 May, the defiant philanthropist reviewed the Monster's latest ravages. On the previous Friday night, the London Monster had attacked a woman in Vigo Lane, dressed in a blue greatcoat with a lighter-coloured coat underneath it, a cocked hat and a cane in his hand. On Saturday night, he had abused and cut a certain Mary Carter, a servant-girl to one of the messengers of the Marquess of Salisbury, in Conduit Street. As she was walking home with some beer for her master, a tall man, dressed in dark brown clothes and with a round hat slapped over his face, had come up to her and insisted upon seeing her home. As she refused, he seized hold of her arm and started to use very indecent language. When she came to her master's door, the Monster 'swore, damn'd, used horrid imprecations, and struck her a violent blow on the side, then looked at her and went away'. Mary Carter had been saved from injury by her strong stays, although her gown had been badly cut. Two days later, on Monday night, she again went out to get beer for her bibulous master, and the same man was waiting for her. He seized hold of her and held her mouth to prevent her from screaming, and then proceeded to cut, or rather claw, the fleshy part of one of her arms with some strange instrument fastened to his hand. She struggled hard and managed to break free; as she reached her home, it was seen that her arm was cut in thirty or forty places, and bled very considerably. Angerstein was again surprised at the Monster's choice of victim: although Mary Carter was just nineteen years old, she was very plain, with a pale and sickly countenance. He was not less surprised by her description of her attacker as very tall, at least six feet in height; some people who had pursued the Monster agreed with this description. A watchman walking up Great George Street had observed a remarkably tall man go by him very fast up the street towards the square, but did not consider this in any way suspicious or connect it with the Monster-hunt.[20]

On Tuesday evening, the Monster continued to wreak havoc. As Jane Hooper, a fair, good-looking servant-girl, was going along Vigo Lane towards Bond Street, a man passed her by and struck her with something on her thigh. Jane Hooper immediately thought of the Monster, and nearly fainted. She reeled into the shop of Mr Trenchard, at No.22 Bond Street, and fell headlong onto the floor. On examination, it was found that she did not have a scratch upon her person, but that all her clothes were cut through. She could not give the least description of the man, though whether this was as a result of her extreme fright, or the consequence of concussion after her heavy fall, is unknown. Later the same evening, the Monster wounded a woman in Marylebone Street. He was wearing a black coat, white stockings, and half-boots; upon one of his stockings was a spot of blood. He also wore a round hat with a high crown, and his hair was frizzed at the sides; in his hand was a fearsome-looking dagger about fourteen inches long. During the attack on Elizabeth Davis the previous Wednesday he had worn a drab-coloured surtout coat and a cocked hat with a cockade. Then on the Thursday morning, as early as eight o'clock, the servant-girl of Mr Vickery, in Cheapside, had been scratched, or rather clawed, by a sharp instrument fastened to the hand of a very short, shabbily dressed man, who had immediately gone away. His diabolical instrument appeared to have at least five prongs or blades.[21]

To digest this highly conflicting mass of evidence would have been a match for Sherlock Holmes himself. John Julius Angerstein probably regretted that he had ever meddled in the Monster business, but it was now too late for him to withdraw. The offer of a reward only seemed to have whetted the Monster's appetite for novel sanguinary outrages. Some imaginative Monster-hunters had brought forth the theory that this fiend in human form was always wearing several coats and surtouts, one over the other, as to be able to discard one of them at will, in order to avoid suspicion. He also had a very large wardrobe of hats, waistcoats and other accessories, in order to disguise his appearance; from this fact, it was apparent that he must be not only a criminal mastermind, but also a gentleman of considerable means. It was speculated that the Monster sometimes wore shoes with very high, stilt-like heels as to appear very tall, and that he possessed a collection of wigs and theatrical props, which he used to alter his appearance. A journalist in *The Times* reminded the public that the actor Charles Price had used seven sorts of false noses, and that the Monster probably did too: 'we would advise all those hardy English Hercules's who are determined to rid London of such a wretch, to pull him hard by the nose!'[22] Mr Angerstein eschewed such idle speculation, however: in his poster of 7 May, he regretfully spoke out that there was not just one Monster, but that 'there is great Reason to fear that more than *ONE of those WRETCHES* infest the Streets'. At least four or five very differing descriptions had been given by the presumed Monster victims, varying with regard to stature, complexion and hair colour, not counting the multiple descriptions of his clothes. He also concluded that 'these unnatural men, these MONSTERS, certainly have some mode of communicating with each other: which evidently appears from the exact similarity of their attacks, as well as from the savage pleasure and delight each of them seems to enjoy in the terror, pain, and distress of the fair unfortunate victims whom they wound.'[23] Angerstein freely admitted that his reward had not yet served its purpose: the cunning and sagacity of the Monsters had enabled them to evade not only the regular police, but also the multitude of vigilantes aroused by the offer of a reward. This was no reason for withdrawing the reward, however, since it had at least served to thoroughly alert the Londoners to the danger that threatened the female inhabitants of the metropolis, who were at the mercy of a ruthless gang of Monsters. In a postscript to his poster, Angerstein added another idea: the Monster must live in a house where the servants could not read; otherwise

Pall-Mall, 7th May, 1790.

Mr. ANGERSTEIN
Informs the Public,

THAT from the Information he has received of the **PERSON** who since
Friday laft, has affaulted and wounded feveral Women, there is great
Reafon to fear that more than *ONE of thofe WRETCHES* infeft the Streets;
it is therefore thought Neceffary to give the following Defcription of *ONE*
who, within this **Week**, has committed many Acts of *Cruelty* upon Women.

HE is generally defcribed to be a Perfon upwards of fix Feet high, thin
made, and thin vifaged; full Eyes, a large Nofe, and is marked with the
Small-pox on his Cheek Bones. On *Friday Night* laft, when he affaulted a
Woman in *Vigo Lane*, he was dreffed in a blue great Coat, with a light
coloured Coat under it; **light coloured Waiftcoat**; cocked Hat; and had a
Stick in his Hand. On *Saturday Night* and *Monday Night* laft, when he
wounded a young Woman in *Conduit Street*, he was dreffed in dark brown
Clothes, and wore a round Hat flapped over his Face. On *Tuefday Evening*, between feven and eight o'Clock, when he wounded a Woman in *Marybone Street*,
he wore a black Coat, white Stockings, and half Boots; and upon one of his
Stockings was a Spot of **Blood**; a round Hat with a high Crown; his Hair
platted behind, and frizzed at the Sides; at this Time he had a DAGGER
about fourteen Inches long. And on *Wednefday Night*, when he wounded a
poor Woman in *Holborn*, he wore a drab coloured furtout Coat, which reached
juft below his Knees; ftriped Waiftcoat; white Stockings; a cocked Hat, with
a high Brim, and a Cockade; his Hair frizzed at the Sides, in a Bufh;
platted and turned up behind; and had a Nofegay in his Hand.

PRINTED BY J. MOORE, No. 134, DRURY-LANE.

Mr Angerstein's second Monster poster, issued on 7 May 1790.

he would have been captured long ago, since all London was out
looking for him. All tradesmen's servants and baker's boys were
urged to spread the word about this fiend in human shape to the
illiterate servant-girls they visited; an extra £20 was offered if this
information would lead to the apprehension of the Monster.

The same day Mr Angerstein's new poster was pasted on the
London walls, several inhabitants of St Pancras held an emergency
meeting at the Percy coffee-house. It was clear to them that the
watchmen were wholly unable to deal with the threat posed by the
Monsters, and fifteen gentlemen undertook to nightly patrol the
streets of the south division of St Pancras, between half an hour

before sunset and eleven o'clock at night; they evidently presumed that any lady who ventured out after that time was not worth protecting. A subscription was taken up for the capture of the Monster, and a set of 'Regulations tending to Female Safety and the Public Peace' drawn up. On 7 May they had a poster of their own printed and pasted up, with the heading 'Whereas an Attack has been made by a MONSTER upon a YOUNG WOMAN', to recruit new vigilantes and subscribers.[24] Some newspaper writers applauded this venture, and urged that this auxiliary anti-Monster police force should be extended to patrol the entire metropolis. Rather than the elderly, stentorian watchmen, whose habit of calling out the time at regular intervals gave the criminals an excellent idea of what part of their beat was safe to operate in, they envisioned a force of active young men, armed to the teeth, dressed in a special uniform and wearing padded shoes for stalking the Monster more effectively.

5

MONSTER-MANIA

Good Angerstein,
Be not so keen,
For WOMEN still will roam:—
Nor wounds nor death,
'Till stopp'd their breath—
Can keep our WIVES at HOME.

> A deplorable poem by 'Benedict' in the *World*
> newspaper, 17 June 1790.

In mid-May, London was in a turmoil. In the *Oracle* newspaper, yet another journalist was complaining about the criminal supineness of the authorities in tackling the Monster or Monsters. The terror caused by the mysterious assailant was now such that women hardly dared to venture outdoors after dark:

> It is really distressing to walk our streets towards evening. Every woman we meet regards us with distrust, shrinks sideling from our touch, and expects a poignard to pierce what gallantry and manhood consider as sacred...[1]

Lady Newdigate wrote to her husband that 'I shall take care & not walk ye streets that you may not find me dead or under ye surgeons hands. The stories in ye papers of this horrid Woman Hater are not exaggerated. Not a night passes that some female is not dreadfully wounded'. The sprightly noblewoman then goes on to describe the dastardly attack on 'Lady Howe's own Woman', who had seen the Monster following her and desperately rung the bell at Lord Howe's house in Grafton Street, but the porter had not been in the hall to let her in. The Monster 'threw her down upon ye steps, kick'd & punch'd her till she fainted away & then stab'd her in ye thigh. In this Condition she was found when ye Door was open'd'. Another Monster victim was but slightly wounded, since the Monster's dagger had gone through a thick bundle of muslins in her pocket. Lady Newdigate concludes by stating that 'A Premium of 100 Guineas is offer'd and subscrib'd but nobody can lay hold of him'.[2]

John Julius Angerstein himself gave a similar account.[3] His reward had brought no other result than that several innocent people had been arrested, and sometimes beaten up by vigilantes, before being hauled off to Bow Street. In spite of the large posters headed 'The MONSTER' pasted up at the corner of every street all over the metropolis, new accounts of fresh victims of the Monster appeared almost every day. Mr Angerstein's eloquent description of the state of London in May 1790 deserves to be quoted verbatim:

> The magistrates were much harassed; all the town, and especially the women were exceedingly alarmed; and the whole business appeared the more extraordinary and astonishing, as every day brought fresh accounts of new victims to the horrid attacks of these ruffians, notwithstanding the bills offering high rewards for their apprehension were pasted up at every corner of every street all over the metropolis.
>
> It became dangerous for a man even to walk along the streets alone, as merely calling or pointing out some person as THE MONSTER, to the people passing, was sufficient to endanger his life; and many were robbed, and extremely abused, by this means.

No man of gallantry dared to approach a lady in the streets after dark, for fear of alarming her susceptible nature.

There was a total suspension of all street amours.

The gentle salutations and the gay blandishments of the *peripathetic* beauties, the soft, easy, accommodating fair ones, were all over; and gloomy jealousy and dark distrust appeared on every female brow.

The whole order of things was changed. It was not safe for a gentleman to walk the streets, unless under the *protection* of a lady.

The German naturalist Georg Forster was in London at the height of the Monster-mania, and in his diary he left an interesting sketch, dated 12 May 1790.[4] For the past four weeks, all London had been talking about the Monster, and Forster recorded that:

> The newspapers are full of him; the playwrights entertain audiences with his exploits from the stage; the ladies are afraid of him; the mob gives every pedestrian a keen look in case he is the Monster; all the walls are covered with posters advertising a reward for the apprehension of the Monster; a fund has been opened to finance the hunt; Mrs Smith, a society lady, has shot him with a pistol behind the ear; he disguises himself, goes about in various different guises, wounding beautiful women with specially invented instruments, with hooks hidden in bouquets of flowers, with knitting pins, etc.

There were rumours, he stated, that the Monster or Monsters, these tigers lusting for the blood of women, were intent on destroying the entire female sex, or at least the beautiful portion of it. There were also rumours that the Monster was an evil spirit, who could make himself invisible to evade detection, that he was a master of disguise, who could change his appearance at will, or that he was an insane nobleman who had vowed to maim every beautiful woman in London. The German J. W. von Archenholtz, another resident of London, was well aware that some ribald prints tried to make fun of the monster-business; nevertheless, he asserted that such a miscreant really did exist, since he had personally spoken to some of the ladies he had assaulted; their descriptions of his language and conduct were 'sufficient to impress the most callous mind with horror!'[5]

There were, at this time, anti-Monster vigilante associations in both Westminster and St Pancras, but all they had accomplished was to arrest several innocent people. The Prince of Wales had himself vowed to detect and expose the identity of the London Monster; whether he actually made any attempt to do so is unknown. Another appeal was made to the Knights of the Order of the Bath, since these crusty Knights were actually bound by their oath to defend all women and maidens.[6] There were frequent calls for a special Monster police force to be recruited, to patrol all the streets of London between seven and eleven o'clock in the evenings. The ladies did not trust even these well-organised guardians, nor had they any faith in the Runners or watchmen. It is recorded that, at the height of the Monster-mania, several ladies instead turned to the London braziers for protection against the Monster: they ordered copper cuirasses or petticoats to be fitted, to shield them against his darting rapier.[7] Less financially well-endowed ladies had to be content with having cork-rumps, or even a large porridge pot, fitted underneath their voluminous clothing, to protect their precious *derrières* against the Monster's various cutting implements.[8] At this time, the Westminster Forum debating society regularly arranged debates on the most interesting topics of the day. A committee of ladies had, for some time, tried to arrange a question to be put concerning the London Monster, but only after the intervention of a public character of renown, who was an advocate for the abolition of slavery, could they come up with an atrocity that paralleled those of the Monster. The May 1790 question was: 'Who is the Greater Disgrace to Humanity, the Monster, who has lately cut so many women in London, or the Slave-trading Wretches, who drag the Unhappy Female African from her family and native country?' The outcome of this singular debate is not known, but considering the prevailing mood in London, anyone backing the

Monster would probably have the odds in his favour. It is known, however, that there were several speakers, and a full house including many Monster-hunters, who sought for novel clues as to his identity; Monster victims, who basked in the glory of having been subject of the Monster's attentions; and supporters of Distressed Female Africans.[9]

The Monster-mania had some decidedly strange side effects when the criminal element in London had assessed the situation, and made plans to capitalise. On 10 May, a gang of pickpockets attacked a wealthy gentleman near Holborn.[10] They hustled him and took his watch, money and hat, but the robbed man showed some spirit, and attempted to run after them and give the alarm. The pickpockets then called out 'It's the Monster, he has just cut a woman!' and pointed at their victim. This dastardly plan was a brilliant success: the pickpockets got clean away, and the gentleman had to run helter-skelter along the London streets, pursued by an ever-growing mob of roughs and toughs, who shouted 'The Monster! The Monster!' Finally, they caught him after a furious chase: he was knocked down, pummelled and jumped on, and surrounded by a howling mob of several hundred people. He would probably have lost his life, had not some gentlemen of his acquaintance seen the bruised, bloody wretch being manhandled in the street. They resolutely broke into the mob and rescued him, dragging his limp body into the Gray's Inn coffee-house. The mob was soon reinforced by other amateur monster-hunters, however, and their assessment of the situation was that the Monster's wealthy accomplices had rescued him from justice. The furious mob, which now numbered nearly a thousand, charged the coffee-house, but the gentlemen managed to hail a hackney coach and escaped to the Brown Bear, a well-known public house situated just opposite the public-office in Bow Street. The mob followed, and attacked the pub. They broke its every window, yelling and cursing the meanwhile. The situation was getting increasingly desperate, but at nine o'clock in the evening, after the siege of the Brown Bear had been going on for some hours, the gentleman's gallant saviours managed to convey him, in disguise, to the Bow Street public office. The mob was still in the street outside, and would have massacred him had they seen him. Sir Sampson Wright lamented that the perpetrators of the original, daring assault and robbery were to go unpunished, but he was at least able to give the gentleman protection against the mob outside, until it had dispersed.

Other low-life elements also benefited from the Monster-mania. At least one man was convicted of calling out 'The Monster!' as an enemy went by, to enjoy seeing him beaten and pummelled by the street mob. In early May, a drunken gentleman returning from an ale-house had his pockets picked and was pushed into the gutter by a gang of thieves. They then called out 'The Monster!' and alerted a furious mob, from which the gentleman barely escaped alive. A braggart who called himself Mr Jon Pieters reported to the *World* newspaper on 14 May that his sister-in-law had been attacked by the Monster and that she had shot him in the neck with one of Mr Pieters' own pistols. This afterwards proved to be a lie, published under an assumed name.[11] On 17 May, a certain Mr Heather was crossing Tower Hill at about nine in the evening, when he observed a well-dressed woman lying on the ground. Her gown and apron were bloodstained, and she said that a very tall man had just wounded her with some sharp instrument, and begged his assistance to get her to a coach waiting nearby, in the Minories. After she had been driven off in this vehicle, the gallant and foolish Mr Heather found, to his dismay, that she had picked his pockets of his watch and three guineas.[12]

In spite of the Monster-mania, the young gallants still went strolling about the London streets, ogling the ladies. But the ladies of easy virtue, formerly so accommodating, now shrank with terror at their approach. Some clever young spark thought of a solution. He formed a club called the 'No Monster' club, encompassing himself and several of his friends who were above suspicion of being the Monster. They all wore a cardboard badge with the text 'No Monster' on the lapels of their coats, and were soon seen sauntering about Oxford Street. Whether this club had any success is unknown, but the newspapers derided this latest ludicrous fad in the Monster-mania. The *St James's Gazette* wrote ponderously that 'The distressed Beauties of Great-Britain present their grateful compliments to *No Monster*, and return him many thanks for reminding them of those noble and valorous knights who are sworn to defend all maidens and widows in want of protection ...' It was also deplored that the 'No Monster' club did not, through cowardice or 'want of chivalry', have as its aim to actually capture this elusive criminal.[13]

At Astley's Theatre, a new theatrical piece called *The Monster* had been getting full houses since late April; it was a full-scale re-adaptation of the entire career of the London Monster, with suit-able musical interludes. Pretty actresses had their buttocks pricked by his rapiers, and their noses wounded by his fiendish nosegay. The final song always produced unbounded applause:

> *When the Monster is taken in the fact,*
> *We'll have him tried by the Coventry Act,*
> *The Black Act,*
> *The Coventry Act!*[14]

On one instance, an intoxicated Irish sailor jumped out of the gallery, with a stout oak stick in his hand, and dashed forward to give the actor playing the Monster's part a good drubbing! This would definitely have happened, had not the stage personnel dropped the curtain hastily.[15] The only way the Drury Lane Theatre could compete with this monstrous hit was to produce a Monster entertainment of its own. On 11 May, a monologue entitled *The Monster Discovered* had its opening night, but it failed to attain the popularity of Astley's play.[16]

In early May, there was much newspaper interest in the tragic story of Miss Barrs, 'a very fine girl, daughter to a Fruiterer in Great Mary-le-bone-street', who had twice been cut by the Monster.[17] On Sunday 2 May, a man came up and talked to her in the most obscene manner, and later stabbed her in the thigh. Not content with this outrage, he came back the next day and cut her in the other thigh. According to the *World* newspaper, the wounded girl was confined to her bed. She became a celebrity for a few heady days, and the fruiterer's shop was busier than ever, since it had become a popular pastime for the well-to-do Londoners to visit the Monster's latest victim. The ladies of fashion heard her tale of woe with a *frisson* of horror: would they themselves be the next victim of this fiend in human shape? The bloods and gallants ogled the fair sufferer with many appreciative comments about the Monster's great taste in choosing his victims. The *World* of 14 May could report, however, that 'the account of Miss B. of Marylebon-street, which appeared in all the Newspapers, having been twice wounded by the *Monster*' was a complete fabrication. The Select Vestry of Marylebone Parish had inquired into the matter, since some kind-hearted parishioners had appealed for the injured Miss Barrs to obtain a *douceur* from the said Parish. A commission led by the Duke of Portland and Lord Somers had inquired into the circumstances, and one particular gentleman immediately suspected a fraud. Miss Barrs was sent for by this commission, and her cut clothes, and even her slight wound in the calf, were closely examined. Although the cut in her petticoat and stockings was three inches long, her wound was just one inch long, and its appearance would suggest that she had scratched herself, rather than having been injured by some sharp instrument. Her account of the incidents when she had been cut was equivocal and contradictory, and the Select Vestry 'was of but one opinion, namely that SHE WAS AN IMPOSTOR'. They could only presume that her purpose in this fraud had been to procure compassion and money from the philanthropists engaged in the monster-hunt.[18] The enterprising Miss Barrs was evidently not alone in trying this caper. The *World* of 15 May condemned this disgraceful business with the trenchant words 'Girls pretending to be maimed, who never were touched, are new kinds of MONSTERS, that should be as severely punished as the real one, who gave occasion to the reward!'[19]

The Times used the Barrs story to launch a frontal attack on the Monster-mania that was rampant throughout London. The Monster was just a pickpocket fiction, the newspaper writer claimed, since the light-fingered brigade had invented various sharp instruments to cut ladies pockets and steal their contents. These instruments were hidden in sticks, nosegays and other implements to facilitate their plans of plunder. Some pickpockets were maladroit in handling these weapons and cut not only the pocket, but also the skin of its owner; this was the true origin of the Monster legend, which had put London in such turmoil. The journalist went on to claim that no woman had ever been seriously injured by the Monster. At a recent meeting of the Companies of Surgeons and Apothecaries, the Monster had been one of the prevailing topics of conversation. When it was asked how many of those present had ever attended a Monster victim, the answer was 'Not one!' although many distinguished surgeons were present.[20] It had been proven by repeated testimonies, the journalist claimed, that several women had fraudulently reported themselves to be wounded by the Monster, in hope of sharing Mr Angerstein's reward. The public had been unnecessarily alarmed by the Monster-mania that had ensued, and the reporter saw it as his public duty to point out the frauds of Miss Barrs and others, in order to lessen the fears of the public, and the Ladies in particular. Ending the article in a light-hearted vein, the newspaper man presumed that Miss Barrs had been scheming to attract customers to her father's shop, but 'such is the force of truth, that the flimsy veil of deceit, is easily seen through'. Indeed, 'the serpent has taken *another* form to tempt mankind to eat an *apple*! If it was not too much like *fun*, we might be induced to say, she has really *Barred* the doors against all customers!'[21]

In mid-May there had been several dubious attacks on women, few of them as convincing as the earlier outrages. On 11 May, a lady had her clothes cut as she passed by the Bank, and the Monster, aware that he was being pursued, turned into the Stock Exchange, where he quickly eluded detection.[22] Some days later, there was a great outcry near St Bride's Church, after a man in the dress of a beggar, who had previously knocked and rang at several doors nearby, had been captured after attempting to stab a woman. He turned out to be an imbecile, a maimed sailor, incapable of articulate speech.[23] Mary Fisher, the wife of a coal meter, who kept a cook's shop in Pye Street, was described as 'a very plain, poor, middle-sized old woman, turned of forty, and very meanly dressed'.[24] As she was walking past Charing Cross about eleven o'clock at night, with a basket of eggs under one arm and a piece of beef under the other, she saw three men coming towards her. She kept out of their way, fearing that they would break her eggs just for the fun of it, but one of them instead suddenly struck her in the face with some sharp instrument he had in his hand, and knocked her down. Her face was badly cut, but she still struggled to her feet to curse her assailants; one of them retraced his steps and knocked her down again; the three 'gentlemen' then gave a loud laugh and made off. Four days later, Mrs Smyth, the very first Monster victim, who had accused William Tuffing, was again attacked.[25] As she was returning from Covent Garden market with her maid, three well-dressed gentlemen came up to her when she was looking at the goods in a shop window. The unsuspecting Mrs Smyth received a blow in the face, and the three men laughed and walked away. Mrs Smyth described the main culprit as a man about forty years old, tall, stout and full-faced, with abundant fair hair like a wig, and a round hat. His two companions appeared smaller and younger. A rather more typical Monster outrage was described a week later: a beautiful girl passing along the Pall Mall in the evening was stabbed several times, and cut under the chin in a dangerous manner by the Monster's nosegay.[26]

There was much uproar in town, and several spurious cases in the newspapers. Even the friends of Mr Angerstein sometimes joked and bantered him very freely on his active involvement in the Monster-business, and told him that they were chasing a mere phantom.[27] A reporter writing in the St James's Gazette confessed that he was 'a little *sceptical* with respect to the many reports of the

Cutting Monster or *Monsters'*. He suspected that malice and mischief had combined to build up this formidable hysteria, and that the Monster-mania had resulted from the actions of a few blundering pickpockets.[28] A journalist in the *Public Ledger* newspaper went even further.[29] He asserted that there did not exist, and never had existed, a London Monster. The entire affair was the result of a few ladies being slightly wounded by pickpockets trying to cut open their pockets with sharp instruments: 'there is nothing *monstrous* here, unless the monstrous impudence of a pickpocket'. The journalist saw it as his duty to free London from the Monster, this ideal animal who had for so long been allowed to scare women and children. The only people to have anything to gain from this fiction gaining universal credence were the pickpockets and the married men of London. The former could easily elude pursuit by calling out 'The Monster!' and pointing at their victim; the latter wanted to keep their wives at home, and the Monster provided them with an excellent excuse. Even Georg Forster lost faith in the Monster, as evidenced by his diary entry:

> the Monster is nothing more nor less than a phantom invented to amuse the bored inhabitants of London town. A pickpocket who may have learnt to turn pockets inside out and empty them with the aid of an instrument, might perhaps have injured a woman, while picking her pocket in this manner; and this insignificant incident created the story of a Monster enraged with feminine beauty.[30]

John Julius Angerstein was adamant, however, and he gathered the entire company of wounded ladies to give testimony to the *Public Ledger* a few days after the offending article appeared. The editor was forced to admit that many ladies had indeed been attacked in circumstances indicating that there was no question of robbing them or cutting their pockets. In two mealy-mouthed apologies to Mr Angerstein and the wounded ladies, the *Public Ledger* had to admit that the Monster, or Monsters, did exist, and that they had certainly attacked several ladies in circumstances indicating that the aim was not to cut their pockets or to rob them.[31] But Angerstein was taken to task by another audacious journalist, who held forth about his own pet theories about the Monster-hunt in the *Gazetteer* newspaper.[32] Mr Angerstein had been a fool, he wrote, to issue such a high reward for the arrest of the Monster. By 17 May, at least thirty innocent men had been apprehended and charged with being this fiend in human form, accused by avaricious amateur Monster-hunters, keen to get their hands on the reward. All that his untimely interference had achieved was to slow down the detective work of the magistrates of Bow Street; the journalist asserted that if these worthies had been allowed to work undisturbed by monster-hunters and crazy vigilantes, the Bow Street police would have captured the Monster in two days.

Much of Angerstein's personal prestige was invested in the Monster-hunt, and he must have been aware that some people in London society, like Horace Walpole, Mrs Thrale and their friends at Strawberry Hill, openly ridiculed his exertions as a crimefighter. Mrs Thrale wrote in her diary that:

> all this Spring a man has gone about London Streets in dark Evenings stabbing pretty girls if he could catch one walking alone; to which Enormity was added by the perpetrator some expressions of a peculiar Cast; cruel, indecent & undeserved. The Offence was first complained of, & then taken up by a rich Merchant John Julius Angerstein of Pallmall, who offered a large reward for the fellow's discovery. This brought forward our natural Spirit of Derision, & the Ladies' Champion became a subject of Ridicule to all the Merry Fellows, – & most of all, to those who visited at Strawberry Hill whence all the Pasquinades came forth to laugh, & sett the whole town a'laughing at poor Angerstein, whose Quixotism was repre-sented on the Summer stages of London with great effect.[33]

In May 1790, after the attack on the British trading station at Nootka Sound, the Royal Navy began to arm in expectation of a war with Spain. Throughout this month, press gangs scoured the streets to recruit sailors, their main method of persuasion being strong bludgeons, and many a London rough woke up with a headache lying in a seaman's hammock on the lower deck of a ship of the line. According to Angerstein, 'a hot press, which continued for many days and nights, cleared the town of disorderly and suspected characters.'[34] The cessation of the Monster's activities in late May could thus be seen as an indication that he had been hauled on board a man-of-war, and that he was now a sailor, on his way to wreak havoc among the Spanish señoritas. One of the sceptical *Times* journalists even went as far as to query 'Where is the MONSTER? Has the Spanish war destroyed him, or Miss *Barrs* put him to flight? – or is he, as a *wonder* of the day, – with Stone Eater, Learned Pig, Muny Begum, Polish Dwarf, Irish Giant, and Cock-Lane Ghost, gone forever to sleep?'[35] Mr Angerstein and the other Monster-hunters considered it too early to celebrate, however: this clever master-criminal was probably hiding from the press gangs in some rookery, ready to resume his reign of terror as soon as the press had abated. In early June, they had to admit that the Monster was no longer an active threat: there had been no typical attacks on women since early May. The alarm was still up, however, and any nervous lady frightened by a threatening drunk or ugly beggar was likely to cry out 'The Monster!' The consequences of this could be dire, as shown by one newspaper report: on the evening of 4 June, a drunken young man was seized by some Holborn Monster-hunters after an outcry had been made. The vigilantes brought him before the Bow Street magistrates, but he made a good account of himself and did not resemble the original description of the Monster. Sir Sampson Wright could not let him leave the public-office, however, since a large and furious mob had gathered outside, and he feared that they might tear the poor man to pieces.[36]

In early June, a man had been accused of being the Monster, and kept all night in the watch-house of the parish of St Margaret, Westminster. This individual had picked up a girl in the street and taken her to a public house. He then invited her to smell a large artificial nosegay he was carrying, but as she took hold of it, she felt something prick her hand. She went away and told some of her friends, and they concluded that he must have been the Monster, with a dagger in his nosegay ready to prick her delicate little nose when she smelt it. Her friends alerted the watchmen, who went back to the public house, where the man was still sitting waiting for his female acquaintance, and they took him into custody. The next day, the man with the artificial nosegay was interrogated, but he was able to show, to their satisfaction, that the girl had in fact pricked her hand with the wire used to bind the artificial flowers together, and the man was discharged.[37] At about the same time, the pseudonymous Humphrey Henpeck wrote a joking letter to the *Diary* newspaper, claiming that the Monster-mania was the result of several husbands in London Westminster making up a plot to keep their wives at home. The idea of a bloodthirsty party of Monsters stalking the streets was enough to effect this purpose, but the gentlemen had since relented, since the domestic ill-humour of their wives had proved too much for them, and they now asserted and declared that there was no such thing as a London Monster.[38]

The newspapers kept on publishing doubtful instances of Monster activity in the metropolis, but often with ribald and incredulous editorial commentary. The most newsworthy story concerned Eglantine Lady Wallace, the sister of the Duchess of Gordon.[39] She was an eccentric lady playwright and poetess, who had, a few months earlier, divorced her husband on account of his cruelty. Lady Wallace's biographer describes her as 'a boisterous hoyden in her youth, and a woman of violent temper in her maturer years', and she was in fact herself summoned at least twice for assaulting people who had annoyed her. In 1788, her play *The Ton* was enacted at the Covent Garden Theatre, but the booing of the audience was so loud that the actors could barely be heard; after a number of bottles and heavy missiles had landed on the stage, the entire party of thespians were put to flight. In 1789, Lady Wallace left London in disgust when her play *The Whim* had been prohibited by the censor, and went to Paris, where she was arrested as an English agent and narrowly escaped with her life. On 27 May 1790, Lady Wallace made a great

outcry: the Monster had come up to her carriage and paid her compliments, and had afterwards tried to enter the carriage with evil
intent. Had her friend Captain Monroe not interceded, and put the
Monster to flight, she would have joined the ranks of Anne Porter
and the other wounded beauties. From now on, she would always
keep a brace of pocket pistols with her. *The Times* journalist was
unimpressed, however. He suggested that the presumed attacker
must have been a disappointed patron of the theatre, who had
observed her sitting in the carriage looking through some *old* books
to find *new* jokes for her plays. Even more insultingly, he concluded
that 'The Monster at last appears, but leaves cherry-cheeked cham-
bermaids for Lady Wallace, a *monstrous* beauty'.

Another remarkable story, occurring at about the same time, was
that of 'Fat Phillis'. Two young gentlemen, Viscount Netterville and
his brother the Hon. Mr Cuffe, had gone to the theatre, where a
very disreputable character, a certain Charley Jones, alias Vaughan,
alias Fat Phillis, whooped, halloed, and made every sign of being
a very close acquaintance of the confused Mr Cuffe, who claimed
that he had never seen him before. 'Fat Phillis', who was dressed
in female attire, then pressed against Mr Cuffe in an indecent
manner several times, to the great embarrassment of the two
prudish young gentlemen, who finally retired from their seats in
confusion. 'Fat Phillis' followed them out into the street, with his
companion George Smith and a young lad in tow. Here, he collared
Mr Cuffe and threatened to call the watch, since he was certain
that Mr Cuffe had made a very improper proposal to the lad, and
that an unnatural offence had been intended. Lord Netterville and
Mr Cuffe were non-plussed, but when 'Fat Phillis' suggested that
they should pay him a certain fee to avoid being prosecuted, they
made a defiant bluster and refused. The dangerous transvestite then
threatened to call out 'The Monster!' and set the mob on the two
gentlemen! At this dire threat, the brothers tore away, trying to
reach Netterville's house nearby. Just outside the house, Mr Cuffe
made a defiant gesture, and was promptly knocked down, pummelled, and jumped on by 'Fat Phillis'. Lord Netterville managed to

drag his brother's limp body indoors, and immediately sent servants to the Bow Street public office to report this outrage to the authorities. Runner Moses Murrant promptly appeared, and made a prompt arrest of 'Fat Phillis' and his two accomplices, to the relief of Lord Netterville and poor Mr Cuffe. When the gang were brought before Sir Sampson Wright, it was recorded that 'Charley Jones, alias Vaughan, is known to the Officers of this Police. He continually frequents Masquerades, and always goes in a Female Habit. He, as well as his companion, are extremely effeminate, and Vaughan was much painted'.[40]

In 1790, there was a flourishing market for satirical prints dealing with famous or notorious people, or with sensational recent events.[41] The Monster-mania naturally inspired several popular prints, the earliest of which was Isaac Cruikshanks' *The Monster Cutting a Lady*, issued on 1 May. The image of the Monster in this print was based on a drawing by one of his victims, and it had been approved by two other wounded ladies. A lady holding a large muff is attacked by the Monster, who grabs her by the right arm and cuts her behind several times; the slits in her dress are stained with blood. Behind her is a street door in Pall Mall marked 'Angersteein', and one of the Monster reward handbills can be seen pasted on the house wall. Thus the purpose of this caricature was not only to assist in the Monster-hunt, but also to make fun of Mr Angerstein by implying that in spite of his reward, the Monster had cut one of his victims just by his front door. The second compartment in this print shows a half-naked lady standing before a kneeling brazier, who is hammering together the back seams of a short copper petticoat. A placard on the wall reads: 'Ladies Bottoms covered on the most Reasonable Terms and kept in repair by the year by Anti:Monster.' In the shop window are three copper petticoats of increasing size, intended, in turn, for young ladies of fifteen, for ladies of thirty, and for very fat ladies. The ribald note struck by this lewd image was improved upon by other caricaturists. In James Gillray's *The Monster disappointed of his Afternoon Luncheon, or Porridge Potts preferable to Cork Rumps*, which was issued

77

on 10 May, the Monster is depicted as an ogre, who lifts up a shapely young lady. He roars in dismay when he sees that her buttocks are protected by a round shallow pot. In another version of this print the pot was erased, and the Monster can be seen ready to plunge his knife and fork into the lady's exposed naked buttocks.

Six days later, on 16 May, the anonymous print *Old Maids Dreaming of the Monster* was published. Two old maids dream of the Monster, since if he attacks them, this will be ample proof that they are still young and attractive, as it was the Monster's habit to attack only fashionable, beautiful young women. The Monster suddenly appears in the guise of a grotesque, three-headed ogre, with the Devil seated on the middle head. One of the old maids hastily tries to get out of bed, but steps in the chamber-pot by mistake. Two days later the similarly anonymous print *Glaucus and Scylla, or The Monster in Full Cry*, appeared. The immensely fat Miss Jeffries, one of the Queen's ladies-in-waiting, is pursued by the Monster in the shape of George Hanger, one of the cronies of the Prince of Wales. He is depicted with a tail and clawed, deformed legs, and aims to prick her buttocks with a long spike attached to the end of his bludgeon. A man lying on the ground tries to pull him back by the tail, and William Pitt races up to the right, armed with a warming pan, to save her honour from this monstrous assailant. In the background can be seen one of the posters of the St Pancras Monster Patrol, beginning 'Whereas an attack was made on a young lady of this parish by a MONSTER…'

On 20 May, James Gillray's *Swearing to the Cutting Monster, or a Scene in Bow Street*, was published. This ribald print shows one of the wounded ladies pulling her skirts over her head and revealing all to the Bow Street magistrates. Gillray was actually a neighbour of the Misses Porter in St James's Street, and the print was probably inspired by the newspaper reports of them and other Monster victims giving evidence at Bow Street. Sir Sampson Wright, in his hat and spectacles, takes a closer look at the lady's posterior; the men on either sides of him are William Addington and Richard Bond. The Monster at the dock bears a marked resemblance to the

controversial politician Charles James Fox. On 29 May, the anonymous print *The Monster Detected* was published in the midst of the
Monster-mania. The verses relate that a certain Devil was allowed
to come to earth on condition that he married a beautiful virgin.
To test virginity:

> *A little Dagger with a Tube, was fill'd*
> *With Juice of Plants, which such a Liquor yield*
> *That when to Womans velvet flesh apply'd*
> *It makes no Entrance if a Maid is try'd.*

The ribald conclusion is that the great scarcity of virgins in
London makes it necessary for the Devil to stab dozens of women,
thus giving rise to the Monster-mania.

On 5 June, another Monster poster made its appearance on the
London walls. It very much resembled those of Mr Angerstein, but
unlike them, it positively identified the Monster as Captain Philip
Thicknesse, an elderly controversialist. Thicknesse had libelled and
blackmailed many people during his lengthy career, and numerous
enemies were eager for revenge. Thicknesse himself suspected a
certain Captain John Crookshanks for libelling him as the
Monster. They were old enemies: after Thicknesse had accused the
Captain of cowardice, and called him 'a broken, deaf, and lame Sea-
Duck', the eighty-two-year-old Captain had challenged him to a
duel, but Thicknesse had declined to fight him. As a revenge,
Crookshanks had given libellous information about Thicknesse
to the caricaturist James Gillray, and had the faked Monster
posters pasted up all over town.[42] Philip Thicknesse was fuming
with rage. He himself commissioned another caricature, entitled
The Monstrous Assassin, or the Coward turn'd Bill Sticker. It depicts the
lame old Captain as he supervises the bill-pasting operation, with
the caption 'This is not the Captain *Straitshanks* who was Broke for
Cowardice, & who afterwards Offered to Enter into the French
Service, & who has kept his wife and two children upon 13 pounds
a year in Wales till the youngest child is 44 years of age'.[43]

6

The Arrest

OF

RHYNWICK WILLIAMS

Good Angerstein
Is not too keen;
For women ought to roam
At perfect ease,
Where'er they please
And Monsters keep at home.

'An Answer to the Monster', published in the
Gazetteer, 24 June 1790

After she had eaten her evening meal on Sunday 13 June, Miss Anne Porter wanted to take a walk in St James's Park. She was accompanied by her mother, two of her sisters and the twenty-year-old fishmonger John Henry Coleman. The latter individual, evidently an admirer of Miss Porter, had his shop in Gray's Inn Passage. In *Bailey's London Dictionary* of 1790, he styled himself 'Fishmonger to the Prince of Wales'; one would suppose that the Prince's penchant for consuming vast amounts of oysters and devilled whitebait must have done his business much good.

As the Porter family group strolled along, the topic of conversation turned, not surprisingly, to the Monster and his cowardly assault on the Misses Porter. Ann Porter declared that just a week earlier, she had actually seen the Monster again, but her fright in observing this figure of dread had deprived her of the power of acting rationally and calling out that he was the man all London was seeking. The Monster had stood outside her window grimacing at her, and making use of his customary foul-mouthed pleasantries, before Sarah Porter observed him and alerted some servants. They ran off after the man, but he had easily dodged these bumbling pursuers, and escaped into some narrow alleys nearby. John Coleman earnestly begged the Misses that, if any of them set eyes on the Monster in the passing crowd, they should immediately point him out. A few minutes later, Ann Porter was seen to stagger and to call out, with much agitation, 'There he is – the *Wretch*!' It then appeared that she fainted, but John Coleman held her limp form and pulled her towards a group of people, imploring her to point out the Monster. With her last reserve of energy, she did so, saying, 'That's him, in blue and buff!' before falling into the arms of her sisters, like a heroine in one of the novels of Mrs Radcliffe.[1]

John Coleman, at first, did nothing at all. Considering the prevailing mood in London, a man of energy would have brought the man down with a rugby tackle before the admiring eyes of the Misses Porter, singing out 'Tally-ho! The Monster!' Like the manly, forthright hero of one of the gothic novels he must have read, he would then have basked in the glory of all and sundry: Monster-hunters, police, magistrates, and last but not least all the ladies of the Metropolis. The Gray's Inn fishmonger was not a man of action, however, but a timid and unadventurous character. It is likely he was frightened that, like his paramour, he would get a taste of the Monster's rapier. Another line of conduct would have been to point out the man and shout 'The Monster!'; this would certainly have led to a swift arrest, but at the price of losing Coleman his claim to the Angerstein reward. Instead of challenging the man, the indecisive Coleman quietly crept after him as he left the Park, down Spring Gardens, and as far as the Admiralty, where the man turned down a narrow passage. The suspect first very steadfastly looked up at a particular house, and then suddenly turned sharply about to stare directly at John Coleman. Unnerved by the man's steely glare, Coleman nearly gave up the pursuit. The man then very quickly walked down the alley and turned back into Spring Gardens. After some deliberation, Coleman followed him at a safe distance. The suspect appeared confused, and made no effort to run away, and Coleman gradually became bolder, particularly as the man was just five feet six inches in height and did not look particularly strong. When they moved into Cockspur Street and along Pall Mall, John Coleman followed him like a shadow, just a yard behind.

In St James's Street, Coleman was relieved to meet a fellow fishmonger. After a brief council of war, they hurried after the man, but he turned sharply into Bolton Street, where he knocked at the door of a house, and was admitted. John Coleman and his colleague were at a loss how to proceed. The two fishmongers stood outside for a couple of minutes, debating whether to follow the man into the house. They eventually found this course of action imprudent, and Coleman's friend absconded from the scene, preferring to ply his trade rather than to chase dangerous criminals through the streets of the metropolis. John Coleman indecisively hung about outside, and had the man stayed indoors, or bolted through the back door, he would have been safe. But after Coleman had waited about three or four minutes, the man came out through the front door and walked quickly back into Piccadilly. He then walked past Pero's Bagnio down St James's Street, and stopped abruptly at a china shop at the corner of Pall Mall, where he knocked violently at the door. Although the shop was about to close, a servant opened the door, and the suspect was seen to ask him a number of questions.

As the man left the shop and went up St James's Street, John Coleman went up to the servant, who was busy shuttering the shop's windows, and asked him whether he knew the man's name, but the china-shop assistant did not know it, or would not say. Poor

John Coleman, who had hoped to obtain the Monster's name without having to tackle this formidable criminal, raced along to catch up with the man, who was disappearing into the crowds in Piccadilly. He was probably acutely aware that if Miss Porter found out that he had followed the man she had pointed out as the Monster round London for half an hour without even trying to challenge or tackle the criminal in any way, he would not stand highly in her favour. Even worse, the professional and amateur Monster-hunters, police, and journalists would jeer and mock his pusillanimous conduct. As the wretched fishmonger was chasing the suspect through the darkening London streets, he desperately pondered how to stop the man and find out his name and address. To shout out 'He's the Monster!' would now be futile, since the streets were becoming empty of people, and the man would find it easy to run away. John Coleman thought of a certain manner to get the man's name and address: to insult him and provoke him into a quarrel. To achieve these means, Coleman overtook the man, turned round and walked straight at him, looking him straight in the face in an insulting manner. When the man stopped at a house in Bond Street, to knock at the door, the leering Coleman crept up near him and said in what he presumed to be a highly insulting manner: 'Why this is an empty house, what do you knock here for?' The suspect, who certainly appeared very unlike a sinister, brutal criminal, meekly begged his pardon and said that he had believed the house to be inhabited by a gentleman of his acquaintance, by the name of Pearce. He then rushed off towards Oxford Street. Coleman walked close behind, and tried to behave as obnoxiously as possible. The crowning touch was that he actually peeped over the man's shoulder, and called out 'Buh!' at the top of his voice.

The suspect only quickened his pace during the course of these shenanigans, and despite the fact that the exasperated John Coleman 'continued his gestures of offence; nay, made a feint to square at him', he passed safely into Oxford Street.[2] He sharply turned down South Moulton Street, knocked at the door of a house and was swiftly admitted. Once more, the dismal fishmonger stood outside pondering what to do. After some minutes, John Coleman gathered what remained of his wits and courage, and knocked at the door. A servant opened, and introduced him to a pitch-dark parlour, where two men awaited him in silence: one of them turned out to be Mr Smith, the owner of the house; the other was the suspect. This encounter must have been fairly sinister, but for once, Coleman behaved coolly and rationally. He took Mr Smith aside and asked him the name and address of the other man. Mr Smith was astonished, and at first refused, but Coleman firmly said that he was determined to find out who he was. Mr Smith said that the man was an old school fellow of his, and that Coleman must assign his reasons if he wanted any kind of information. The fishmonger replied that he would give his reasons when he saw the man, and demanded that some candles were brought in. John Coleman's relief, when Mr Smith meekly ordered his servant to fetch some candles, can easily be imagined; surely, it must have been the most exciting moment in his life when he had faced two unknown men, one of whom he believed to be a dangerous and desperate crimi-nal, in the dark room. He again demanded the man's name and address, and declared that since he suspected that Mr Smith's visitor had grossly insulted a lady of his acquaintance in St James's Park, he was fully determined to have satisfaction. The suspect suggested that he should go to a coffee-house nearby, and wait there for Coleman to bring the ladies, but the prim fishmonger replied that he thought a coffee-house a very improper place for ladies to visit. Mr Smith then called for pen and ink, and wrote, at his strange companion's direction, 'Mr Williams, No. 52, Jermyn Street'. Through either shrewdness or oversight, the word 'Monster' had not been mentioned in the conversation, and all three men became visibly more relaxed as John Coleman pocketed the paper, and gave his own name and address to the suspect.

The situation then again descended into farce. Suddenly, at the flicker of a candle, Coleman leant forward and exclaimed, 'Good God, Williams, I think I know you!' The mysterious Mr Williams replied, 'I think I know *you*!' It turned out that the two had previously met several times at certain assembly-rooms and public houses, among the throng of young London pleasure-seekers; John Coleman even recollected that Williams had formerly been a theatre violinist, and that his brother was a well-known London apothecary. Both were similarly astounded that they had not recognised each other earlier during the mad chase through the London streets. Knowing that Williams, or at least his brother the apothecary, was a respectable person, made John Coleman even more reluctant to try to arrest him. Happy to have come so creditably out of his encounter with the man pointed out as the London Monster, he seems to have imagined that every one would applaud his conduct when he brought the suspect's name and address to the knowledge of the police. The dense fishmonger took his farewell of Mr Smith and Mr Williams, and started walking back towards Pero's Bagnio, to meet Anne and Sarah and break what he imagined would be the good news that he had met the Monster and knew his identity. Suddenly, as he was walking down Bond Street, his sluggish brain still working over the sensational recent events, he was struck, as if by a thunderbolt, with the realisation that a man capable of attacking and stabbing at least thirty women would not stop short of giving a *false name* and a *false address* to his pursuer!

The distraught John Coleman raced back to Mr Smith's house, but this gentleman told him, gleefully, one would imagine, that their mutual acquaintance had left some minutes ago. For about ten minutes, Coleman ran around the dark streets like a man possessed, looking everywhere for the elusive Monster. Finally giving up, he ran back into St James's Street, but at the top of the street, completely by accident, he almost ran into the mysterious Mr Williams. The man did not try to run away, but merely said, 'We meet again.' After some gasping for breath, Coleman blurted out, 'Yes, Williams, we meet again ... I think Williams I have some knowledge about you – did we not meet at a Ball in King-Street, Covent Garden?' After Williams had answered in the affirmative, Coleman cunningly suggested that since they were actually old acquaintances, he was no longer certain that Williams really was the man that had insulted his lady friends; perhaps they should visit the ladies in question to have him cleared of this accusation? Mr Williams objected that it was very late, but Coleman pointed out that their house was very nearby, and Williams then came along without any demur. When Coleman and Williams were approaching Pero's Bagnio, Sarah and Martha Porter crossed the street, and they hastily rushed into the Bagnio when they saw their fishmonger friend return with his prey. When Williams perceived where they were going, he called out, 'Why, that is Mr Porter's!' which Coleman found odd. Without further ado, they went in through the front door of the Bagnio, and walked into the parlour where the ladies were sitting. The moment Williams came into the room, Anne and Sarah Porter clasped their hands together, screamed, 'Good God, that is the *Wretch*!' and fainted away at the sight of this figure of dread. Surveying their lifeless, recumbent forms, Williams turned to Coleman and said, 'The conduct of the Ladies, Sir, is extremely odd; I hope they do not take me for that Person who is advertised.' Coleman coolly told him that they certainly did.

Mr Williams protested his innocence, and asked leave to send for his mother and sister. He also claimed that he had been working the entire evening of the Queen's birthday, when Anne Porter had been cut, and asked to be allowed to fetch some of his workmates, who could easily prove his alibi. Coleman did not move to restrain him as he went up to leave, but Mrs Elizabeth Porter, a strong and active woman who was the mother of the Misses and the chief bath attendant at Pero's Bagnio, promptly collared the mysterious Mr Williams, and waved her huge red fist in his face. She swore a horrid oath that if the Monster moved a muscle, she would give him ample reason to be sorry for it. Williams sank back into his chair.[3]

A servant was sent to the Bow Street public office, and after about an hour Runner John Macmanus, a grizzled veteran who had acted as the bodyguard of George III after the attempt on his life by the madwoman Margaret Nicholson in 1786, came pounding up to the Porter residence. Macmanus took Williams into custody, and he was committed to the New Prison, Clerkenwell.

The man gave his name as Mr Rhynwick Williams and his trade as an artificial flower-maker. Macmanus also promptly searched his lodgings. The address given earlier proved not to be strictly correct. Rhynwick Williams did not live at No. 52 Jermyn Street, but his mother and sister lived nearby, in Duke Street. His own lodgings were at a dismal-looking ale-house, where six men lay every night in three contiguous beds, situated in the same small room. Both these premises were searched by Runner Macmanus; at the ale-house, a suitcase containing the worldly belongings of Rhynwick Williams was forced open, and a suit of clothes, with a light-coloured coat and a pair of half-boots, were seized, since they resembled the garments worn by the Monster on earlier occasions. No knife, rapier, or other sharp cutting implement was found.

7

RHYNWICK WILLIAMS

AT

BOW STREET

Now the naughty Monster's fast,
Beauty stands no more aghast
At the terrifying word,
Milk of nature turn'd to curd.
Some, as yet, can scarce believe it,
Others, as a dream receive it.
What, that man of woman born,
Woman, fairer than the morn:
Woman, nature's choicest flower,
Soft as rose-buds in a shower,
Sent in pity to mankind,
To allay and ease his mind,
Could uplift his impious arm …

W.H., 'The Monster', from the
New Lady's Magazine, July 1790.

On 14 and 15 June, several newspapers carried the sensational news that the London Monster had finally been apprehended: he was Rhynwick Williams, a native of Wales, twenty-three years old, and an artificial flower-maker.[1] His odd occupation caused some merriment: that the London Monster, the terror of the capital's female world, was making artificial flowers for his living was considered as inappropriate as Attila the Hun being a needlepoint embroiderer, or Ivan the Terrible a ladies' hairdresser. *The Times* was alone in not naming the prisoner as Rhynwick Williams; they merely referred to him as 'a person whose name with regard to his family we shall at present forbear to mention'. *The Times* journalist evidently had some personal knowledge of Rhynwick Williams and his family, and described him as a

> young man of genteel appearance, who unfortunately for his family has been in very dissipated habits of life, which have led him into expenses among women, and a line of conduct extremely injurious to his own character. The misfortune is the greater, as his friends are persons of character and reputation, who most severely feel for the excesses and wanton behaviour of this thoughtless young man, whose person is extremely well known about town.[2]

Many people were amazed that the Monster was not a rough, coarse brute of a man, but young, not unpleasant-looking, and apparently of better than average breeding. Newspaper correspondents soon managed to elucidate that Rhynwick Williams had received a reasonably good education. At an early period of his life, Rhynwick's affectionate parents had put him into the care of a gentleman friend in London, where he received further education at a respectable school. This gentleman, apparently a patron of the theatre, found that young Rhynwick was a pleasant-looking lad, with a supple, graceful body and an a talent for music. At his advice, Rhynwick was articled as an apprentice to Giovanni Andrea Battista Gallini, who was the most famous dancing master in Britain.[3] A native of Florence, Gallini had made his debut as a ballet dancer at the Opera House, Haymarket, in 1753, and achieved such a brilliant success that he was soon the director of the dances, and finally stage-manager of the theatre. While on a tour of Italy, Gallini

Rennick Williams,
Commonly Called
The MONSTER.

Rhynwick Williams, as portrayed in the *New Lady's Magazine*, July 1790. This portrait bears little likeness with the more reliable portraits of Williams – see the illustrations on pages 109 and 111.

so delighted the Pope with his dancing that he was made a Knight of the Golden Spur; this went to his head, and on his return to London, he assumed the title of 'Sir John Gallini', although the Papal knighthood granted him no such right.[4]

Sir John was a brilliant dancing-master, and in his school Rhynwick Williams could not, as eloquently expressed by one of his newspaper biographers, 'fail to acquire those personal graces with which all his manners seem to be tinged; but the trammels of art were too great a confinement to the effervescent spirit of gaiety and expense which soon marked his conduct'.[5] In other words, young Rhynwick seems to have taken on the habits of a scapegrace and rascal during his period of service at Sir John's establishment. This did not preclude him from learning both ballet dancing and playing the violin; he seems to have been active in the theatre orchestra in the latter capacity, and also to have acted as a dancing master both in private houses and at least one school. A Mr Williams is listed among the second violinists at the Handel Memorial Concerts at Westminster Abbey and the Pantheon in 1784.[6] Not only in ribald eighteenth-century novels was a private dancing master considered a serious threat to chastity: the dashing *danceur*, while guiding the movements of the limbs of his pupil, had unique possibilities to seduce the trembling high-born maidens in his charge. Sir John Gallini himself had not eschewed these opportunities. When, according to his rather disapproving biographer, he had been 'admitted into the house of the third Earl of Abingdon', he rapidly won the affections of Lady Elizabeth Peregrine Bertie, the Earl's eldest daughter and a wealthy heiress. Although the Earl was aghast that his daughter wished to elope with a common little Italian mountebank, they later married. Rhynwick Williams, although not as fortunate as Sir John, also became, or at least aspired to be, quite a ladies' man.

Some time in the late 1770s or early 1780s, Rhynwick Williams' entire family came to live in London. His father, Thomas Williams, was a Member of the Society of Apothecaries, and had his pharmacy in Broad Street, Carnaby Market.[7] He was not a mere druggist, but an educated man and an apothecary of some distinction. He died, at a relatively young age, on 9 June 1785. In his will, he left £100 in old South Sea annuities and the rest of his worldly goods to his wife Mary Williams.[8] The apothecary's father, John Williams, who was still living in Beguildy in the county of Radnor, Wales, had to be content with a bequest of one guinea per annum for life. In 1785, the apothecary's eldest son Thomas Williams, who had also pursued his father's profession, took over his position as Member of the Society of Apothecaries by patrimony.[9] There are hints that although the old apothecary and his son Thomas were well off, Rhynwick's mother and sisters soon ran into financial difficulties, having to fend for themselves in the metropolis after the untimely death of the family breadwinner.

In the autumn of 1785, Sir John Gallini became the proprietor of the King's Theatre, where he wanted to stage his own ballet dancing shows. Since his finances were stretched to the limit, he had many difficulties in finding suitable professional dancers, and it is very likely that his apprentice Rhynwick Williams was on the stage; indeed, one of Rhynwick's newspaper biographers states that he was once 'a public dancer on the boards of the Opera-house'.[10] The experience is very unlikely to have been a happy one, however. Not even Sir John's esprit and dancing skills could put some fire into the bumbling amateurs he had to employ. The London stage was, as it is now, a highly competitive arena; but the pitfalls for any one attempting a second-rate routine were somewhat more dangerous than today. A review of one of Sir John's shows in the *World* states that 'the dance, if such it can be called, was like the movements of heavy cavalry. It was hissed very abundantly'. On a later occasion, the dissatisfied audience charged the stage and put the dancers to flight. Sir John Gallini had to fight for his life against a burly assailant, who tried to throw him into the orchestra pit, but the nimble dancing master dodged his blows and managed to knock his antagonist down. Sir John, along with Rhynwick Williams and the rest of the crew, then rapidly made themselves scarce, since the audience was threatening to murder them. The mob proceeded to sack the entire theatre, and destroyed everything that could be broken.[11]

Rhynwick's happy, if somewhat perilous, existence at Sir John's dancing academy soon came to an end. There was an incident when Sir John Gallini suspected his scapegrace apprentice of having stolen a watch belonging to him, and Rhynwick was summarily discharged. This, according to his own admission, occurred not long after the death of his father, and thus probably in 1785 or 1786.[12] He soon ran into serious financial difficulties, since he continued to visit the dancing-parlours, restaurants and assembly rooms of the metropolis. According to the florid newspaper writer quoted earlier, he was 'continually in the company [of], and probably supported by women to whose gratification he sacrificed all his time and talent'. He continued in this way of living for some time, but then apparently made an effort to redeem himself: he managed to obtain the position of clerk to an attorney who aspired to become a Member of Parliament. This gentleman was unsuccessful, although it is recorded that Rhynwick discharged his duty fully satisfactorily; after this failure, the young Welshman was again out on the street, without any employment. By this time, one of his sisters was employed as an artificial flower-maker at Monsieur Aimable Michelle's establishment in Dover Street. She managed to persuade the Frenchman to giver her errant brother a chance in this profession. Rhynwick started learning the artificial flower business in early 1789, and made rapid progress. In consequence of his superior workmanship, M. Michelle gave him a permanent position on his workforce, with a decent salary, from the month of September 1789 onwards. For reasons undisclosed, Rhynwick Williams' employment at the artificial flower factory was terminated in early June 1790.[13]

At the time of his arrest, Rhynwick Williams was not only unemployed but also in dire financial straits. He was lodging at a mean-looking public house in Bury Street called the George, where he had been sleeping in the same bed as another man for some time. Some said that this arrangement was due to reasons of penury, others made a more sinister interpretation of the Monster's preference of male company in bed, and linked this circumstance to his crimes against the female sex. The German chronicler J.W. von Archenholtz, who described Rhynwick Williams as a short man with a dark brown complexion, a long nose and a wild look in his eyes, was aghast when he found out that Rhynwick had slept together with other men, whom he said he did not know! This was indeed an 'inference of horrid propensities, only too consentaneous with his recent practice.'[14]

On 14 June, Rhynwick Williams was taken from Clerkenwell Prison to be examined before Justices Sir Sampson Wright, William Addington and Nicholas Bond at the Bow Street public office.[15] The rumour that the Monster had been caught had spread like wildfire, and a huge, clamorous mob had gathered outside. The inside of the public office was completely crowded with spectators, one of whom was the Duke of Cumberland. A cacophony of boo-ing, shouts and insults from the mob outside announced that the London Monster had arrived, and two sturdy Runners, cordoned by several Bow Street patrols, accompanied the frightened little man in his threadbare blue coat to his seat at the dock.

Anne and Sarah Porter were the first to give evidence. In marked contrast to their earlier vague descriptions of the culprit, they now declared themselves absolutely certain that Rhynwick Williams was the Monster who had attacked them. They also volunteered the damning evidence that already before he had assaulted them on the evening of the Queen's birthday, they had both known him by sight, since he had for some time been in the habit of stalking them in the streets and making them extremely indecent proposals.[16] Their younger sisters Rebecca and Martha had also been accosted by him. According to Sarah, his *modus operandi* was to walk closely behind them, with his head almost leaning over one of the girls' shoulders, all the time talking 'the most dreadful language that can be imagined'. With as much feeling, Rebecca and Martha Porter respectively described his conversation as 'the most horrible lan-guage I ever heard in my life' and 'the most horrid, dreadful words imaginable'; indeed, they had never heard this foul-mouthed fellow utter a decent sentence.

Anne Porter had first seen the *Wretch*, as he was known among the Porter sisters, a year and a half earlier. She was walking back to the Bagnio with her sister Sarah, when she perceived somebody pulling her gown. She turned round and saw a big-nosed little man, and stopped short believing he wanted to pass them, but he stood as still as they did, looking at them. They believed that he was drunk, and made haste homewards, but the man followed them all the way to the Bagnio door, making use of the most horrid, shocking language, too bad to be repeated. Shortly after, when Anne and Sarah took an airing in the Green Park, they saw the mystery stalker standing nearby, grinning at them. They ran home as quickly as they could, but the Wretch pursued them at a distance short enough for them to be entertained by his usual foul language. The third time, Anne Porter was walking in the Haymarket, when the Wretch caught up with her and actually put his head over her shoulder, thus giving her no chance of escaping his pleasantries, which were of the same coarse and sanguinary variety as on their previous encounters.

When, in May 1789, Anne was walking in St Martin's Lane with her sister Martha, she heard someone muttering behind her; she could perceive enough words to form an opinion of who was uttering them, and sure enough, when she turned round, the Wretch stood there grinning at her. Young Martha was very much frightened, and they both sought protection with a gentlewoman who was passing along St Martin's Lane, telling her who they were and that a strange man was following them with evil intent. She let them walk along with them, but the stalker was intrepid enough to stand in front of them and laugh loudly in their faces. Anne Porter then thought they had managed to get rid of the Wretch, but when they were walking on the pavement of St James's Street itself, they saw him racing along the opposite pavement to intercept them. They managed to reach Pero's Bagnio first, however, and immediately told their parents about their harrowing experience. Thomas Porter sent a servant in pursuit of this mysterious stalker, but the Wretch easily evaded this bumbling menial.

After this sensational new evidence had been presented, John Coleman was called to testify. His account of his pursuit of the Monster was received with some derision, and it was commented that the young fishmonger had showed more caution than was perhaps necessary on such an occasion.[17] Numerous other wounded ladies had been called to give evidence, but their testimony varied widely. Miss Reynolds, the companion of Miss Toussaint who had been cut the same evening as Anne Porter, said that Miss Toussaint's recollection of this incident was too vague for her to identify the culprit, but that she herself had seen him clearly, and that he was definitely not Rhynwick Williams. Nor could three other ladies, whose names we do not know, point out Rhynwick Williams as the Monster. The magistrates must have been somewhat relieved when Mrs Franklin boldly spoke up and positively identified Rhynwick as the man who had insulted her with his foul, blasphemous language on seven or eight different occasions. Ann Frost, whose clothes had been cut by the Monster in November 1789, did not give the same good impression. There was much laughter in court when she demanded that a round hat should be placed on Rhynwick Williams' head. 'Whatever for?' asked Sir Sampson Wright, and Ann Frost replied that since he had worn a round hat when he attacked her, she could not swear to him without a round hat! The magistrate told her, in no uncertain terms, that the man's face should be more distinctive than the cut of his hat, and refused her request. Despite the absence of headgear, she then rather easily identified Rhynwick Williams as the Monster, although the attack had taken place seven months before, on a dark winter night.[18] The next witnesses were more prudent. Miss Elizabeth Baughan thought that Rhynwick Williams resembled the man who had cut her in December 1789, but he was not as tall as she had believed. Her sister Frances was more positive about his identity, and rather hesitantly swore that he was the Monster.

Rhynwick Williams himself spoke up only once during this interrogation: he said that he was an artificial flower-maker, and at the time Miss Porter was cut, he had been working at Mr Amabel Mitchell's artificial flower factory in Dover Street, where he had remained until nearly one o'clock in the morning. He thus had a clear alibi for the offence against Anne and Sarah Porter, and if he had been allowed to do so, he would have brought Amabel Mitchell and his staff into the public office to provide evidence that he had been hard at work in the flower factory at the time when the Misses Porter had been attacked in St James's Street. He also volunteered the damning information that he had twice before 'been challenged for the Monster, particularly once at the *Play-House*'.[19] It does not give credit to the detection ability of the police and magistrates that this lead was, apparently, not followed up. It must have been a quite alarming experience to have been pointed out as the Monster in a crowded assembly room, but fortunately for Rhynwick, this incident, which can be traced through Mr Angerstein's thorough chronology of the Monster's outrages, had happened quite some time before the proper Monster-mania. He was identified by Miss Mary Forster, who had been wounded in September 1789, and actually taken by some friends of her, who later released him after he had given his address.[20] The other instance on which Rhynwick had been challenged may well have been the one reported in the *Oracle* newspaper: a man with an artificial nosegay was arrested after a girl had pricked her finger when she smelt it, but he had been able to show that the girl had in fact pricked her hand with the wire used to bind the artificial flowers together, and he was again discharged.[21]

Rhynwick Williams was extremely frightened when the time arrived for the prisoner's van to leave the public office; this was not without reason, since the mob surged forward as soon as the carriage appeared. The Bow Street patrols had to form a cordon to keep them at bay, and the prisoner's van was quickly reversed back into the yard. At five o'clock they made another attempt to leave the public office, with many policemen on each side of the prisoner's van to ward off any attacks. The mob charged nevertheless, and it was said in the newspapers that the immense crowd were so exasperated, that they would have torn Rhynwick Williams from the coach and destroyed him, if it had not been for the courage and determination of the Bow Street patrolmen.[22] Even these brave constables could not prevent a rotten vegetable of some description, thrown by some individual in the mob, from scoring a direct hit in poor Rhynwick's face.

On 16 June, Rhynwick Williams was again brought before the magistrates. Quite a crowd of wounded ladies were now present. The spectators were as numerous as the day before: among them the Duke of Cumberland, the Duke of York, Prince William of Gloucester, the Earl of Essex, Lord Beauchamp, and many others of rank and fashion. The mob was again very much in evidence: according to the *World* newspaper, 'Charles James Fox's coalition at the Hastings, and the Monster in Bow Street, were the two attractions of yesterday: and the crowds were immense'. According to another newspaper account, the Duke of Cumberland was becomingly solicitous on the occasion, but the behaviour of some of the other young sparks and toffs left much to be desired. The levity with which these individuals treated the proceedings, with many loud jokes and guffaws of laughter, was 'neither creditable to their humanity or their GALLANTRY. It being the fashion to treat the affair with ridicule, has not been a little instrumental in shedding the blood that has been spilt, and exciting these outrages in a NEST of unnatural banditti that calls aloud for their extermination!'[23]

Miss Aride, who had been abused and cut in Jermyn Street, was first to give evidence. She told the usual story about the man who had stalked her in an attempt at seduction, then abused her with his customary foul language. When asked by Sir Sampson Wright to point out the culprit, she declared that he was not there. Nor could four other of the wounded ladies positively identify Rhynwick Williams as the Monster. They either thought he was unlike the man who had wounded them, or were unable to identify him due to either fright or darkness (many of the attacks had taken place late at night). Miss Toussaint, who had previously said that she could not recall her assailant at all, now appeared in the box, eager for her moment in the limelight as one of the wounded beauties. She said that Rhynwick much resembled the man who attacked her, and that he was the right height and size, although she could not swear that he was the Monster. Nor could Charlotte Payne, the lady's maid of the Countess of Howe, swear positively that Rhynwick Williams was the man who had assaulted her before

Lord Howe's front door. She thought that he very much resembled the culprit, however, although she was not positive. The stupid Rhynwick Williams, who was unaided by any counsel, made another very damning admission: he 'did not deny being in the place mentioned, and said the accident might have happened from something in his pocket'(!)[24]

Next, plain little Elizabeth Davis was brought up. All accounts agree that she identified Rhynwick Williams as the man who had assaulted her, but the details differ in important respects with regard to exactly *how* the confrontation between the two had been staged. According to Rhynwick Williams himself, he was standing in the yard, surrounded by a circle of Bow Street patrolmen, expostulating with them as to how he was to be saved from the mob, whose behaviour was as threatening as the day before. Suddenly he heard, from above, the words 'Is that him without the hat?' Rhynwick looked up towards a window, to observe Elizabeth Davis with some of the Runners, who congratulated her with the words 'Yes, that is him, in blue and buff!' Rhynwick wrote that since his dress was quite different from that of the Runners, and since he was the only person present not wearing a hat, the identification of him as the prisoner would not have been difficult. According to the *World* newspaper, Williams stood in the middle of the office, with people all around him. Elizabeth Davis was asked to look around to see if any one of those present resembled the man who had cut her, and 'she immediately and without hesitation fixed upon the prisoner, whom, in the most positive manner, she swore was the man who wounded her'.[25] It should be noted that Elizabeth Davis's original description of the Monster was as unlike Rhynwick Williams as it could be, and the query must be raised whether the Runners had found it prudent to 'coach' her beforehand.

Next, there was time for more histrionics as Miss Mary Forster positively identified Rhynwick Williams as the man who had stabbed her in the thigh. She pointed him out among fifty other men, with the passionate words: 'This is the man! – I'll swear to him! – Nay more, if I were upon my dying bed, I would take the Sacrament this is the man!'[26] Rhynwick Williams objected strongly to her identification of him. He claimed that on the day she claimed to have been attacked, he had been in Weymouth, 130 miles from London. Runner Macmanus, who had virtually been Rhynwick's neighbour when the latter had lived in Bow Street, could corroborate this story, since he had actually seen him there. This caused much consternation on the part of Mary Forster and the magistrates; the lady faltered and had to admit that she was by no means certain which day she had been attacked, and that it may well have been a week earlier.[27] She knew for sure it was on a Sunday, however, and that the attack had happened at about eight o'clock in the evening. Sir Sampson Wright then asked her how she could identify the man responsible at such a late hour. 'From the bright lights in the shop windows', she replied. There was laughter in court, since no shops were open on a Sunday evening, and Mary Forster again had to retreat. The imprudent Rhynwick Williams did not deny that Mary Forster had later pointed him out as the Monster at the Playhouse; indeed, he willingly admitted that this was the case, and that when taken, he had given his address as No. 36 Bow Street, where he was living at the time.[28]

After Mary Forster had been bound over to give evidence, Miss Kitty Wheeler identified Rhynwick Williams as the man who had several times insulted her with his foul language, and from whom she had once been rescued by the intervention of her father. A poor young servant-girl then appeared; she was the one who had been stabbed near the eye with the knife concealed in the artificial nosegay. According to the newspapers, this girl was shockingly disfigured by the cut she had received. She thought Rhynwick Williams was like the person who had wounded her, but could not swear positively as to his identity, since three other ruffians had been in the Monster's company at the time.[29]

After this second session, the mob outside the police office was even more threatening than before, and Runner Macmanus saw that many tough-looking ruffians had armed themselves with stones and bludgeons. He was a veteran of Lord George Gordon's 'No Popery' riots in 1780, and this experience had given him a healthy respect for what an enraged London mob was capable of. Macmanus was unwilling to let the prisoner's van, containing the terrified Rhynwick Williams, run the gauntlet of this vicious crowd, and waited for more than an hour before deciding to move. Cleverly, he ordered some Bow Street patrolmen to open the main doors, and the mob surged forward, eager to see if the Monster was taken out that way. Macmanus then swiftly had the side gates opened, and the coachman whipped up the horses as the prisoner's van pulled out. The mob pursued it, but some patrolmen armed with long staffs acted as a rearguard, and the van got a good head start. Suddenly, three roughs dashed out from a public house, alerted by the shouts of 'The Monster!'; they jumped up onto the running-boards, where two Bow Street constables were riding, and tried to push them off the vehicle. One of the roughs reached inside the prisoner's van, and poor Rhynwick gave a terrified cry as the man collared him with a hearty goodwill. The situation would have been a desperate one had not Macmanus, with admirable presence of mind, kicked the door open with great force. The rough was forced to release his grasp of the wretched prisoner, and was catapulted off the vehicle. The other ruffians were also thrown off, and Macmanus shouted, 'Whip up, man! Whip up!' to alert the coachman of the danger. Driving at breakneck speed, they arrived safely at Clerkenwell Prison, and it was found that Rhynwick Williams had sustained no other injury than a swollen and bloody nose, which had come into contact with the woodwork of the carriage during the fracas. When the other prisoners saw that the Monster was injured, they whooped with delight.[30]

On 18 June, Rhynwick Williams was brought before Mr Nicholas Bond, the sitting Bow Street magistrate, for a third and final time.[31] First, Mr Joshua Williams, a relation of the prisoner, who 'appeared greatly interested in his favour', spoke as a character witness. His evidence had the diametrically opposite effect, however, since he declared on oath that he had often heard Rhynwick say that he had chased women about town, and abused and blasted them with very obscene language if they refused to take him home and go to bed with him.[32]

As if this ill-judged appearance from his kinsman had not been enough bad news for Rhynwick, Mrs Sarah Godfrey, who was described by a susceptible journalist as 'a Lady of uncommon beauty' was introduced by Mr Bond and told the story about how she had been assaulted in May 1789. Rhynwick Williams was standing in a circle of upwards of thirty men, all wearing their hats, but Mrs Godfrey pointed him out as the Monster with the words: 'If it be any one in this company, this is the man'. But when Rhynwick removed his hat, she almost wanted to withdraw her identification of him, and said that he looked quite unlike her recollection of the Monster. The magistrates promptly ordered Rhynwick to put his hat back on, however, and Mrs Godfrey, relieved, said that she had very little doubt that he was the Monster who had wounded her.

A third, resounding blow to Rhynwick Williams' flagging spirits came when Mr Bond informed the court of the statutes of law under which he was to be committed for trial. At this time, there was a sharp difference between felonies and misdemeanours. The former category consisted of 'serious' crimes, punishable by death or transportation; the latter were relatively milder offences, punishable by prison, pillory or a public flogging. For example, grand larceny was a felony, minor larceny a misdemeanour. More than 200 crimes were punishable by death, but the felons often received a pardon. Murderers were of course hanged, as were hardened thieves, highwaymen and street robbers, but the other felons were more often transported to a prison colony abroad. Common assault, even with intent to maim or kill, was a misdemeanour, and Rhynwick and his friends had hoped that the Monster's crimes would be categorised as such.[33]

But, on the other hand, the authorities were under pressure to find a legal statute that made the Monster's crimes a felony, since they feared a public outrage in London if he was charged with a mere misdemeanour. One of the debating societies suggested, 'Ought not the Legislature (in protection of the ladies of Great Britain) immediately pass an act rendering the Crime of Rhynwick Williams, commonly called the Monster, a capital offence?', but the magistrates and judges did not follow their advise, despite being hard pressed to find any Act in the present legislature that covered the Monster assaults. The Coventry Act, named after Sir John Coventry, whose nose and ears had been slit by the Duke of Monmouth and his accomplices, made it a felony to lie in wait to maim or disfigure some person. But it could not be proved that the Monster had actually been lying in wait for his victims, and this Act was thus not applicable. The Black Act made it a felony to go armed while under disguise, but this was again not applicable to the Monster's crimes.

However, the magistrates and judges had discovered an ancient statute from 1721, intended to repress the activities of certain weavers who objected to the importation of Indian fashions, which were purchased by the public in preference to the weavers' own goods. The weavers actually poured *aqua fortis* on the clothes of people wearing these foreign fashions, and, to stop these outrages, it was made a felony, punishable by transportation for seven years, to 'assault any person in the public streets, *with intent* to tear, spoil, *cut*, burn, or deface, the garments or cloaths of such person, provided *the act* be done in pursuance of such intention'.[34] There had obviously been some debate among the judges as to whether the Monster should be charged under this ancient statute, as the first case ever: although Sir Peter King believed that this statute was fully applicable to the Monster's crimes, other judges were hesitant, since the Monster had actually cut the clothes to make way to the flesh underneath.[35] Sir Peter quoted a case from the Lent Assizes for Suffolk, in which two men were prosecuted for having cut the nose of another. They were charged with deliberately cutting his nose with intent to maim and disfigure him, which was a capital crime. The men claimed, in order to escape becoming felons for deliberately deciding to disfigure him, that they had cut his nose in an attempt to kill him, but the court convicted them nevertheless and they were both executed.

In the newspapers, there was much gloating that the Monster should be tried as a felon. One newspaper correspondent considered that he was actually lucky to be considered as a felon, since if he was put in the pillory, the mob would tear him to pieces. There was no question of Williams being allowed bail. Seven ladies (Anne Porter, Sarah Porter, Elizabeth Davis, Mary Forster, Frances Baughan, Sarah Godfrey and Ann Frost) were bound over to testify against him. It was hoped that, if Rhynwick Williams was found guilty on each of the seven indictments against him, he would have to spend seven times seven years as a convict labourer at the Botany Bay penal colony. When Rhynwick, accused of having cut so many women, was taken back to Clerkenwell Prison, all the other felons were disposed to *cut him*: not a single man would speak to the London Monster. The prejudice against him was such that even his local Member of Parliament found it necessary to insert the following notice in *The Times*: 'The Party denies that the man taken as the Monster voted for Lord John Townshend in the late Westminster Election.'[36]

The only newspaper to disagree was the *Morning Chronicle*, where a writer asserted that although Williams might well be guilty, the descriptions of the Monster, lodged by various wounded ladies, disagreed in many particulars. The ruffian's hair colour had been stated to be in every shade from black to fair, and the reports of his height varied from the tallest to the most diminutive stature. Rhynwick Williams was just one member of a ruthless gang of Monsters, and the journalist urged that the plans to establish a special anti-Monster police force should not be abandoned: 'Let a proper association be formed: let proper regulations be adopted; and, where is the man of gallantry, humanity, or spirit, who will decline to wear the uniform?'[37]

8

It is of a Monster I mean for to write,
Who in stabing of Ladies took great delight;
If he caught them alone in the street after dark,
In their Hips, or their Thighs, he'd be sure cut a mark.

The poetry quoted in this chapter is from
The Monster Represented, an illustrated set of
doggerel verses published just after the
first trial against Rhynwick Williams.

On 8 July, Rhynwick Williams was to stand trial at the Old Bailey.[1] He arrived there in a wretched state, fearful of more rough treatment from the anti-Monster ruffians. As he cowered in one corner of the prisoner's van, he could see angry, red-faced thugs wave their cudgels at him, and hear men, women and children scream abuse. He became even more frightened and dejected when he heard the boos and insults from the vicious mob standing outside the Old Bailey, baying for his blood. The Bow Street patrols again had to shield the trembling little man from the mob as he was led up towards the courtroom.

Rhynwick's respectable brother, the apothecary Thomas Williams, had tried to help him arrange his defence, but it had not been easy to find any legal counsel willing to represent the man accused of being the London Monster. Through the offer of a considerable fee, Thomas Williams had been able to recruit Mr Chatham, a solicitor of renown, to handle Rhynwick's case. The day before the trial, after he had made the acquaintance of Rhynwick and heard him speak, this gentleman threw down his brief and left, for reasons undisclosed.[2] Only in the nick of time had Thomas Williams managed to find another solicitor, Mr Fletcher, and a barrister named Newman Knowlys who was to argue the case. Although these two gentlemen were experienced lawyers, they had only one day to learn the case, and from Mr Chatham's sudden departure, if nothing else, they must have suffered considerable prejudice against their notorious client. There was only one indictment: that of wilfully and maliciously cutting Anne Porter's cloak, gown, stays, petticoat and shift. The somewhat embarrassing fact that the Monster had cut not only the aforementioned articles, but also the lady's buttocks, was disregarded by the legal luminaries in charge, as was the fact that forty or even fifty women had been assaulted in a very similar manner. Already before the trial, some learned judges had been overheard to comment that the law had been stretched too far to make the Monster a felon, and that this circumstance might backlash as soon as the trial was over.[3]

The judge in the trial of Rhynwick Williams was Sir Francis Buller, Bart.[4] He had been called to the Bar in 1772, and in 1778 had become, at the age of thirty-two, the youngest judge in England. His unfortunate assertion, at a trial in 1782, that any husband could thrash his wife with impunity provided that the stick was no thicker than his thumb, has caused some ridicule, and inspired James Gillray's amusing caricature *Judge Thumb*. Judge Buller had also been in trouble after being accused of having helped members of his family to line their pockets from public funds; this scandal had prevented him from being appointed Chief Justice, but as a solace, he had been made a Baronet on 13 January 1790.

The mainstay of the defence Mr Fletcher and Mr Knowlys had prepared was that Rhynwick Williams had been at work at the artificial flower factory when Anne Porter was attacked. Rhynwick's brother Thomas Williams had ascertained that Amabel Mitchell and his colleagues from the factory were ready to testify that this story was true. He had also done a good job in locating many previous acquaintances of Rhynwick Williams who were ready to testify as to his good character. Rhynwick himself later claimed that several wounded ladies, namely, Miss Marlow, Miss Fenton and Mrs Burney, were all standing by, ready to give evidence that he was not the Monster who had wounded them. Miss Reynolds, the companion of Miss Toussaint, who was cut on 18 January just like the Misses Porter, was also ready to testify that Rhynwick was not the culprit. None of these ladies were called as witnesses, however. Nor was any attention given to the fact that at Bow Street, many ladies had declared that Rhynwick was not the Monster who had cut them; it does not reflect creditably on Rhynwick Williams' counsel that none of them were called to give evidence.[5] It is a fact, however, that at least one wounded lady had come to give evidence on his behalf: the notorious Lady Wallace came forward on her own accord and declared that Rhynwick was not the man who had frightened her, and that she was prepared to testify about this at any court of law. Thomas Williams thanked her very much for her kindness, and ushered her to her seat in the front row of the courtroom.[6]

The head counsel for the prosecution was Mr Arthur Leary Pigot, an eloquent, highly talented gentleman who had thirteen years of experience at the Bar. After his associate Mr Cullen had read the indictment against Rhynwick Williams, and Rhynwick had pleaded Not Guilty, Mr Pigot opened the case against the prisoner in ringing tones. During his many years at the Bar, he had never seen a case blacker than this: the Monster-business was 'the most extraordinary case that ever called for the attention of a Court of Justice'. Rhynwick Williams' 'unnatural, unaccountable, and, until now, unknown offence' was 'a scene so new in the annals of mankind; a scene so unaccountable: a scene so unnatural to the

KENWICK WILLIAMS.
'Commonly called The Monster —'

A drawing of Rhynwick Williams at the
dock in the Old Bailey, by Nixon.

honour of human nature that would not have been believed ever to
have existed, unless it had been demonstrated by that proof which
the senses cannot resist'.[7] It was, indeed, a melancholy lesson that
no depravity, and no unnatural offence, however atrocious, could
be considered impossible and contrary to human nature: during
this trial, he warned the court, they would have to listen to 'enormities without any precedent'. Mr Pigot then went on to describe
the Monster's assault on Anne and Sarah Porter on the evening of
the Queen's birthday. He trod lightly when describing Coleman's
pursuit of the Monster. When he mentioned that Rhynwick
Williams did not lodge at the address given, but that his mother
and sister did, many people seemed astonished that the Monster
had female relations. Mr Pigot went on to claim that Rhynwick's
mother and sister knew very little of him. Another interesting new
snippet of information appeared when he described how John
Coleman had finally managed to persuade Rhynwick Williams to

go with him to Pero's Bagnio: Rhynwick had been 'unable to refuse it in the state in which he then was' – that is, he had probably been drunk. Either he had already been intoxicated when pursued by Coleman, or he had gone to some ale-house to fortify himself immediately after his escape from the fishmonger turned Monster-hunter, only to have the ill-fortune to run into this same gentleman just after his drinking session. Arthur Pigot vowed to prove, beyond any doubt, that Rhynwick Williams did purposely slit and cut the clothes of Anne Porter. He understood that Rhynwick Williams' counsel would attempt to prove an *alibi*, and urged the jury to observe closely the testimony of the alibi witnesses, and how much they could be relied on, hinting at possible perjury on their part. Mr Pigot's eloquent opening address was the subject of much admiration. The *London Chronicle* found his address 'as pathetic as it was humane', the *Oracle* spoke of his 'elegant exordium on the mysterious nature of the charge' and the *New Lady's Magazine* admired his 'very elegant language'.[8]

> He met Miss Anne Porter, who chanc'd late to stay,
> At the Ball at St James's the Queen's last birthday.
> Coming home with her sister Miss Sarah we find
> He struck Miss Sally's head, and cut Nancy behind.

Anne Porter was the first witness for the prosecution. She was elegantly dressed in grey muslin, and wore a veil as protection from the rude and profane glances of Rhynwick Williams. Mr Shepherd, another associate of Mr Pigot, questioned her, and she recounted how she had left St James's Palace at a quarter past eleven. Suddenly, her sister had desired her to make haste, and shouted something that she did not quite hear. They all ran as fast as they could, but as she passed the corner of the rails before Pero's Bagnio, she felt a violent blow on her hip. She turned round to see who had struck her, and observed Rhynwick Williams stooping down. She

RYNWICK WILLIAMS,
Commonly called
THE MONSTER!

Rhynwick Williams in the dock at the Old Bailey, a drawing purported to be by James Gillray, yet 'not by Gillray' according to a note at the Department of Prints and Drawings at the British Museum.

had seen him three or four times before, when walking with her sisters in the middle of the day: 'he insulted me and my sisters with very gross and indelicate language; he walked behind me and muttered'. Rhynwick did not run away after assaulting her, but walked up to the top of the steps of the house next to the Bagnio. He stood as close to her as he possibly could, and gave his victim an excellent opportunity to observe his countenance. Mr Shepherd pointed at Rhynwick Williams and asked her: 'Look at him as he stands – there – have you any doubt of that being the person that struck you the blow?' She answered: 'No, Sir, I have not the smallest doubt; I could not have been positive, but I saw him three or four times before; I suffered so much from the insults I received, that it is impossible I could be mistaken; I could never forget him.'

Anne Porter then brought out the clothes she had worn on the fateful evening of the Queen's birthday, and showed them to the court; they certainly seemed to have been slashed by some very sharp instrument. Finally, she described how she had pointed Rhynwick Williams out to John Coleman, and how the valiant fishmonger had returned to Pero's Bagnio with his prey.[9]

When Newman Knowlys, the barrister employed by Rhynwick Williams' relations, rose to cross-examine Anne Porter, he first asked her pardon if any of his questions might confuse her; he assured her that no man in this court could sympathise more with her sufferings, and that his duty was the only reason why he questioned her at all. Rhynwick later described how his heart had sunk within him as he heard this remarkable speech; it was now painfully clear to him that even the legal counsel his relations had employed believed him to be guilty.[10] Mr Knowlys' other questions to Anne Porter were in a similar vein: polite, superficial and easy to answer. In all of her alarm and flutter, did she really have time enough to observe Rhynwick Williams? She did. Was there enough light in the street for her to see him clearly? There was. Anne Porter's clothes were again produced. When Mr Knowlys suggested that her gown could easily be put in a wearable state, the injured lady replied 'No, Sir.' After this feeble questioning, Miss Sarah Porter was sworn in as the second witness for the prosecution. Under the skilful direction of Mr Pigot, she described how she had, at least four times, been stalked through the London streets by the bugbear Rhynwick Williams, who had walked closely behind her 'with his head quite leaning over my shoulders, and talking the most dreadful language, that can be imagined.' He was thus well known to her, and it was easy for her to recognise him, since he had impudently stared her in the face before shouting, 'Oh ho! Is that you!' and striking her on the head. The street was very much illuminated, and she had also observed him, at a closer distance, when he ran up to her sister and struck her on the hip with his hand closed round some object. Sarah Porter also told the court that she had observed Rhynwick Williams just a week before he had been taken into custody. Sitting at work by the front window, she had observed Rhynwick walking down St James's Street. She called out to her sister: 'Good God, Nancy, look over this way!' and Anne Porter immediately came to the window and said

'There is the wretch that wounded me.' They sent two men after Rhynwick Williams, but they had followed another man by mistake. Like Anne Porter, Sarah was perfectly certain about the identity of Rhynwick Williams as the man who had assaulted them; at Bow Street, she had pointed him out when he was standing indifferently in a crowd of people. Knowlys again did not distinguish himself in the cross-examining: many of his questions were just echoes of Pigot's own. He tried to make Sarah admit that there were many people in the street at the time, but she resolutely replied that there were very few. Next, Martha and Rebecca Porter testified that Rhynwick Williams had several times stalked them and their sisters in the streets. Mr Knowlys objected as to the relevance of this evidence, but without success.

The fishmonger John Coleman then gave a lengthy, ruminating account of how he had pursued Rhynwick Williams through the London streets. He was certain that the man must have noticed that he was being followed, and that he was well aware for what offence he was being pursued; Rhynwick Williams had clearly seen Anne Porter point him out in St James's Park, he said. Coleman made a boast of his martial attitude during the Monster-hunt: 'I did everything that laid in my power to insult him, by walking behind him, walking before him, looking at him very full in the face, making a noise behind him; I used every art I could to insult him, he would not take any insult, he never said a word, I followed him behind, and I behaved in this kind of way, (peeping over his shoulders, and making a clapping with my hands), and I was going to knock him down once or twice.'[11] It is not known how many were taken in by this feeble bravado. Coleman also claimed that he had at first been prevented from entering Mr Smith's house in South Moulton Street by its owner. Later, when introduced to Rhynwick Williams in the pitch-dark room, Smith had refused to fetch a candle until Coleman had insisted that this should be done. As soon as the room was lit up, Smith wrote down Coleman's address and also the name and address given by Williams. To his astonishment, John Coleman then discovered that the two had actually met before; this was not

denied by Williams, who asked if Coleman had not been introduced at a ball in Bond Street to which he belonged. Outside Mr
Smith's house, the two men went different ways, but Coleman fortunately changed his mind and managed to overtake Williams.
Coleman had to admit that the Monster was a cool customer:
when brought before the fainting Misses Porter, he 'did not conduct himself in any particular way. I thought he possessed very
great resolution in case he was the guilty man.' He had said, 'Good
God! I hope they do not take me for the person about whom there
has been so many Publications', which was considered damning,
but John Coleman had to admit, at the prompting of Mr Knowlys,
that Rhynwick Williams had not seemed in the least embarrassed
when they went to Pero's Bagnio.

Runner Macmanus was next sworn. He recounted how he had
gone to the George public house, which Mr Pigot had described
in such derogatory terms, and taken a coat, a hat and a pair of
boots from a box belonging to Rhynwick Williams. Interestingly,
Macmanus had a personal knowledge of Williams, since the latter
had previously lodged not far from the Bow Street public office, and
he had himself seen Rhynwick Williams wear this coat. Mr Knowlys
made an effort to rehabilitate the landlord of the George, and suggested that although these lodgings were not particularly expensive,
the public house was a decent one, and run by good people. 'As
good as any that keep a public house', Macmanus answered guard-
edly. Mr Knowlys had better luck with Rhynwick Williams' grey
coat. It was evident that it was not, as had been previously alleged, a
surtout coat; its fit was quite close-bodied, even around Rhynwick's
slender frame. This threw suspicion over the Misses Porter's identification of this garment as the coat worn over another coat by the
Monster, but Knowlys made no attempt to pursue this advantage.
Nor did he press the point that Macmanus had found no cutting
implements at the lodgings of Rhynwick Williams, or those of his
mother. Judge Buller himself asked the Runner a series of important questions. He wanted to rule out the possibility that the address
Rhynwick Williams had given, No. 52 Jermyn Street, might apply to

the George public house in Bury Street, a crossroad to Jermyn Street. Macmanus replied that it did not, but that it might apply to Rhynwick Williams' mother's dwellings in Duke Street, another crossroad of Jermyn Street.[12] He was quite out of his depth to explain the topography of these streets, however:

> 'What number did the mother live at?'
> 'I do not know.'
> 'Nor do you know what the number of the house was that you searched?'
> 'No.'

After the Runner had been dismissed, somewhat petulantly, by Judge Buller, Surgeon Tomkins was sworn. He testified that Anne Porter's wound was nine or ten inches long, and that its middle part had penetrated the skin to the depth of three or four inches. Mr Knowlys asked him 'Whether a cut with a sharp instrument, merely to cut the cloaths, would have wounded so deep as that?' The Surgeon answered in the negative: but for the bow of the stays, the wound might even have penetrated the abdomen. After this important admission from the Surgeon, Mr Knowlys turned his attention to Runner Macmanus, who again had to hold forth on the topography of Jermyn Street. He willingly admitted that the dwellings of Rhynwick Williams' mother had been at the corner of Duke Street and Jermyn Street, and that one entered through a door in Jermyn Street. He could not recall if it was No. 52, however.

At this point, there was a defection from the witnesses for the defence. Lady Wallace, who had come into court at her own initiative offering to testify that Rhynwick Williams was not the Monster who had threatened her, called the counsel for the defence and said that the whole thing had just been one of her little jokes. She had never been attacked or insulted by the Monster, and was not prepared to give evidence. She would be pleased to retain her front-row seat at this fascinating trial, thank you very much, since it would be interesting to see that wretched little man being convicted.

The wound that he made in this young Lady's hip
was Nine Inches long, and near Four Inches deep;
But before that this Monster had made use of force,
He insulted their ears with obscene discourse.

After a brief recess, it was time for Rhynwick Williams to make his defence. One of his biographers wrote that, 'When it is considered what universal alarm the depredations of the man, denominated *The Monster*, have excited in the metropolis, need we wonder that the moment in which he is about to make his defence, should be considered an interesting one, by a splendid and numerous auditory! Silence and attention pervaded every corner!'[13] Rhynwick Williams was a disappointment, however. The big-nosed little man in the shabby blue coat, who was the cynosure of all eyes, from those of the Duke of Cumberland to those of the lowliest court servant, endeavoured to speak from memory, but his shrill, thin voice did not carry; he soon lost recollection and was unable to proceed. He then seized up a bundle of papers and read the following pathetic speech:

My Lord, and Gentlemen of the Jury, I stand here an object deserving of your most serious attention, from conscious innocence of the very shocking accusations brought against me, I cannot but hope that just and really liberal minds will have reason to commiserate my situation, and must feel me deserving pity and compassion. As my case has been multiplied in horror, though, with submission, I think, in compassion, far beyond even the sufferings of my accusers, I admit in justice that I should have experienced the hardships I have suffered in the process of the law against me, till my innocence could be proved, but while I revere the law of my country, which presumes every man to be innocent till proved guilty, yet I must reprobate the cruelty with which the Public Prints have abounded, in the most scandalous paragraphs, containing malicious exaggerations of the charges preferred so much to my prejudice, that I already lie under premature conviction, by almost an universal voice, I chearfully resign my case into the hands of this tribunal, whose peculiar province and character is to reason on evident motives and circumstances, and which, I trust, will not suffer the fate of a fellow creature to be determined by popular prejudice ... I most seriously appeal to the Great Author of Truth, that I have the strongest affection for the happiness and comfort of the superior part of this creation, the fair sex, to whom I have, in every circumstance that occurred in my life, endeavoured to render assistance and protection. I have nothing, my Lord and Gentlemen, further to say, but that, however strange and aggravated this case may appear to you, I solemnly, and with the utmost sincerity, declare to you all, that this prosecution of me is founded in a dreadful mistake, which I hope the evidence I shall bring will prove to your satisfaction.

Rhynwick Williams sat down amid a torrent of hisses from the audience.

The witnesses for the defence were then brought up. It was an unpleasant surprise for Mr Pigot and his associates to observe that an entire crowd of people were prepared to give evidence on behalf of Rhynwick Williams. The first and foremost of them was his former employer, the Frenchman M. Aimable Michelle, proprietor of Mitchell's Artificial Flower Factory at No. 14 Dover Street.[14] He had lived in London for four years, and had decided to anglicise his surname to Mitchell; his Christian name was a more difficult case in this respect, and in the newspaper accounts of the trial, he is variously referred to as 'Amabel' or 'Amarvel'. His prolonged residence in London had not induced Amabel to learn to speak proper English, however; he was such a poor linguist that he had to be interrogated through an interpreter. At the direction of Mr Knowlys, Amabel Mitchell testified that Rhynwick Williams had worked at the artificial flower factory for about nine months at the time Anne Porter had been attacked. His normal working hours were from nine in the morning until nine in the evening, but the evening of the Queen's birthday, 18 January, had been an exception. There had been particularly many orders for artificial flowers, and Williams had stayed at work until midnight. Amabel Mitchell then had the decency to offer his tired labourer, who had been making artificial flowers for nearly fourteen hours, some supper; Williams finally left the factory at half past midnight. Mitchell was adamant that Rhynwick Williams had not been absent from his workbench at any time between two in the afternoon and midnight. He credited Williams with 'the best character a man could have' and added that he had always treated the female workers with civility and good nature.

It was then Mr Pigot's turn to cross-examine the Frenchman, who gave all his replies through the court interpreter. He was amazed at the booming business of the flower factory, which had forced Mitchell to keep both Rhynwick Williams and several of his other employees at work nearly around the clock. The Frenchman replied that a large order from Ireland had forced him to keep his entire workforce doing extra hours for at least nine days before the Queen's birthday. In addition, on the afternoon of 18 January, he had received a last-minute order for a lady's gown to be decorated with artificial flowers, after three of his workforce had already sought, and obtained, permission to go out and enjoy the festivities of the day. Amabel Mitchell himself, his sister Reine Michelle, Rhynwick Williams and two workwomen who lodged in the house had to finish this gown by the following morning. Suddenly, Mr Pigot tried to bully the Frenchman into making an admission:

> 'Upon your oath, had not you and the prisoner at the bar been out that day together?'
> 'Certainly not.'
> 'You had!'
> 'I had not.'

Mr Pigot then reverted to his former careful probing into the workings of the flower factory and the comings and goings of its staff, and in particular everything that Mitchell could remember about what had happened during that evening half a year earlier, which the Frenchman appeared to recall so perfectly. He hoped to shake the inscrutable Amabel's testimony, or at least to demonstrate contradictions in the other alibi witnesses that were to follow. Mitchell patiently told him that during the eight or nine months Rhynwick Williams had been in his employ, he had been a model worker: he had never been absent from work, except once or twice when given leave. It was very rare that he was sent out on errands: on a typical day, he just sat quietly at his desk beavering away at his work on the artificial flowers. Mr Pigot asked Mitchell whether he had looked at his watch or clock just when Rhynwick Williams had left the factory, since he was so sure it was exactly at half past midnight. The Frenchman replied that he had not, and Mr Pigot pricked up his ears; how could he then swear so positively that it was half past twelve at night when Rhynwick Williams had quitted him. Mitchell replied that his maid Molly had, just that instance, heard the watchman cry out the time; she had remarked to her sister Catherine how well the flower factory clock in Amabel Mitchell's parlour kept the time, since it exactly agreed with the watchman's shout. The sister later repeated this observation to Amabel's sister Reine. She had, in her turn, reported it to her brother two or three weeks later.

Rhynwick Williams had come to work early the following morning, and had remained with Mitchell's establishment until 4 June. The great order from Ireland for a massive amount of artificial flowers had come from a certain Mr Crowe, who was apparently an artificial flower wholesaler; he had come to London in person to bring the order. Mitchell's brother-in-law M. Jean Jerseaux (alias John Jerso), who was taking care of business at the factory while Mitchell was away, had written proof of all this. At this time, while Mr Pigot was ending his questioning, Lady Wallace, who was still sitting among the witnesses for the defence, sent a scribbled note across the court. Its contents were startling: the day before, she had been accosted by a strange, threatening man in Green Park, and later outside Lord William Gordon's house in

Piccadilly.[15] She was certain that this man, or rather Monster, was none less than Amabel Mitchell! Mr Pigot immediately went in for the kill. Did the witness know Lord William Gordon's house? Yes, he had been there. Had he happened to pass this house, or pass through Green Park, yesterday evening? The bemused Amabel replied that he had not.

> 'And all the rest that you have sworn today, is just as true as the last,
>   that you were not in Green Park yesterday evening?'
> 'Just as true.'
> 'Then, not being in Green Park, I need hardly ask you whether you
>   accosted any ladies in the Green Park yesterday evening.'
> 'No, I did not accost any ladies in the Green Park.'
> 'Or near Lord William Gordon's house?'
> 'I was not near that way.'

Mr Pigot ended his cross-examination by calling out, in a menacing way, 'Let that witness not go out of court!' He intended, of course, to call Lady Wallace as a witness, and thus win a brilliant legal victory: he would not only incriminate Mitchell as the possible accomplice of the Monster, but also discredit his entire testimony in favour of the prisoner. But when he asked Lady Wallace to testify, she again flatly refused: the whole thing had just been one of her little jokes, and she was delighted it had been taken so seriously! Poor Mr Pigot probably wished that the Monster had really cut this skittish lady's behind; his attempt to discredit Amabel Mitchell had fallen flat.

Mlle Reine Michelle (alias Miss Raines Mitchell), the flower-maker's sister, was next sworn. Examined by Mr Knowlys, she confidently swore that, on the evening of the Queen's birthday, Rhynwick Williams had been at work from dinnertime until twelve o'clock, and that he had not left the factory until half past midnight.[16] His behaviour towards her and the other female workers had always been perfectly good-natured. Mr Shepherd next took over the cross-examining. Raines Mitchell repeated her brother's testimony: the flower factory had had a great deal of work for Ireland for several weeks, and at six o'clock on the Queen's birthday came an order for a gown for the celebrated actress Mrs Abingdon, who was to perform and wear it the night after the birthday.[17] Mr Jerso had come to the factory with a pattern of floral decoration that Mrs Abingdon had given him, and Amabel Mitchell ordered his workers to set about making the flowers and pasting them onto the dress. Of the normal workforce of at least eleven people, only Rhynwick Williams, the sisters Molly and Catherine Alman, who lodged in the house and thus could not escape extra-time work, the workwoman Frances Beaufils, and the workman Typhone Fournier, had been available to finish the work on the gown, and both Amabel and his sister had helped as well. With his own hands, Amabel Mitchell had pasted Rhynwick's artificial flowers onto the gown. Raines Mitchell repeated her brother's story about Molly the maid's comment about the clock. When Rhynwick Williams had been taken as the Monster, the Mitchells had gathered their servants and workers to see what they recalled about the night Miss Porter had been attacked. Molly then told her story about the watchman and the clock. Probably impressed by the quality of Rhynwick Williams' alibi, Judge Buller demanded that Mr Jerso should be called as a witness, and an officer was to accompany Amabel Mitchell back to the flower factory to get his books of trade.

In the meantime, the forewoman Catherine Alman, sister of the maid Molly who was so observant about the time, was sworn.[18] Interrogated by Mr Knowlys, who was becoming increasingly active during the course of the trial, she verified Amabel Mitchell's story in every respect: she was absolutely positive that Rhynwick Williams had been at work in the flower factory from two in the afternoon until half past twelve on the Queen's birthday, and that he had not been absent one moment during this time. Her sister had told her that, at the time she opened the door to let Williams out, it was half past twelve, and she was equally certain about the date. It was her convinced opinion that Rhynwick Williams was a very good-natured man, and very sober and attentive in his habits. Mr Pigot rose to cross-examine her. She maintained that she could well recollect that on the night in question, her sister Molly had come into the workshop where they had supped, saying that it was half past twelve, and that she was afraid Williams might be too late to get into his lodgings. At the time, Rhynwick was lodging at Mr Williams the china-seller, in Duke's Court not far from the flower factory. Amabel Mitchell, his sister and the French artificial flower-maker Typhone Fournier had been present when Mary had told them about the watchman, the clock and the time being half past twelve. Mr Pigot pricked up his ears, sensing a contradiction, but the witness calmly told him that she had spoken in English, a language which the three French people did not normally speak, and they probably did not understand her. Normally, the conversation in the flower factory was in French, but Molly was a bad linguist just like her employer, and preferred to speak English whenever possible. After Molly had shut the door after Williams, she had come straight back into the back shop and made the remark in question. Catherine Alman had not recollected this observation of her sister until Rhynwick Williams had been arrested as the Monster, but at that time, she remembered it to perfection. She also recalled that the following morning, Rhynwick had told her that he had managed to get into his lodgings after all, and that the clock had struck one when he finally went to bed.

Molly Alman was the next witness for the defence. Questioned by Mr Knowlys, she repeated her sister's testimony almost verbatim. Mr Shepherd then took over the questioning. The strength of Rhynwick Williams' alibi was surprising, but this witness did not appear to be particularly clever, and he took considerable care in examining her testimony. She had just been staying with Mitchell one or two months at the time. The flower factory was a large one, and had been very busy for some time. Contradicting her colleagues, she claimed that Rhynwick Williams never stayed long at work, and that this was the longest she had ever observed him to work. Molly had been in the workshop all afternoon, but had never observed any person come in to deliver an order. At Judge Buller's prompting, she later corrected herself and said that Jerso had been at the factory at about four in the afternoon, but she had not paid any attention to what business he was about. Nor could she recollect Amabel himself leaving the factory for any period of time. She herself, Rhynwick Williams, Amabel Mitchell and his sister had worked on a gown all evening: there had been no other people in the room at the time. Shepherd then moved on to the most important point of all: the time when Rhynwick Williams had left the flower factory. Molly declared that just as she had let Mr Williams out, *he had asked her to look at the clock*! Mr Shepherd asked her why Williams could not have looked at the clock himself, but she simply replied that he told her to look. Her sister Catherine had appealed to her about three weeks before to recall the events of the Queen's birthday, at the time when Rhynwick Williams was taken up as the London Monster. She freely admitted that she had told her sister that she had looked at the clock because Williams had asked her to do so, and for no other reason. She also denied that she had, at any time, said that she was afraid Rhynwick would be late back to his lodgings.

Next, the workwoman Frances Beaufils was sworn. Questioned by Mr Knowlys, she testified that she had been employed at the flower factory six weeks before that fateful Queen's birthday on 18 January. She had been working there that day until half past eleven, and Rhynwick Williams (a very good-natured man) had been there all the time. She knew the time since she had asked the watchman when she got home in Coventry Court (off Coventry Street near the Haymarket) and he had told her it was half an hour past eleven. Cross-examined by Mr Pigot, she said that Amabel Mitchell had not been out at any time after two o'clock. Neither had, she said, any order for a dress come in during this period of time; nor could she remember Jerso having made an appearance. The Frenchman Typhone Fournier agreed with his fellow workers that Rhynwick Williams was a very good-natured man, and that he had been at work at the factory at least until eleven o'clock in the evening. Mr Shepherd then extracted the information that this witness had only worked for Mitchell's flower factory from Christmas 1789 until 14 February 1790: for a kingpin of the London artificial flower business, Amabel Mitchell certainly had a dangerously rapid turnover of his workforce! At about eleven o'clock, Fournier had left the factory to go to his own lodgings off Great Windmill Street; at this time, Rhynwick Williams was still at work. In a faltering way, the Frenchman swore that Amabel Mitchell himself had also been at work from two in the afternoon until late at night. The clever Mr Shepherd then made him swear that he was just as sure about Amabel Mitchell's whereabouts (bearing in mind that Mitchell had earlier claimed to have been out in the afternoon) as he was about any other circumstance, and Fournier readily obliged.

Runners Macmanus and Townsend then returned, together with the excited Amabel Mitchell and his colleague Jerso. The latter was questioned by Mr Knowlys, and testified that he had certainly called upon his brother-in-law Amabel Mitchell on the Queen's birthday to give him an order for a gown for Mrs Abingdon; he had drawn the pattern for it at Mitchell's house at some time after seven o'clock that evening. Amabel himself had been out at the time, and Jerso was not even sure that he had come home an hour later, when Jerso had visited the factory to see how the work on the gown was proceeding. The entry for this gown was in the books, just as Amabel Mitchell had predicted.

> She met with this Monster one day in the Park,
> As she walk'd with Mr Coleman, who notic'd the spark,
> She told him how much from this wretch she'd endur'd
> So he follow'd the Monster, and had him secur'd.

After the alibi witnesses were done, no less than seventeen character witnesses testified on behalf of Rhynwick Williams. Sarah Brady, a former workwoman at the flower factory, had known him for six months and pronounced his character to be very good-natured, with no single instance of a spiteful disposition. Sophia Cameron, who had known Rhynwick Williams no less than eight years, and who had later worked five months at the flower factory, also pronounced him 'truly good-natured'. Mr Pigot, who was apparently more than a little mystified by Rhynwick Williams' strange ways and the company he kept, did what he could to disparage the clouds that seemed to obscure the prisoner's shady past. He asked Sophia Cameron if she had known Rhynwick Williams when he lived with Sir John Gallini, but she gave a non-committal reply, evidently understanding that this topic was not a suitable one to be further probed into. A certain Mr Terry, who worked in the Navy office, and in whose house Rhynwick Williams and his family had previously lodged for an entire year, also gave the prisoner the 'most amiable character for good nature, amiable behaviour and politeness'. He had left Sir John Gallini, whom he used to assist in teaching in some boarding schools, some time before Mr Terry met him in 1786. He had then had no other work except to assist his sister in making artificial flowers, and Mr Terry had often seen him sitting hard at work late in the evenings. The next character witness, Mr Thomas Williams, a respectable china-seller in St James's Street, was quick to point out that the prisoner was no relation of his! He had known Rhynwick Williams for nearly six years, and the prisoner had actually lodged in his house at one time. Thomas Williams pronounced Rhynwick a very good-natured young man; in fact, his main fault was that he 'liked the ladies too well' (laughter in court)! Rhynwick Williams had quitted Sir John Gallini in 1785, and had been making artificial flowers for nearly two years at the present time; when asked how Rhynwick had earned his bread during the intervening period of time, Thomas Williams just replied, 'I know no more than you.'[19]

Another character witness was Miss Sarah Seward, of Seven Dials. A plain, inelegantly dressed woman, she swore that she had known Rhynwick Williams for four years, and that he was an honest, manly young man, for he had once *saved her life*! This later statement did not have the desired effect, however. Miss Seward may have appeared ridiculous in her dress or person, or it may be that the idea that the Monster had saved a woman's life appeared exceedingly funny to the audience; it remains a sad fact that there was a great laugh in the courtroom, in which Mr Pigot and the other prosecuting counsel heartily joined in. Poor Sarah Seward retreated from the witness-box in confusion, amidst lewd and villainous insults from the more rowdy members of the audience. Rhynwick Williams himself was, for some reason, particularly indignant about the brusque treatment of his premier character witness. He wrote that although she did not possess 'a silver toned voice, a delicate painted face, nor habited in white muslin, nor declaiming the fashionable cause of the day', she had deserved a better treatment. He contrasted the laughter at poor Sarah Seward's expense with the great empathy and compassion shown to the Misses Porter and their apparent sufferings: 'while telling their tale, did they excite a laugh? Was the audience merry then? No! no! no! certainly not!'[20]

Many other character witnesses followed, and according to the newspaper reports, they often had precious little to tell about the elusive Rhynwick Williams. William Baker, in whose house Rhynwick had lodged for four months, had nothing to say except that he believed the prisoner to be an honest young man. According to one of the pamphlets about the trial, a certain Mr Smith (the man of mystery from South Moulton Street?) 'produced nothing in addition to the character of his old acquaintance, whatever might have been his intention.' Many in the audience were shocked and outraged that several beautiful women appeared in court to testify to Rhynwick Williams' fondness of the fair sex. The evidence of these ladies is not contained in any transcript of the case, but one pamphlet writer sneeringly remarked that '*several* young women, whose appearance, however, did not bespeak them of the highest class, but rather of the inferior kind' had appeared in favour of the prisoner.[21] A susceptible journalist in the *Oracle* newspaper wrote approvingly of these 'very beautiful females', and considered that their testimony had proved to everyone's satisfaction that far from having any aversion to the female sex, Rhynwick Williams was 'in habits of fond, constant, and manly intercourse with them'![22]

Judge Buller then addressed the jury.[23] He presumed that every person in the crowded audience knew about the London Monster and his heinous crimes. Considering the prejudice any honest man must feel who entered a court where such enormities were discussed, he strongly urged every member of the jury to totally disregard every thing they had heard about the Monster business before they had entered the Old Bailey: they should disregard all prejudice and consider the case with patience and attention.

Judge Buller pointed out to the jury that all four Misses Porter were well acquainted with the Monster's appearance: according to their testimony, he had stalked them through the streets on several occasions, and there was little chance they were mistaken as to his identity. The judge ruminated at length about the assailant's uncouth way of making himself known to Sarah Porter: 'Oh ho! Is that you!' – this was a particularly vulgar and distasteful expression, and truly befitting to a Monster. This singular address surely indicated that the Monster had previously met the Misses, and that the circumstances of their meetings had not been amiable; it thus served to support the testimony of the Misses Porter that Rhynwick Williams had previously stalked them. Judge Buller also put much emphasis on the fact that Williams must have known that he was being followed by Coleman, and that he made several attempts to dodge his pursuer, a circumstance in itself indicative of guilt. He then recapitulated the great fainting scene in the front room of the Bagnio – 'a more distressful or melancholy scene could hardly be exhibited' – and the fact that Williams was himself the first person to suggest that they took him for the London Monster. When Coleman had affirmed that this was the case, Williams had said nothing, and did not attempt to clear his name. These were all circumstances that gave additional credence to the oaths of all four Misses Porter, who had identified him without reservation.

Judge Buller then discussed the testimony in favour of the prisoner. No less than seven people had appeared to give Rhynwick Williams an alibi for the evening in question. It was evident that Mitchell had gathered his servants and workforce in June, after

Williams had been taken as the Monster, to try to recollect what had happened on the evening of the Queen's birthday and how long Williams had stayed at the factory. The judge considered this a very loose way of making up their minds, with ample opportunity for a mistake with regard to the date, the time and other circumstances. Amabel Mitchell's testimony did not have the same candid appearance as that of the Misses Porter, and there had been some contradictions: in particular, the stories of the sisters Molly and Catherine Alman disagreed in several important particulars.

Judge Buller left it to the jury to decide which side to believe: the artificial flower-makers, who swore that Williams had been at the factory at the time Anne and Sarah Porter were attacked, or the very positive testimony of the four Misses Porter, who identified Williams as the Monster. If they decided to believe the Misses Porter, the next thing was to consider his intent. If Williams had intended to cut Anne Porter with intent to murder, he must be innocent, for this was not a felony but a mere misdemeanour. On the other hand, if he had cut her with intent to cut and tear her clothes, then he was a felon according to the Sixth Act of George I, and must be punished accordingly. The judge then made the important admission that he himself had some doubts about this indictment, and whether this ancient statute was really the proper one; if Rhynwick Williams was found guilty, he intended to reserve the case for the consideration of the Twelve Judges of England. In the mean time, the jury should consider whether it might indeed have been Rhynwick Williams' intent to cut both the clothes and the flesh: in that case, he must be found guilty as charged. He cunningly pointed out that the instrument used by the Monster was of a particular construction, both very long and very sharp, and that the witnesses had said that their clothes were extremely badly cut. It was of course impossible to strike Miss Porter's person without cutting her clothes, but the damage to the clothes was certainly much worse than could have been expected. Whether this constituted an intention to cut her clothes was for the jury to decide: 'I can only leave the case, on both points, for your consideration; it is for you alone to discuss, and pronounce the prisoner, GUILTY or INNOCENT; as you shall judge the truth of the case to be.' The jury immediately pronounced Rhynwick Williams guilty as charged. Judge Buller recommended that the sentence was to be respited until the December sessions, for the opinion of the Twelve Judges to be heard in the meantime.

On the Eight of July, at the Old Baily try'd
After Eight Hours hearing the Jury decide
That he was found Guilty, but sentence defer'd
Until the Twelve Judges opinion is heard.

In May 1790, John Julius Angerstein had decided to collate his abundant material on the Monster assaults into a pamphlet. Whether Ang-erstein wrote the pamphlet himself, or whether he employed some journalist to do so, is uncertain, but it contains material available only to Angerstein himself or someone in his close circle. This pamphlet was clearly intended as a complete handbook for the prospective Monster-hunter and contained a detailed summary of all Monster attacks until May 1790; his *modus operandi* in each case was reviewed, and every wounded lady gave evidence, as well as she could, as to his dress and appearance. The pamphlet was ostentatiously entitled *An Authentic Account of the Barbarities lately practiced by the Monsters! Being an unprecedented and unnatural Species of Cruelty, exercised by a set of Men upon defenceless and generally handsome Women.* It also contained a brief pen-portrait of each of the wounded ladies, since Angerstein thought that 'a description of the person of each of the fair victims of this novel species of barbarity must be interesting'; in this way, he would also be certain of a considerable number of subscribers from London's female world.

The great ballyhoo about the arrest of Rhynwick Williams made this pamphlet obsolete before it had even been published. Although it was advertised in the papers, it is unlikely that any books were actually printed. Angerstein saw fit to revise it and include a couple of lengthy chapters about the arrest and trial of Rhynwick Williams. In spite of all the work he had put into this pamphlet, its philanthropic author had not thought it befitting to put his name on the front page; the reason may well be that he was already ridiculed by some for his obsessive anti-Monster activities.[24] This revised edition was not published until late July, and by that time the market was already saturated with Monster books. Just like after the trial of some notorious public figure in our own time, several catchpenny publishers had decided to make some money out of the Monster-mania and publish an account of the crimes and trial of Rhynwick Williams. The first of these publications, *The Remarkable Trial of Rhynwick Williams*, had been taken down in shorthand by a student in the Temple, and printed with all possible haste to be ready at the booksellers' shelves at noon on 9 July, the day after Rhynwick Williams had been found guilty. This student was probably dismayed to see that someone else had had exactly the same idea; later on 9 July, another catchpenny pamphlet entitled *The Trial of Rhynwick Williams* made its appearance. Its contents had been taken down in shorthand by L. Williams Esq. This latter pamphlet had an advantage not only in its low price – one shilling – but also in that it was illustrated with an engraved portrait of Rhynwick Williams 'taken on the spot by a capital Artist'. It was cleverly advertised all over London with huge posters labelled 'The MONSTER' which mimicked those of Mr Angerstein.[25]

Two more pamphlets appeared shortly after: the anonymous *Authentic Trial of Rhynwick Williams* and the *Full Account of the Trial of Rhynwick Williams*, written by Mr Nath. Jenkins. Mr E. Hodgson, the official Short Hand Writer to the Old Bailey, had been completely overwhelmed by his numerous and mercenary competitors. Although he and his publishers did what they could to make haste, his *The Trial at Large of Rhynwick Williams* was not out in the bookstalls until 13 July. Although he had published newspaper advertisements warning the public that 'as there are spurious and Catchpenny trials now publishing, to be particularly careful to order E. Hodgson's *Trial at Large*', much was lost in terms of sale. Mr Hodgson's pamphlet is by far the most extensive, as well as the most accurate, account of the trial, and the only one to give the testimony of the alibi witnesses verbatim. It was illustrated with an excellent print of Rhynwick Williams at the Bar of the Old Bailey. In spite of the competition, it is, along with the Williams volume, the most common Monster pamphlet to be met with today. It is interesting that Hodgson's pamphlet was the only one to take the Monster-mania over the Atlantic: an American edition was printed by Thomas Greenleaf in 1791, and sold by the bookseller Andrew Marschalk in New York.[26]

The trial of Rhynwick Williams also inspired another spate of satirical prints. Already on 9 July, two good likenesses of Williams, by Nixon and (possibly) Gillray, could be purchased in the print shops. *Representation of the Monster*, which was published on 12 July by W. Dent, is a good indicator of the amount of prejudice against Rhynwick Williams. This caricature had several frames: one depicted a villainous-looking Rhynwick Williams on trial at the Old Bailey, another showed him prowling about in one of his disguises; the grand scene of him cutting the Misses Porter was in the middle. Its text boldly agitates that Rhynwick Williams should be hanged, and not transported, since the latter punishment would give him an opportunity to exercise his cruelties on the females of another country. In another of Dent's prints, *Spanish Rupture*, the Monster takes a hand in politics: Prime Minister William Pitt is depicted as the Monster. He dashes his diabolical nosegay into Britannia's face with gusto, and stabs her in the behind with his rapier. A violent diarrhoea has burst his breeches; the torn parts are inscribed Sudden – War. The rival politician Charles James Fox stands looking on aghast, calling out that had she trusted to him for protection, 'he would have her on such a BOTTOM that none would have dared to insult you'. Pitt had been unjustly accused of truckling to Spain over the Nootka Sound affair, and this was but one of the several satirical prints lampooning him.

The unfortunate Mr Angerstein was quite outclassed, in terms of sales, by this unexpected competition. His thick pamphlet of 166 pages cost two shillings and had no illustrations at all. Along with Hodgson's *The Trial at Large of Rhynwick Williams*, it is by far the best account of the Monster-mania and the arrest and trial of Williams, however. Angerstein was *the* expert on the Monster business, and it is particularly interesting to read his opinion of the case against Rhynwick Williams. At the time he was writing, he was apparently not entirely convinced that the right man had been convicted. He was very much impressed with the solidity of Rhynwick Williams' alibi, which had, after all, been sworn to by seven different witnesses. The contradictions in their stories could be explained from the fact that the foreign witnesses gave their evidence through an interpreter, and were unable to explain or correct any mistakes or misconceptions that might have occurred. Angerstein also queried why Mrs Miel, the chaperone of the Porter sisters, and their brother John who opened the door to them, had not been called as witnesses; how could the prisoner's counsel have allowed this to happen, since their testimony was of the utmost importance? The Editor of the *Rambler's Magazine* shared his doubt about Williams' guilt, claiming that many Londoners who had attended the trial were impressed by the alibi; there were 'serious apprehensions entertained by many, that the ladies have mistaken the person of their inhuman assailant.'[27]

John Julius Angerstein was also convinced, from the dissimilarity of the descriptions of the culprits, that 'there are SEVERAL of these *unnatural wretches*, these inhuman MONSTERS, ... or rather *creatures in the shape of men*, a disgrace to society, the outcasts of the creation.' Moreover, he was certain that these unnatural men, these Monsters, were in league with another. He particularly noted an article from the *Morning Chronicle* of 25 June, claiming that a man had been apprehended in Birmingham for deliberately wounding one of the ladies of that town. It was said that he had been identified as a Londoner, and that he had fled the metropolis in consequence of the measures taken by the authorities to bring to justice the *accomplices* of Rhynwick Williams.

As Rhynwick Williams sat in his cell in Newgate Prison, he is likely to have been the most wretched man in London. Even before he had been arrested as the Monster, his existence had not been an enviable one: he had been penniless, with hardly any friends; indeed, he had been shunned even by his own relatives, and lived under the most dismal circumstances with not even a bed to himself. Now he was the most hated man in London. Had the mob not been restrained, the anti-Monster ruffians would literally have torn him to pieces. Newgate served him as a safe haven rather than a prison. There were calls in the newspapers to have him hanged, flogged, pilloried or at least transported, but most people seemed content to let him rot in prison. Sir Sampson Wright and the other magistrates were very much relieved to be rid of this spectre of a Monster, which had put the metropolis into such a turmoil. Mr Angerstein was receiving congratulations from his many new friends in London's female world, gloating that he had been right all the time: there had really been a Monster, and he had been instrumental in the apprehension of this human fiend. The exulting John Coleman could not wait to get his hands into Angerstein's money-coffers, and the swooning Misses Porter heaved a communal sigh of relief to be saved from their monstrous assailant. Although no less than seven people had sworn, upon oath, that Rhynwick had been elsewhere at the time of the assault on Anne Porter, he had been convicted by an unanimous jury; not even his own legal counsel had believed in his innocence. Like in some bizarre pagan ceremony, he had been dragged through the streets to be jeered and pelted by the Londoners celebrating the end of the Monster's reign of terror. If there was ever a man in need of a doughty champion, a valorous knight-errant, that man was Rhynwick Williams.

9

THE
MONSTER'S
Champion

I loath my own and every wedded wife –
I'll drag connubial secrets into day,
Stranger myself to all domestic peace,
Distracted matrons my revenge shall fear –
With phrase obscene I'll wound each delicate ear –
Infants with screams my furious threats shall hear,
And never shall my efforts cease
'Till I have agonized each College dame
Blasted her comfort – sneered away her fame –
My great revenge shall laugh her griefs to see
And RHYNWICK WILLIAMS' self shall be outdone by me!

Theophilus Swift, *Prison Pindarics* (1795)

It must have come as a surprise to the Londoners when, in
September 1790, as Rhynwick Williams was languishing in
Newgate, the Irish poet and controversialist Theophilus Swift
appeared as his champion. In a startling pamphlet entitled *The
Monster at Large*, he advanced the theory that Rhynwick Williams
was innocent and that the real Monster was still free and unpunished.

He also claimed that Misses Porter and John Coleman were a gang of impostors, who had deliberately planned the arrest and subsequent downfall of poor Rhynwick Williams.

Theophilus Swift was born in 1746, the son of Deane Swift of Dublin, an Irish gentleman of some fortune, and a descendant in a collateral line of Jonathan Swift. Theophilus was educated at Oxford, and graduated with a BA in 1767. He was called to the Bar at the Middle Temple in 1774, and practised law for a couple of years. In 1783, his father died and Theophilus inherited his estates in Limerick. A forthright, eccentric character, he spent a good deal of time in Dublin, and became involved in much controversy. Nichols' *Literary Anecdotes* tells us that that a certain Captain Ayscough, a timid military man with literary ambitions, was several times insulted by Theophilus Swift, who treated him as a poltroon.[1] Theophilus married an Irish wife, with whom he had many heated quarrels. He himself later wrote that 'I am the quietest, best-tempered man, but she was a very termagant'. Once, when Theophilus teased her by reading aloud a lewd and satirical poem he had written about 'The Female Parliament' – insane women who imagined themselves equal to men[2] – his wife seized up her own infant, young Deane Swift, from his cot, and took a swing at her tormentor. Many years later, Theophilus still remembered the resounding knock as his head met that of his son in full swing. After this incident, he decided that he and his wife would do much better living apart.[3]

It took until 1789 for Theophilus Swift to become more widely known. That year, Colonel Charles Lennox had challenged the Duke of York to a duel after they had had a heated argument in the regimental mess room. They exchanged shots at Wimbledon Common, and Lennox's bullet grazed one of the Duke's curls. The Duke then fired in the air. Afterwards, he refused to say that Lennox was a man of honour and courage, apparently being firmly convinced to the contrary. Theophilus Swift took great exception to this scandalous duel. In a pamphlet entitled *A Letter to the King on the Conduct of Colonel Lennox*, he abused and blackguarded the Colonel as 'a hot-headed young man, who had conceived his own polluted person insulted by Royalty'.[4] He even advanced the audacious theory that Charles Lennox was a secret agent in the employ of Prime Minister William Pitt, on a mission to murder all George III's sons – this dastardly attempt on the Duke's life was just the first in an intended series of assassinations masked as duels. As a result of this pamphlet, Charles Lennox, who was the son of Lord Charles Lennox, and grandson of the Duke of Richmond, challenged Theophilus Swift to a duel. It took considerable courage for anyone to face up to a man like Charles Lennox: a tough, ruthless character who fancied himself as a crack shot. Theophilus Swift, from sheer obstinacy if nothing else, nevertheless went through with the duel. His shot missed, but Lennox's did not: Theophilus was hit in the belly, and his life was several times despaired upon. Theophilus said farewell to his friends, made his will, and bequeathed to the Duke of York his gold snuffbox. According to a contemporary account, both gentlemen had behaved with great coolness and intrepidity during the duel.[4] While finally recovering from his bullet wound, Theophilus wrote another venomous pamphlet: in his own words, 'When confined with the wound I received from Lenox in the cause of my country, nothing gave me so much pleasure as writing the charming little pamphlet I published on the occasion.'[5] He also spread a rumour that he had originally wanted to fight with swords, but that Lennox had preferred pistols; had they fought with swords, Theophilus would have carved the Colonel like a turkey, he boasted. He even hinted that as soon as he recovered from his bullet wound, he would challenge Lennox to another duel, with swords, but *The Times* acidly remarked that the Colonel would have the choice of weapon if challenged, and 'Mr Swift, we believe, has *had enough of that*'.[6] Theophilus had obviously hoped to gain some preferment by this quixotic adventure, but all he got was that the Duke of York once sent his compliments and condolence.[7]

The same year, 1789, Theophilus Swift had made the acquaintance of Rhynwick Williams, whom he later described as 'a very ingenious artist and my particular friend'. Although Rhynwick's profession was, at the time, that of an artificial flower-maker, he was also an excellent engraver and had a remarkably good hand at frontispieces; Theophilus claimed that he had several times employed him in these capacities.[8] Theophilus Swift was much surprised when he saw the name of Rhynwick Williams in the newspapers, after he had been arrested as the Monster. The exact motivation for him to appear as the Monster's Champion is unclear. It may be that he felt inclined to defend his old acquaintance when Rhynwick Williams was accused of being the Monster, but this is not particularly likely, since they were by no means close friends. Another possibility is that Rhynwick's respectable brother Thomas had paid Theophilus to defend him. In his pamphlet, Theophilus Swift particularly denied that the apothecary had had anything to do with it, and that he had not been bribed to defend the London Monster; if one knows his character, this is in itself an indication that the accusations in question might well be true. The most likely explanation is that Theophilus Swift did it all for self-seeking motives, or for the sheer fun of it. He wanted to outrage the mealy-mouthed and sanctimonious Mr Angerstein and his fellow Monster-hunters; a male chauvinist even by the standards of the day, he felt free to attack the characters of the wounded ladies, and to enjoy the ribald aspects of the Monster's crimes to the full. He also wanted to keep his own name before the public after his attack on Colonel Lennox the year before, and to meddle in the Monster-business seemed a certain way to achieve this. Theophilus Swift rather fancied himself as a satirical pamphleteer: 'Writing is my Hobby-horse – speaking also I am fond of – Reading is too dull for me. I have always been thought to have remarkable talents for Satire, and thank God I have never hid them in a napkin!'[9]

In the beginning of his pamphlet *The Monster at Large*, Theophilus Swift emphasised that he was not defending the Monster; his only purpose was to prove that this arch-villain, still on the prowl, was not Rhynwick Williams. Well knowing the unpopularity of his cause, he expected that he would soon share Rhynwick Williams'

sad fate in being depicted with horns and other monstrous attributes in the print shops, but this did not stop him in his quest for the
truth. He depicted Rhynwick as a poor, helpless, illiterate criminal,
whose counsel had been his only hope. Theophilus Swift was outraged by the way Mr Knowlys had let Rhynwick Williams down
by his feeble defence. Mr Knowlys had even found it necessary to
apologise to Miss Porter for defending his client, thus indicating his
own belief in Williams' guilt, something that Theophilus himself
would never have done. Theophilus contrasted Mr Pigot's flowing
oratory with the faltering efforts of Mr Knowlys; had the eloquence of Mr Pigot been employed to defend Williams, instead of
most fatally to accuse him, Rhynwick Williams would certainly
have been acquitted. In particular, he was astonished that neither
Mrs Miel nor John Porter had been called to give evidence: clearly,
they must have been held back by the scheming Misses Porter and
their friend the Dastardly Fishmonger. Mr Knowlys had committed a serious mistake when he had not called these two as witnesses: had this been the case, Theophilus asserted, they would have
testified that Rhynwick Williams was not the Monster, and it
would not even have been necessary to establish an alibi.

Poor Rhynwick Williams was the victim of another, deadlier
Monster, the one known as Prejudice. Such was the feeling against
him that the Runners had barely been able to shield him from the
mob after the examinations at Bow Street: 'To what country is our
Virtue fled? Where has Humanity taken her flight? Has Reason, has
Religion altogether forsaken us? Let us no longer boast the light of
the present age, in which a man, *before he has been tried*, with difficulty escapes to Newgate; and finds, in a Land of Freedom, his best
asylum in a Jail!'[10] The authorities had played along with the popular
feeling against him, and were glad to punish the first man that had
fallen into their hands to end the Monster-mania. The law had been
stretched beyond its limits to make poor Rhynwick Williams a
felon, and Theophilus had a field day ridiculing the odd charge
made against him: why, he could just as well have been indicted on
the Window Act of William III for *peeping up* Miss Porter's petti-

coats, or on the Tobacco Act for *smuggling* Mrs Miel! Theophilus Swift claimed, whether with any foundation is not known, that Sir Sampson Wright himself was convinced that Rhynwick Williams was not the London Monster; nor had the Bow Street Runners ever suspected Rhynwick in any way. He had had occasion to examine the various accounts of the trial of Rhynwick Williams (all partial and badly written, he claimed) and also the testimony given by the Misses Porter at Bow Street and the complaint lodged by their father just after the assault. It is a great pity that he does not reproduce, or at least properly abstract, this latter document, which is clearly of the greatest interest. In his long and rambling narrative, Theophilus refers to it from time to time, and claims that Anne Porter had never, at that time, indicated that she knew the Monster or that this individual had been in the habit of stalking her and her sisters. Instead, she had said that the assailant was probably a pick-pocket, who had tried to cut her pocket open but misjudged his strike. Importantly, Theophilus Swift also claimed that the description of the Monster in Mr Porter's original complaint did not match Rhynwick Williams at all. The Misses Porter had described him as being thirty years old (Rhynwick was twenty-three), six feet tall (Rhynwick was five feet six inches in height), with fair or very light brown hair (Rhynwick's hair was 'as black as Coleman's conscience', according to Swift), very thin made (Rhynwick was stoutly built, Theophilus claimed, although the available portraits do not support this), and an ugly, prodigiously large nose (not even Theophilus could explain away Rhynwick's prominent 'smeller', but he elegantly added that it was cast in a Grecian mould). But although the Misses had originally sworn to the identity of another man, the real London Monster, as the man who had attacked them, Mr Angerstein's reward had tempted them to change their story and point out Rhynwick Williams as the Monster.

Theophilus had also found several contradictions between the Misses Porter's account of the Monster at Bow Street and their evidence at the Old Bailey. Firstly, Anne Porter at Bow Street said that she had seen Rhynwick Williams following them very close in

St James's Street before he had struck her; at the Old Bailey, she swore that she did not see him until after he had cut her. Also, and more strangely, both Anne and Sarah Porter had sworn, at Bow Street, that Sarah was struck on the head in front of the Bagnio itself; at the Old Bailey, as in the original report, they swore that she had been struck at the bottom of St James's Street. At Bow Street, Theophilus claimed, Anne Porter had said that she had observed her sister Sarah 'change colour' at the Monster's approach, but since the time was after eleven o'clock at night, it was feared that this part of her tale would be *too high-coloured* for the Old Bailey, and the cunning minxes gave *a new complexion* to the story, and an alteration of colour became merely an 'agitation'. At Bow Street, Anne Porter had also rashly sworn to the identity of Rhynwick Williams' coat as that worn by the Monster, but at the Old Bailey it was clearly demonstrated that this close-bodied coat bore no resemblance to the greatcoat that fell across the shoulders of the Monster, according to Anne Porter herself, and even covered another coat under it.

What were the conditions of light in St James's Street, and had it been possible for the Misses Porter to identify the Monster on the night of the Queen's birthday? To see for himself, Theophilus Swift went to the 'Bagnio of Shame' on the evening of the birthday of the Prince of Wales, when the streets were brightly illuminated. With him was his son, the seventeen-year-old Eton schoolboy Deane Swift. Theophilus found that the front of the old Bagnio 'does not advance itself; it modestly retires; it goes back, as all such houses should'! The houses on either side of the old Bagnio had large bow windows, and however brightly lit the street was, these windows put the entrance in deep shade. Theophilus asked Deane to stand in the position supposed to have been occupied by Miss Porter, and he himself stood where the London Monster had taken his stand after the assault (but exactly where this was, he did not state). Deane Swift protested that, had he not known his father's face and figure, he would not have known who stood there. The two changed positions, and the situation was the same, according to

Theophilus, although this was in August, when the streets were much brighter than they had been in January on the evening of the Queen's birthday.[11]

It had been used as an argument in favour of the guilt of Rhynwick Williams that no women had been assaulted after he had been taken into custody. Theophilus Swift, with some reason, pointed out that, at the height of the Monster-mania, many ladies had falsely declared that they had been assaulted; he audaciously went on to claim that 'many are *now* wounded, who fear to acknowledge it'. The women, incapable of independent thought, were ashamed to swear to any other man after Williams had been convicted as the Monster: 'There may be two *Monsters*, but they know there never can be two *The Monsters*.' Nevertheless, Theophilus Swift had found two cases of women being attacked in a way rather resembling the Monster's *modus operandi*, both occurring after Rhynwick Williams had been arrested. One of these concerned Mary Sudbury, a servant of Mr Holden, a whip manufacturer in St Sepulchre's Yard. Late in the evening, a man had made a stab at her hip with a sharp instrument, but she was saved by a large cellar key that she had fortunately kept in her pocket. She could not describe this man in any way. A rather more sinister tale was that of Miss Zubery, of Old Palace Yard. Since the arrest of Rhynwick Williams, this unfortunate young lady had been attacked by the same man no less than seven times, and wounded during four of these assaults. The first attack had, according to Theophilus Swift, taken place 'four days after the dastard Coleman had received the first wages of his cowardice.' According to Miss Zubery, his appearance much resembled the original Monster of Mr Angerstein's posters, both with regard to his build, the colour of his hair, and the size of his prominent nose. His behaviour, also, had resembled that of the Monster. During one of the attacks, he had shouted 'Oh ho! I know you!' and stooped down to look into poor Miss Zubery's face as he struck her, just as during the assault on the Misses Porter.[12]

The arguments presented thus far are nothing but reasonable; had they been brought up in the Old Bailey, they would have caused consternation among the Misses Porter, and may well have shaken the jury's conviction that Williams was the Monster. Theophilus Swift was not a controversialist for nothing, however; just like in the Lennox affair, he saw things only in black and white, and if Rhynwick Williams was innocent, his accusers must be villains of the blackest hue. Some of the arguments that will follow must have seemed almost as ludicrous to the Londoners of 1790 as they do to the modern reader; it must be remembered that they were written by a man who had, just three years previously, accused the Prime Minister of Great Britain of a conspiracy to murder the entire royal family.

In his pamphlet, Theophilus Swift drew a picture of Rhynwick Williams as an honest, innocent, prejudged man, torn from an aged and weeping mother to stand trial for a loathsome series of crimes. He was dragged in irons before a hostile mob that jeered him as *The Monster*. Theophilus claimed that Rhynwick Williams was a manly, forthright and chivalrous character; after all, he had saved the lives of two women! He recounted the pathetic story of Sarah Seward, who had once been saved from drowning by the valorous Rhynwick Williams, and who had been so shamefully treated during the first trial, and added that of Mrs Smith, the Matron of Magdalen Hospital. Some time in 1788, this venerable lady had been taking a stroll in St George's Fields. Suddenly, she fell down and sprained her thumb, and was unable to proceed further; Theophilus leaves it unexplained how such a calamity could have deprived her of the power of locomotion. The noble, strong and manly Rhynwick Williams had found her, picked her up and carried her a considerable distance to a nearby house. The grateful old Matron afterwards took an interest in Rhynwick Williams, and always called him her *son*, Theophilus claimed. He considered it a physical impossibility that a man capable of such worthy, humane acts as these would be the inhuman, brutal Monster, even if fifty ladies swore as to his identity.[13]

Theophilus Swift went on to admit that Rhynwick had lived a vicious life for the past four or five years. He was obsessed with sex, and his self-indulgence in this respect had 'not only hurried him into expenses of which he repents, but into excesses of which he is heartily ashamed'. He never saw a beautiful woman without approaching her with his wicked wishes. Sometimes he was successful; other times, his chase was fruitless. In one of his dreadful puns, Theophilus Swift commented, alluding to the tale of Mrs Smith who had been carried to safety by her noble rescuer, that such was Rhynwick Williams' constant attachment to the female sex that when no young women chanced to come his way, he instead *picked up* an old one. But lately, Rhynwick Williams had repented of his wicked ways. To save money, he had moved out of his old lodgings at Bow Street, and instead moved into the ale-house where he was sharing a bed at the time of his arrest. Exactly how he was employed, if at all, after leaving the artificial flower factory was again unstated; Theophilus was content with commending Rhynwick Williams for his thrifty way of life. Mr Martin, the keeper of a respectable hatter's shop in Chandois Street, informed Theophilus Swift that Rhynwick Williams, at the time he was apprehended, was in the course of paying him one shilling a week of the debt he owed; a tailor named Barrington had his bill discharged by the same mode of payment. This was made possible only by Rhynwick finding cheaper lodgings, and that was why he had moved to the George public house. Theophilus was particularly outraged by the groundless insinuations of some newspaper men that Rhynwick Williams was a homosexual, just because he had slept in the same bed as another man at this public house. This venture had just been another of this thrifty young man's money-saving ventures; in fact, all the beds at the George were so occupied by their penniless tenants.

After having spoken to Rhynwick Williams and his brother the apothecary, Theophilus Swift obtained quite a different version of the events that had led to Rhynwick being apprehended as the Monster.[14] Rhynwick Williams had certainly observed Coleman following him through the streets, but he had taken little notice of him since he had 'presumed him to be a catamite'! Coleman's various gestures of offence, and his strange way of walking immediately behind Rhynwick Williams shouting 'Buh!' in his ear and clapping his hands, had been taken as an attempt at seduction. Theophilus Swift commented that it was quite natural to believe such a person to be one of the Beasts of Gomorrah. When he himself met with this kind of behaviour in the streets of London, he used to lay about him with his stick, but he could not blame Rhynwick Williams for his decision to ignore the buffoon cavorting around him. After this amusing exposé of the gay scene of London in the 1790s, Theophilus Swift goes on to scrutinise Coleman's story of his pursuit of the Monster. Coleman had reported that Rhynwick Williams had looked very steadfastly *up at a house*; this was another *untruth* by the dastardly fishmonger, since Williams had in fact been looking *into a house* through the window, hoping to see his mother and sister in there. Such, exclaimed Theophilus Swift, was Rhynwick Williams' affection for his female relations! Coleman was also very much mistaken to presume that Rhynwick Williams had attempted to enter Mr Williams' china shop in St James's Street in order to escape his pursuer: in fact, he had come to speak to Mr Williams about his prospects of finding work and employment. Theophilus also lambasted Coleman for his story of the other fishmonger who had joined in the hunt: Who was he? Why had he not given evidence? The whole story is a lie, since it is impossible to find another fishmonger as cowardly as Coleman! Had anyone else been there, he would have arrested the Monster on the spot, and dragged him into the Bagnio, instead of behaving as a buffoon!

Rhynwick Williams had then repaired to a house in Moulton Street, but not, as Coleman had presumed, in order to escape his pursuers. Rhynwick had in fact visited a 'fille-de-joie' of his acquaintance, who lived on the first floor. Coleman stated that he had remained there for three or four minutes, and Rhynwick himself maintained that he had stayed there five minutes; the sources thus agree that his rendezvous with the Moulton Street prostitute had not been a lengthy one. Theophilus Swift does not dwell upon exactly what may have had occurred in there, but he took the opportunity to praise Rhynwick Williams for his manly love for the opposite sex! The fact that Coleman, when he knocked on the door, had received no information about where Rhynwick Williams had gone, was airily explained by that experienced man-about-town Theophilus Swift: Men who visited *Nuns* living on the *First Floor* were not in the habit of using *visiting cards*. It should be noted that the epithets 'Nun' and 'Vestal' were, in those days, euphemisms for 'prostitute'.

Theophilus Swift went on to describe Coleman's *valorous* conduct at the rails of the house of 'Mr Pearce' in Vere Street. Only the house was not owned by any person of that name, but by a respectable merchant named Mr Pearson. Theophilus had visited Mr Pearson, and had been informed that Rhynwick Williams had approached Mrs Pearson with the request that she would offer for sale, in their shop, a quantity of ornamented chip-hats manufactured by his own hands. Such was Rhynwick's devotion to the female sex and its proper adornment! Theophilus had also spoken to the mysterious Mr Smith, who had come to the Old Bailey to testify about the circumstances of Coleman entering his house in pursuit of Rhynwick Williams; the muddled Mr Knowlys had not called him, however, and only employed him as another character witness. Mr Smith emphatically denied that he had in any way prevented Coleman from entering; in fact, he had himself invited the timid fishmonger to come in. John Coleman had never accused Williams of being the Monster, but merely said, with 'indications of a mind labouring with Guilt and Cowardice', that Williams had several times insulted some ladies of his acquaintance, and that he wanted the satisfaction of a gentleman. Again, the veracity of Coleman had been cast into doubt, Theophilus wrote: 'To say that Coleman was a witness as pure, and unexceptionable as Mr Smith ... would be as absurd as if it should be maintained that the Abortion of Manhood were the Perfection of Human Nature; or that Miss Porter herself were the Flower of Nun's Flesh.'[15]

Theophilus Swift wrote that the fact that Rhynwick had gone with the fishmonger back to Pero's Bagnio without resistance was another clear indication of his innocence. Rhynwick Williams was, he claimed, an accomplished boxer, and men of superior boxing skill were not apt to take fire at every 'gesture of offence' that a street buffoon, or something worse, may chance to practice. Even at 'the Door of Prejudice', the entrance to the Bagnio, it was within his science and ability to make papier-mâché of a better man than Coleman. Just before they reached the Bagnio, Miss Rebecca Porter and one of her sisters crossed St James's Street with Coleman's brother; they rushed back into the Bagnio to report that the fishmonger was returning with his prey. This, Theophilus claimed, would have given the Misses Porter ample time to prepare for poor Rhynwick's reception at the Bagnio. So little notion had Rhynwick Williams of where the fishmonger was leading him, that he was quite surprised when he saw the inscription over the door they were about to enter. 'What here? Why this is Pero's Bagnio!' he said, according to Theophilus Swift, being greatly surprised, and meaning: 'Is it here you bring me? Sure you don't want me to fight for the Girls of *this* house?' About the great fainting scene inside, Theophilus was scarcely less eloquent: the only species of *Fits*, exhibited by these ladies, were of that sort that are known by the name of *Counter-feits*!

Theophilus Swift went on to accuse the Porter sisters and John Coleman of having staged an elaborate conspiracy against poor, innocent Rhynwick Williams. Mr Pigot had treated the court to 'a most pathetic and distressing picture of a bleeding lady, attended by a train of sisters, weeping, fainting, terrified!' but in reality, the Misses were nothing but a gang of conniving minxes who had deliberately and wrongfully accused Rhynwick Williams of being the Monster, to lay their hands on Angerstein's reward. This philanthropic gentleman's exertions to capture the London Monster, Theophilus wrote, had only led to the downfall of Rhynwick Williams, and the filling of the pockets of the conspirators, Anne and Sarah Porter, and their dismal accomplice John Coleman: 'Or was it the *Poverty* of Mr Angerstein that bribed the Valour of Coleman, and purified the Veracity of his Mistress?' Even if Angerstein would devote the remainder of his life to philanthropy, this would not repair the injury to society caused by his disastrous meddling in the Monster-business. He was not the only one to offer a reward, and Theophilus speculated that Anne Porter and her lover Coleman had, 'by their late jobb, touched to the tune of *fourteen hundred pounds!*' He went on to make the startling claim that the departure of Mr Chatham, who had been employed as the counsel of Rhynwick Williams, had been because Angerstein had approached the law partnership Mr Chatham belonged to, and threatened to withdraw his business from them if he did not abandon his client. Mr Fletcher had been the only solicitor prepared to disregard Angerstein's threats: 'For myself ... I had rather possess the *Humanity* of Mr Fletcher than the *Gold* of Mr Angerstein. It was Gold that conducted the pious Aeneas through a *world of lies.*'[16]

What, then, had prompted Anne Porter to set her eyes on poor Rhynwick Williams as the victim of her evil plot? In fact, Theophilus claimed, they knew each other ten times better than she was willing to admit. He boldly stated that Anne Porter had once had an illicit affair with 'Captain' Crowder, 'who, though he might not enjoy the rank of Captain, was nevertheless a Soldier of honour, and a distinguished member of the honourable gang of street-robbers that recently infested Westminster'. Anne Porter had once eloped from the Bagnio, and spent several weeks in the arms of this Captain. She was finally dragged back to Pero's Bagnio by her father, in deep disgrace. After Captain Crowder had been arrested, he was sentenced to be 'dropt into another world', but the sentence was finally mitigated to transportation. Theophilus Swift claimed that the brazen hussy Anne Porter had visited him several times as he was held in Newgate before embarking on his one-way journey to the Antipodes. Like many young men about town, Rhynwick Williams knew about Anne Porter's past indiscretion. In his usual pursuit of cheap sexual thrills – 'it was seldom that he saw a beautiful woman, to whom he did not lay siege' – the dissolute Rhynwick had several times approached the Porter sisters. In particular, he tried to seduce Anne Porter, but she was always disdainful towards him. Finally, he said 'Madam, I do not see that my person is not as good as the Captain's, with whom you went off from the bagnio.' This insult highly enraged Miss Porter, and when the stupid Rhynwick Williams afterwards renewed his attempts on her virtue, his advances met nothing but 'oppobrious appellations': Anne Porter called him a rascal, a wretch and a scoundrel. The foul-mouthed Rhynwick Williams replied by calling her a whore and a bitch; this particular insult, Theophilus claimed, this vindictive, malignant woman never forgave him. Driven by 'two of the most infernal passions that ever debased the human mind, AVARICE and REVENGE', she decided, there and then, to denounce him as the Monster once the opportunity arose.[17]

In Theophilus Swift's pamphlet, Anne Porter and her family came in for a torrent of abuse. She was something of a social climber: unwilling to admit her humble background, she had claimed to have been present in the ballroom on the night of the Queen's birthday. The snobbish Theophilus Swift heavy-handedly reminded her that 'the *Ball-room* is appropriated to persons of *one* description; the *Gallery* to persons of *another*. It is sufficient to say, that Miss Porter has not yet been introduced at Court'. Theophilus went on to claim that it had been inappropriate of Judge Buller to allow the Misses Porter to wear veils during the Old Bailey trial: the reason was not, of course, to shield them from the unwelcome stare of Rhynwick Williams, but to 'conceal the changes which the emotions of guilt may happen to throw upon the female cheek'. He made some ribald comments about the depth of Anne Porter's *décolletage* at the Old Bailey: surely, it had influenced the jury in her favour! He was something of a classical scholar, and could well remember the story of how the 'Pigot of Athens', the silver-tongued Hyperides, had defended the 'Miss Porter of his day': when his arguments failed to impress, he snatched the veil from his client's bosom, and this 'well-timed oratory, this silent rhetoric' won over the court. Surely, it had also been a highly inappropriate, not to say indecent, moment when she displayed her damaged petticoat: 'has the display of a *Shift* nothing moving or persuasive in it? Does it conceal no *Magnet of attraction*? Have the wounds which it covers no *Center of sympathy*?'[18]

Theophilus Swift claimed that Pero's Bagnio, the home of the Misses Porter, had a very low reputation indeed; it was little better than a common brothel. Both sexes were admitted promiscuously, and the place was a well-known haunt of prostitutes. Theophilus Swift went on to claim that the Misses Porter, 'The Nuns of the Bagnio', were resident prostitutes in this tavern of ill-repute. He ridiculed Anne Porter's fainting fits with the words, 'Miss Porter is not apt to faint at the approach of a man'! Many a classical quotation, and many a heavy-handed pun was brought to bear on Pero's Bagnio and its unfortunate inhabitants: 'The question has been asked, Whether any man may take a *Fille-de-Joye* into Pero's Bagnio? The answer is this: I do not know whether you may *take* a Fille-de-Joye into the Bagnio, but I know that you will *find* one in it.' He made much of an unwise statement of Anne Porter's (or perhaps rather of her father giving evidence on her behalf at Bow Street), that she had observed Rhynwick Williams from the 'steps' of the Bagnio's front entrance; in fact, there were no steps to this door. Theophilus's trenchant rejoinder deserves to be given in full:

> 'It is not necessary to *ascend* the Bagnio of Beauty, although the Beauty of the Bagnio has *sworn*, that you approach it by 'steps'; and that for a man to enter it, he must "walk up to the top of them!" The reverse turns out to be the *truth*: whoever enters *that* Bagnio, DESCENDS to go into it!'[19]

Theophilus Swift also grossly insulted the wretched fishmonger John Coleman: he was called a *Dastard*, a *Frog-blooded Coward*, a *Despicable Buffoon*, and *Miss Porter's Puppy*, with an added, eloquent quotation from 'an old poet':

That cow-hearted Coleman,
Pray, is he a half-man, or is he a whole-man?

It was rumoured, Theophilus Swift claimed, that after his successful part in the Monster-business, John Coleman had risen from his plebeian calling as a fishmonger, and that he had recently become the hackney-writer of an attorney. Theophilus made another of his tasteless puns about the fishy smell of this 'Pimp of the Law'. A quotation from Hamlet was also brought to bear on the luckless Coleman:

> *Polonius:* Do you know me, my Lord?
> *Hamlet:* Excellent well: you are a Fishmonger.
> *Pol.:* Not I, my Lord.
> *Ham.:* Then I would you were so honest a man.

The other wounded ladies did not escape Theophilus Swift's abuse: several of them were roundly accused of being harlots of ill-repute, bribed by the fiendish Misses Porter to aid in her conspiracy against Rhynwick Williams. Mary Forster, 'one of the Greffe-Street Vestals' had lied to Macmanus about the date she had been cut, but conveniently changed her story. Ann Frost, another 'daughter of sanctity', had also perjured herself at Bow Street. 'Kitty' Wheeler, who had positively identified Rhynwick Williams as the man who had insulted her, and who had been saved from the Monster's attack by the intervention of her father, was '*another* Tavern-Vestal in St James's Street'. Piling sensation upon sensation in one of his footnotes, Theophilus went on to claim that 'The character of this Vestal is said to be as pure as that of her Sister, who slept in the arms of Molloy, the Highway-man, on the night before he was apprehended'! The father of these sisters of ill-repute, 'Parsloe' Wheeler, was an arsonist, who had burnt down his own tavern to get the insurance money; he had then implicated a poor innocent boy, who was transported for life.[20]

Surgeon Tomkins received his share of Theophilus Swift's ire, due to the excessive sense of propriety in his report on Anne Porter's wound, which left unanswered the bold Irishman's question as to exactly what part of her body was injured. At Bow Street, he had placed her injury at the thigh; at the Old Bailey, at an unspecified region *higher up*. Theophilus Swift speculated at length about the anatomy of Anne Porter's thighs and pelvic region, and found it most likely that she had been cut in the buttocks. With his usual caddishness, he considered it a shame that 'the Captain', who must have been in the know, had not been questioned to give his opinion of the anatomy of Anne Porter's most private parts. From the Surgeon's inept description, Rhynwick must be more than a Monster, 'whose *Instrument*, through Shift and all, could penetrate *four inches* into a *Virgin!*' More relevantly, he questioned why the surgeon had appeared at all, since Rhynwick Williams was not on trial for assault, but for wilfully cutting and tearing Miss Porter's clothes. Surely, a tailor should be employed as an expert witness in such a case, not a medical practitioner.

In Theophilus Swift's pamphlet, the low morals and malicious falsehoods of the Monster victims were contrasted with the impeccable, spotless behaviour of Rhynwick Williams' alibi witnesses, who had come into court tutored only by Truth, and uninfluenced by any hopes of a reward. The Porter gang had threatened them, Theophilus claimed, and sworn that the bread would be taken from their mouths and those of their families, but the loyal, uncomplaining artificial flower-makers still appeared in court to testify. At the Old Bailey, Amabel Mitchell and his staff had come through their ordeal at the hands of Mr Pigot with flying colours, in spite of the interpreter being partial and trying to mislead them: 'Perjury they leave to the idle, the dissolute, and the debauched; to *Coal-men* and to *Porters*, whose hearts the music of a *Bribe* alone can soften, and whose consciences acknowledge no Monitor but *Revenge*.'[21]

Theophilus Swift claimed that it had been the height of fashion among the feather-brained, easily-led ladies of all ages and all social classes, to claim that they had been wounded by the Monster.

The reason for this was, of course, that the Monster was presumed only to attack well-bred, beautiful ladies; indeed, it was something of a social ostracism not to have been given attention by him. Like a flock of sheep, the ladies had followed one another to swear against Rhynwick Williams, and enjoy their day in the limelight as one of the dreadful Monster's lovely, tearful victims. Mr Sybley, the Turnkey of Newgate, had told Theophilus an amusing story. A woman of decent appearance had called on the Turnkey to get a view of Rhynwick Williams *before* she went to swear to his person as the Monster who had wounded her. The Turnkey, a man of ready wit, asked her to sit down, and then went to fetch one of the other prisoners, who was to impersonate the Monster. At the sight of this prisoner, she called out, 'Aye, aye! You are the man: I know you, you villain: it was you who wounded me, and I'll swear it in any Court of Justice!'[22]

Theophilus Swift's pamphlet caused quite a furore. In the *New Lady's Magazine*, previously a firmly anti-Williams periodical, his theories were quoted with respect, and it was acknowledged that Rhynwick Williams must be the innocent victim of a conspiracy.[23] One of the London debating societies went as far as to propose the question: 'Did the late extraordinary conduct ascribed to Rynwick Williams (commonly called the Monster) originate in an unfortunate Insanity – a diabolical inclination to injure the Fair Part of the Creation – or in the groundless apprehensions of some mistaken Females?' Monster-hunters, Monster victims and a leading lawyer with strong opinions on the case (was it Theophilus?) were promised to be in the audience.[24] There was also a spate of newspaper articles in response to Swift: some claimed that Williams had been falsely accused on the basis of a mistaken identity, and that his actions when arrested were certainly not those of a guilty man; others criticised the indictment under which he had been made a felon; yet others were outraged by Swift's vile insinuations against the Porter family.[25] Although the Twelve Judges of England were not scheduled to meet until November 1790, it was becoming increasingly clear that the Monster's offence could not, under any circumstances, be considered to be within the statute in question. This meant that Rhynwick Williams was not to be considered as a felon, but that he was to face a retrial for misdemeanour at the sessions of the peace at Hick's Hall. This meant that he was no longer in danger of being transported: the maximum punishment for a misdemeanour was imprisonment.

According to a scurrilous rumour, Rhynwick Williams decided to celebrate this unexpected victory in a singular manner.[26] He sent fifty cards of invitation to his various relatives, the alibi friends, numerous other prisoners, and 'other night hawks of varied trades'. At four o'clock in the afternoon, this large party sat down to tea. Afterwards, two violins struck up, accompanied by a drum and fifes, and the Monster's Ball began. In the merry dance, the cuts and entrechats of the Monster were very much admired. At about eight o'clock in the evening, the company sat down to dine, and a sumptuous meal and a variety of wines and spirits were produced. At nine, the guests departed, since this was the usual hour for locking up the prison. In the newspapers, the Monster's Ball was deplored as brazen and vulgar; it was considered a sign that Rhynwick Williams must have friends (or even accomplices) in high places that this degraded being could revel in such a way while still a prisoner. The *British Mercury* found something mysterious in the Monster's extravagance and dissipation, and suspected that some character of opulence, as well as depravity, must be the mastermind behind the entire business.[27] *The Times*, a perhaps more reliable source, commented that 'The paragraph inserted in several morning newspapers, of Rhynwick Williams having given a ball and entertainment to several people in Newgate, is without the smallest foundation. His friends are sufficiently unfortunate without having such idle reports to increase their uneasiness'.[28]

Theophilus Swift's comment, as punning as ever, was that he rather regretted that Rhynwick's case did not constitute a felony: 'An airing to New-Holland, I had considered as preferable to an Airing in New-gate, or preferable perhaps to a more elevated

Airing in another place. Poor Williams is at sea again. Madam Prejudice is once more his Pilot...' In an eloquent sentence, he recounted the plight of poor Rhynwick Williams: 'When the Bloodhound REVENGE snuffs his prey, and FALSEHOOD fastens on the Game which PREJUDICE has started, the Law becomes the snare of Innocence, and Justice is but a gin in the hands of the unlicensed Poacher!'[29]

On 10 November 1790, the judges finally met at Serjeant's Inn Hall, to discuss whether the indictment against Rhynwick Williams was within the statute regarding the wilful cutting of clothes. Nine of the eleven judges present considered that, notwithstanding the verdict of the jury at the Old Bailey, the offence of Rhynwick Williams was not within this statute, and that the indictment was bad in point of form. Rhynwick Williams would thus face a retrial at the Hick's Hall sessions house for the misdemeanour of wilfully and maliciously cutting people with intent to kill and murder them.[30]

On 8 December, Rhynwick Williams was again put to the Bar at the Old Bailey. Judge Ashurst ordered him to be discharged of a felony, but detained him to undergo a new trial for a misdemeanour. Rhynwick then produced a manuscript and read a pathetic speech. Theophilus Swift was his only friend in a world full of enemies, he said. In his pamphlet, this learned gentleman had pointed out the weaknesses of the case for the prosecution in no uncertain manner. 'Good God! for what am I reserved?' he called out, wringing his hands, 'without friends, without money ... to stand another trial against those who *reward has enriched*, and whose cause has made friends of all men.' Another remarkable sentence was: 'My Lord, I stand an instance of singular misfortune, that while my passion for the sex had nearly ruined me, a sanguinary charge of a nature directly opposite should complete my destruction...'[31] According to the *Argus* newspaper, a pro-Williams publication, Rhynwick delivered his speech with much energy, and made a lasting impression.[32]

10

THE
Second
TRIAL

But the Monster now is fast –
Thus when surly Winter's past
See the primrose deck the vale,
Hark, the music of the dale;
See, what crowds of nymphs appear;
Cheeks, no longer pale with fear;
Assignations, long suspended,
And by conscious night befriended;
Scandal and quadrille renew'd…

W.H., 'The Monster', from the
New Lady's Magazine, July 1790.

Before the second trial, the fortunes of Rhynwick Williams at last seemed to have taken a turning for the better. He would be tried for a misdemeanour, not for a felony, and there was no question of him being transported to Botany Bay. At the first trial, he had had the useless Mr Knowlys as his barrister; now, he would have the formidable Theophilus Swift. The popular interest in the Monster business had abated, and no mob was standing outside the courtroom baying for his blood. Several papers and magazines had mentioned Theophilus Swift's pamphlet, and some of them had seriously discussed the probability that Williams was innocent, or that there were several Monsters.

The main question was whether Anne Porter would survive an interrogation by Theophilus Swift, a man well known for his cleverness and audacity. She was reputed to have been greatly put out by his scurrilous pamphlet, which had vilified her entire family, and cast a slur on her own good name. Had she been in possession of a gentlemanly protector, who had treated this vile pamphlet as a matter of honour, this gentleman would, according to the morals of the time, have been perfectly justified to deliver a horsewhipping to its author, or to challenge him to a duel. Neither Coleman nor Thomas Porter felt *quite prepared* for such heroics, however, and neither of them dared to openly challenge a man widely known for his violent and quarrelsome disposition, who had once stood for the fire of Colonel Charles Lennox in a duel.

Theophilus Swift's main strategy, as already outlined in his pamphlet, was to shatter the evidence of Anne Porter, and to present her and John Coleman as a pair of impostors, who had 'framed' Rhynwick Williams in order to claim the huge reward for bringing the London Monster to justice. Once the evidence of this pair, the star witnesses for the prosecution, had been discredited, Mr Pigot's case would fall like a house of cards, and Theophilus would have a comparatively easy task to demolish the evidence of the other wounded ladies.

At ten o'clock on Monday 13 December, Rhynwick Williams was brought down from Newgate to the Hick's Hall sessions house on Clerkenwell Green by Runner John Macmanus and a Bow Street patrol.[1] He was tidily dressed in his blue coat lined with buff. The court was crowded with 'a number of very respectable persons', some of whom had been there since an early hour to secure a good seat. The judge presiding was William Mainwaring, who had been one of the leaders of the opposition against the Police Reform Bill in 1785. His reputation was somewhat tarnished by the fact that he was also a banker, and that he had transferred considerable sums of public money, through accounts controlled by the Middlesex Sessions, into his own bank. He and his friends ran these Sessions through a policy of ruthless patronage, bestowing valuable appoint-ments to themselves, their friends and families.[2] After Judge Mainwaring had taken the Chair, the jury, consisting of twelve respectable men, was called over and sworn. Normally, Mr Pigot would then have opened the case, but Rhynwick Williams, show-ing much agitation, applied for permission to address the court. The little man at the prisoner's dock produced a paper from the pocket of his infamous blue coat, and read another set of overblown, pathetic harangues aloud. In hopeless, despondent tones, he begged the jurors to disregard the immense prejudice against him, which had been so evident at the first trial. This preju-dice had been such that he had despaired of getting a fair trial, and he had been so despondent that he had informed Theophilus Swift that he wanted to plead guilty to all charges. Earlier that very morning, he claimed, his relatives had managed to change his mind, and Mr Swift had immediately offered to defend him in court. Rhynwick Williams made a solemn oath before God that he was not 'that savage *Monster*, from whom I would this moment, at the risk of my own life, rescue even the very woman who has so barbarously pursued me'. His speech ended with the bitter words, directed to the jury: 'My confinement has been long and painful; yet, not content with this, the purse of my prosecutors is still open against my poverty, and against my innocence; but to your candour and impartial justice, which will not suffer Falsehood to triumph over Truth and Innocence, I am sure I may look with confidence.'[3]

Just as Rhynwick Williams sat down, Theophilus Swift stood up. He deplored the prejudice and injustice that had made young Rhynwick Williams a prisoner, and pointed out that, since he had only accepted his brief a few hours earlier, he would alone be opposing the four counsel for the prosecution (Mr Pigot was assisted by Mr Fielding and Mr Shepherd, and also received occasional advice from Mr Garrow) armed only with his own strong conviction of poor Rhynwick's innocence. Since the dejected prisoner had wanted to give up and plead guilty, no witnesses for the defence were ready, and he asked leave to call all the alibi witnesses from the artificial flower factory 'as he understood the case of Miss Porter was to be brought forward'.

The prosecution counsel reluctantly had to agree to this scheme, although there were (probably well-informed!) people saying that Theophilus Swift had planned the whole thing beforehand, and that it was *he* who had written Rhynwick Williams' pathetic speeches. This suspicion is supported by the fact that the whole gang of alibi witnesses, and some other individuals, repaired to the courtroom very quickly after being summoned by Mr Swift. There were rumours that they had all been waiting at a disreputable public house near Hicks' Hall. They poured into court just as Mr Pigot was opening the case for the prosecution, with a motley crowd of children, relatives and interpreters in tow. Theophilus ushered them to their seats with a contented smile, before returning to his chair, where he sat fixing pretty Anne Porter with his basilisk stare.

After a brief pause, Mr Pigot went on with his case. Although the early phases of the trial, with Rhynwick Williams squeaking away at will, and Theophilus Swift throwing his weight about without restraint, must have been something of a shock to him, he delivered his opening address with dignity and restraint. Like everyone else, he saw nothing absurd in that Rhynwick was not charged with the heinous felony of wilfully destroying people's clothes, but merely with the misdemeanour of cutting human beings with the intent to kill and murder them. Although, he said, some members of the jury might find the construction of the prisoner's offence as a mere misdemeanour inadequate, there was no reason to blame the law of the country, since 'the Legislature could not foresee all the depravity of the human heart; this is a crime with which they were unacquainted – a crime which the Legislature, past or present, could never foresee – a crime baffling all human speculation, confounding all the chronicles of this court, and all other courts, in all ages of the world'. Mr Pigot lacked words to describe the dreadful barbarity, the shocking brutality and the infernal ferocity of Rhynwick Williams as he attacked Anne Porter: the prisoner must lack all morality and all claims to manhood. He solemnly read the definition of 'monster' from Dr Johnson's *Dictionary*: 'any thing out of the ordinary course of human nature'; surely, such had been the enormities committed by the London Monster. Even more solemnly, he reminded Rhynwick Williams that he had just called his Maker to witness his innocence; it was a melancholy thing that he had thereby added one more vice, namely cant and hypocrisy, to those he already possessed. His witnesses stood ready to identify Rhynwick Williams as the Monster: they remembered him well, since 'a man who talked of "drowning them in their blood", who "blasted their eyes", it was natural for them to take particular notice of'.[4]

Anne Porter was the first witness to be called. As she took her seat in the witness box, she had her sister Sarah close behind her, and John Coleman was also nearby to give support. But before she could even answer the first question from Mr Pigot, Theophilus Swift called out, 'Holt, Madam!' Leering at her, he requested that all the other witnesses were to leave the court, so that they could not influence each other. At the sign of the judge, both prosecution and defence witnesses rose and left the courtroom. Anne Porter showed obvious agitation when her sisters left her alone to face the loathsome Theophilus Swift. Again, Mr Pigot started his examining, but he was once more interrupted. This time, it was Rhynwick Williams himself, who agitatedly pointed out that he had detected that creature John Coleman peeping and listening through a broken pane, and demanded that he should be removed. The judge first tried to ignore him, but Rhynwick was adamant: his shrill vociferations were received with a cacophony of hisses and catcalls from the audience. Theophilus Swift joined in, and demanded that Coleman be removed. Judge Mainwaring ordered silence in a stentorian voice, and reproached both Rhynwick Williams and his counsel for their obstreperous conduct.

The audience laughed and jeered. The judge also ordered that Coleman was not to be allowed to eavesdrop on the trial, and the fishmonger was told to make himself scarce. Mr Pigot was allowed to proceed with his examination of Miss Porter's evidence; this time, Judge Mainwaring said in a menacing voice, there would be *no interruptions.* Mr Pigot started to question the distressed Anne Porter, and she replied in faltering, insecure tones, but gradually gained confidence. The audience took a lively part in the proceedings, and Rhynwick Williams was distressed to observe that 'many persons around me were exclaiming "Oh, the villain!" "Oh, the wretch" and looking towards me with indignant eyes' as Anne Porter described her sufferings at the hands of the Monster.[5] Judge Mainwaring wrote that the court was crowded with various rowdy spectators, who even stood all around the prisoner's bar; Rhynwick Williams was almost hidden by them. When Anne Porter was told to identify the man responsible, she had to approach the Bar, but as soon as she saw the face of Rhynwick Williams peeping out at her, she called out 'Oh! That is the man!' and appeared much agitated.[6] Theophilus Swift energetically objected to some of her statements, and accused her of having changed her testimony from that originally delivered at Bow Street. In particular, he pointed out that her original description of the Monster did not match Rhynwick Williams at all, and she did not deny that she had originally described him as a man of twenty-eight or thirty years of age.[7]

When Anne Porter had concluded her evidence, Mr Pigot reluctantly had to surrender her to the leering Theophilus Swift, like a shepherd leaving a tender lamb before the slavering jaws of a wolf. Theophilus immediately went in for the kill. With a torrent of very unpleasant questions about the gay goings-on at 'the Bagnio of Beauty' ('is this, Madam, or is it not, the name by which Pero's Bagnio is known among men about town, on account of the *Vestals* to be found within?') and her elopement with Captain Crowder, he had her literally 'at the ropes'. She appeared to have swooned, and was unable to give any coherent replies.

Miſs. Ann. Porter,

Who was so Barbarously treated by the Monster.

1 Miss Anne Porter, as she was portrayed in the *New Lady's Magazine* of July 1790.

2 *Above*: A view of St James's Street in 1800. On the right is the west side of the street, with Brook's Club as the first building. Just after the street is No.61, and No.62 is the house with the large bow windows and the tall chimney. Immediately behind it, hidden by the bay windows in this engraving, is Pero's Bagnio and the entry to the narrow stable yard behind it.

3 *Left*: Pero's Bagnio, a drawing made after the year 1800, when this establishment had been taken over by Francis Felton. It still carried its old name, and was probably not greatly changed from the time it had been run by the Porter family.

FENTON'S late Pero's HOTEL.

JOHN JULIUS ANGERSTEIN, ESQ.

St. PANCRAS, MAY 7th. 1790.

WHEREAS,

An ATTACK,

HAS BEEN MADE BY A

MONSTER,

UPON A

YOUNG WOMAN,

WITHIN THE

SOUTH-WEST DIVISION OF THIS PARISH

AND THE

INHABITANTS of the faid DIVISION, affembled at a general Meeting this Day, at *Percy Coffee-houfe*, have entered into an *ASSOCIATION*, for the Prevention of fimilar *Affaults* in future. Such of the Inhabitants, Houfeholders, as were unable to attend the faid Meeting, are hereby earneftly invited to become Members of fuch *Affociation*, the *Articles* of which may be feen and fubfcribed, at the Bar of *Percy Coffee-houfe*.

BARTLETT AND CO. PRINTERS, No. 3, JOHN-STREET, GEORGE-STREET, TOTTENHAM-COURT-ROAD.

Clockwise from top left:

4 John Julius Angerstein, a portrait by his friend Sir Thomas Lawrence.

5 The original list of subscribers at the forming of the St Pancras Monster patrol at the Percy coffee-house, from the Monster scrapbook of Miss Banks in the British Library.

6 The first poster of the St Pancras Monster patrol, from Miss Banks' Monster scrapbook in the British Library.

the MONSTER Cutting a Lady

This likeness of him was Drawn by a Lady who he had wounded and Approved by two others.

7 *Left: The Monster Cutting a Lady*, a print by Isaac Cruikshanks published on 1 May 1790. The face and figure of the Monster was reconstructed from the evidence of several wounded ladies, and they afterwards approved of the drawing, thinking it a good likeness. Note the diabolical spikes on his knees; this was after the ferocious assault on Mrs Payne. Also note the door marked 'Angersteein' and the Monster reward poster pasted on the wall.

8 *Below: The Monster disappointed of his Afternoon Luncheon, or Porridge Potts preferable to Cork Rumps*; a bawdy cartoon published at the height of the Monster-mania.

The MONSTER disappointed of his Afternoons Luncheon - or Porridge Potts preferable to Cork Rumps.

9 *Right*: *Copper Bottoms to Prevent being Cut*, another print by Isaac Cruikshanks, issued at the same time as *The Monster Cutting a Lady*. A lady wearing only a chemise and a hat is standing before the kneeling brazier, who is hammering together the back seams of a short copper petticoat. A placard on the wall reads: 'Ladies Bottoms covered on the most Reasonable Terms and kept in repair by the year by Anti:Monster'. In the shop window are three copper petticoats of increasing size, intended, in turn, for young ladies of fifteen, for ladies of thirty, and for very fat ladies.

10 *Below*: *Old Maids Dreaming of the Monster*. An anonymous satirical print that ridiculed the London Monster's propensity to attack fashionable, beautiful young women. Two old maids dream of the Monster, since if he attacks them, this will be ample proof that they are still young and attractive. The Monster suddenly appears in the guise of a grotesque, three-headed ogre, with the Devil seated on the middle head. One of the old maids hastily tries to get out of bed, but steps in the chamber-pot by mistake.

COPPER BOTTOMS *to Prevent being Cut*.

J. Cruikshanks
1 May 1790

OLD MAIDS DREAMING OF THE MONSTER.

Pub May 18 1790 by S.W.Fores N 3 Piccadilly. Where may be seen the compleatest Collection of Caricatures in the Kingdom also the head & hand of count Strensee & M:rust

GLAUCUS and SCYLLA or the MONSTER in full CRY

11 *Glaucus and Scylla, or The Monster in Full Cry*, a satirical print by Isaac Cruikshanks published on 18 May 1790. The immensely fat Miss Jeffries, one of the Queen's ladies-in-waiting, is pursued by George Hanger, one of the cronies of the Prince of Wales. He is depicted with a tail and clawed, deformed legs, and aims to prick her with a long spike attached to the end of his bludgeon. A man lying on the ground tries to pull him back by the tail, and William Pitt races up to the right, armed with a warming pan, to save her honour from this monstrous assailant.

Swearing to the Cutting MONSTER or A Scene in Bow Street

12 *Swearing to the Cutting Monster, or A Scene in Bow Street*, another ribald engraving by James Gillray, showing one of the wounded ladies revealing all to the Bow Street magistrates. Sir Sampson Wright, in his hat and spectacles, takes a closer look; the men on either sides of him are William Addington and Richard Bond. The Monster at the dock bears a marked resemblance to the controversial politician Charles James Fox.

13 *The Monster Detected.* Another satirical print, with verses, published in midst of the Monster-mania. The verses relate that a certain Devil was allowed to come to Earth on condition that he married a beautiful virgin. To test virginity:

> *A little Dagger with a Tube, was fill'd*
> *With Juice of Plants, which such a Liquor yield*
> *That when to Womans velvet flesh apply'd*
> *It makes no Entrance if a Maid is try'd.*

The ribald conclusion is that the great scarcity of virgins in London makes it necessary for the Devil to stab dozens of women, thus giving rise to the Monster-mania.

The MONSTER.

Mr. ARGENSTEEN, takes the earlieft opportunity of informing the Nobility and the Public, of the MONSTER's re-appearance in Town on Friday laft June 4th. He is dreffed in a Scarlet Coat, wears a prodigious Cockade, and bears in every refpect a Striking Likenefs to that much refpected Character

PHILIP THYCKNESS, Efq.

He has already frightened a Number of Women and Children; made feveral defperate attempts upon different Noblemen; and, has attempted to cut up his own Children.

Since his laft arrival in London, he has affumed the name of Lieutenant Governor G A L L S T O N E; and, as it is ftrongly fufpected that his prefent Journey to Town, is in Order to devour all Editors of Newfpapers, Book-fellers, Engravers and Publifhers of Satiric Prints, and evey other Perfon who has dared to arraign his Conduct, the Public are cautioned to be upon their Guard.

N. B. The Reward for his Apprehenfion ftill remains in its full force.

14 Captain Thicknesse is accused of being the Monster in this spoof of Angerstein's posters. From Miss Banks' Monster scrapbook in the British Library.

Take Care your feet don't get into them there holes Captain.

MONSTER Detected

Sr S. Meadows & The Public are requested to take notice, this is not the Captain Straitshanks who was Broke for Cowardice, & who afterwards Offered to Enter into the French Service not to fight against his Native Country, & who has Kept his Wife & two Children upon 13 pounds a year in Wales till the youngest Child is 44 years of age, & who with one Leg in the Grave is Endeavouring to do all the Mischief he can with the other — this is not that their Captain Straitshanks

1788

MONSTROUS ASSASSIN or the COWARD turn'd BILL STICKER

15 Thicknesse gets his own back on the 'Monstrous Assassin, or the Coward turn'd Bill Sticker'. A satirical print by Isaac Cruikshanks, from Miss Banks' Monster scrapbook in the British Library.

16 The Bow Street public office in 1808, a plate from Ackermann's *Microcosm of London.*

17 The Old Bailey sessions house in 1790, an engraving by J. Ellis.

18 A late eighteenth-century interior of the Old Bailey.

A Representation of Rynwick, alias Renwick Williams, commonly called

THE MONSTER,

cutting Miss Porter, in St. James's Street, on her return with Mr. Neil and his Sister from the Ball at the Palace, on the Queen's Birth Day, Jan.ʳ 18.ᵗ 1790.

NB. An ex post facto Law was made to hang Jonathan Wild, whose attacks were on the Property only, but the above Criminal for attacking the Persons of the fairest of the Creation, is subject to no more than Transportation for Seven Years, a punishment by no means proportioned to the Crime nor fit, as it may afford the Wretch an opportunity of exercising his cruelties on the Females of another Country.

The MONSTER as he appeared in DISGUISE.

The MONSTER as he appeared on TRIAL.

The way the MONSTER ought to be mann.

The way the MONSTER ought to be framed.

THE MONSTER.

Represented as Wounding Miss Ann Porter, in company with her Sister, and another Lady, at her Father's door, on their return from the Ball on the Queen's Birth Day; at half past Eleven at Night.   18. Jan.ʳ 1790.

1
It is of a Monster I mean for to write,
Who in stabbing of Ladies took great delight.
If he caught them alone in the street after dark,
In their Hips, or their Thighs he'd be sure a mark.

2
He met Miss Ann Porter, who chanc'd late to stay,
At the Ball at St James's, the Queens last birthday,
Coming home with her sister Miss Sarah we find,
He struck Miss Sally's head, and cut Nancy behind.

3
The wound that he made in this young Lady's hip,
Was Nine Inches long, and near Four Inches deep.
But before that this Monster had made use of force,
He insulted their ears with obscene discourse.

4
She met with this Monster one day in the Park.
As he walked with Mr Coleman, who noted the spark.
She told him how much from the wretch she'd endur'd,
So he follow'd the Monster and had him secur'd.

5
On the Eighth of July at the Old Baily try'd,
After Eight Hours hearing the Jury decide
That he was found Guilty, but sentence defer'd,
Until the Twelve Judges' opinion is heard.

London. Published July 13, 1790, by C. Sheppard N.º 19 Lambert Hill Doctors Commons.

---

19 *Above: Representation of the Monster*, a satirical print by W. Dent that is a good indicator of the amount of prejudice against Rhynwick Williams. This satirical print by Dent depicts Rhynwick Williams on trial (right) and prowling about in one of his disguises (left), with the grand scene of him cutting the Misses Porter in the middle. It is clearly published in the interval between the two trials, while the Twelve Judges' opinion was awaited. Its anti-Monster author boldly agitates that Rhynwick Williams should be hanged, and not transported, since the latter punishment would give him an opportunity to exercise his cruelties on the females of another country.

20 *Left:* A drawing of the Monster attacking the Misses Porter on the (non-existent?) steps of the Bagnio, with doggerel verses underneath. This was a cheap print issued just after the first trial to cash in on the great ballyhoo about the Monster.

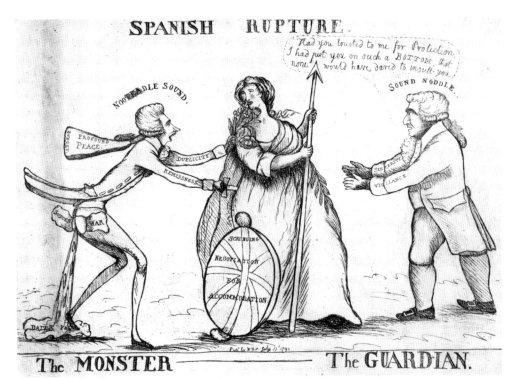

SPANISH RUPTURE.

NOOTKADLE SOUND.

SOUND NODDLE.

Had you trusted to me for Protection, I had put you on such a BOTTOM, that none would have dared to insult you.

SPOILT PROFOUND PEACE.

DUPLICITY

REMISSNESS

SINCERITY

VIGILANCE

SCROUGING

NEGOTIATION FOR ACCOMMODATION

WAR

DATES

The MONSTER —————— The GUARDIAN.

21 *Above*: Prime Minister William Pitt is depicted as the Monster in the satirical print *Spanish Rupture: The Monster – The Guardian*. Pitt dashes his diabolical nosegay into Britannia's face with gusto, and stabs her in the hip with his rapier. The rival politician Charles James Fox stands looking on aghast, calling out that had she trusted to him for protection, he would have her on such a BOTTOM that none would have dared to insult her. Pitt had been unjustly accused of truckling to Spain over the Nootka Sound affair, and this was but one of the several caricatures lampooning him.

22 *Right*: Rhynwick Williams cutting a lady, a print issued just after the first trial.

RENWICK WILLIAMS
commonly called
THE MONSTER.

23 *Essay in Duelling*, a satirical print by Collings, issued on 10 July 1789. Colonel Lennox, brandishing a pair of murderous-looking pistols, shoots Theophilus Swift in the stomach with one of them and shoots a curl off the Duke of York's head with the other. The startled Duke exclaims 'There goes the best part of my poor head!' The Prince of Wales stands far right, armed with blunderbusses, rapiers and pistols, saying 'Never mind your head I am your *corps de reserve*!' George Hanger, in the attitude of a pugilist, says 'Blast my eyes, I'll tip him Ward's damper in no time at all!'

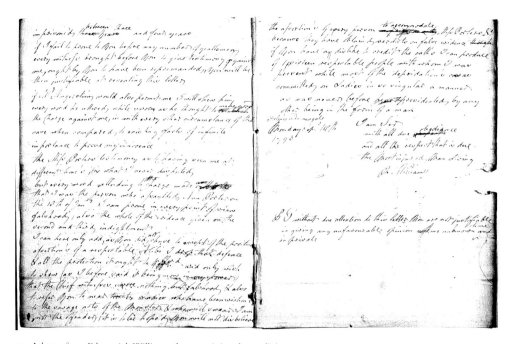

24 A letter from Rhynwick Williams, the most injured man living.

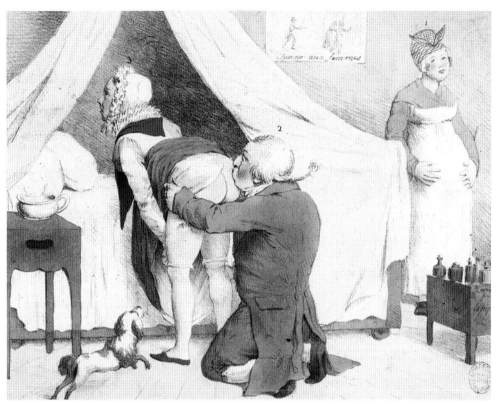

25 *Le danger d'être femme ou la suite des piqûres*, a satirical print published at the height of the Piqueur craze in Paris 1819.

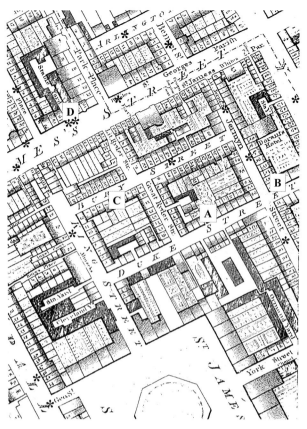

26 *Left*: A map of the London Monster's hunting grounds, with Rhynwick Williams' former dwellings in Duke's Court (A), his mother's house in Jermyn Street (B), the George public house where Rhynwick Williams lived (C) and Pero's Bagnio at No.63 St James's Street (D) marked. The nearby Monster assaults have also been plotted.

27 *Below*: A contemporary map of London, with all possible Monster assaults plotted.

Mr Pigot and Mr Fielding rushed up with a glass of water and some smelling salts, like two seconds trying to restore the flagging spirits of a severely mauled boxer. They objected that Mr Swift's questions were improper and insulting to the witness, and had little to bear on the case itself. The judge agreed, and called Theophilus to order. He had to beg the court's pardon, and requested that they would attribute his conduct to his strong conviction that Williams was innocent, and the 'natural impetuosity in his nature'. He then went on unabashed, and tried to make her repeat the foul language that Rhynwick Williams had whispered in her ear when he had stalked her in the street. She was most reluctant to do so, but the caddish Theophilus persisted, and finally managed to draw her into repeating his words verbatim. 'Blast your eyes, you damned bitch, I will murder you, and drown you in your blood!' said the blushing, embarrassed Anne Porter. Theophilus realised that this particular line of questioning, although amusing, was not exactly in favour of his client, but rather the opposite. He decided to torment Miss Porter in another way, and rapidly changed the subject. Now he tried to make her admit that there was not enough light outside the Bagnio for her to recognise Rhynwick Williams as the man who had cut her. He also asked her if she had been very frightened at the time. 'Yes,' said Anne Porter with feeling, 'I was almost insensible.' Then, being in such a state, Theophilus continued, how could she know Rhynwick Williams? She replied 'that however agitated she might be, she should have always known him, as his features were more impressed on her recollection, than those of her most intimate friends'. This gave Theophilus another opportunity to dig into her past, and he inquired *exactly in what way* she had previously been acquainted with Williams. She again became very agitated, and seemed totally deprived of the power of speech. The audience was making threatening noises, and Mr Pigot strongly objected to Mr Swift bullying and insulting her. Theophilus's passion was up, however, and instead of apologising, he called out 'Your agitation, madam, always seems to occur at the *most convenient time!*'

'Withdraw, Sir!' called out Mr Pigot.

'*I* will not be influenced by stage effects!' replied Theophilus Swift.

'Shame! Shame!' shouted Mr Reynolds.

'Boo! Boo!' roared the audience, who were getting increasingly rowdy.

At this time, Rhynwick Williams himself tried to make himself heard, but his shrill voice was almost drowned out by the furious hissing of the audience, as if he been sitting in midst of a nest of vipers.

Despite the attention of Mr Reynolds, who was holding the smelling salts to her nose, poor Anne Porter seemed almost to have fainted away, and her limp body was only held upright in the chair by the help of Mr Pigot.

Theophilus was unaffected by this drama, however. In a stentorian voice, he bawled out:

'A *certain kind* of ladies can faint at any time, as easily as the crocodile sheds tears!'

At this time, the opposing counsel were loudly appealing to the judge to have Mr Swift called to order, and the audience was most uproarious.[8] As Theophilus turned towards the spectators, with a satisfied smirk on his face, a young man had to be restrained not to leap over the barriers and assault him.

After the judge had calmed down all the participants, and once more reproached Theophilus Swift for his clamorous and undignified behaviour, the trial continued. Mr Pigot may well have taken the opportunity to brief Anne Porter about Mr Swift's probable next line of attack, since her forthcoming answers were much more clever than her earlier ones. Theophilus asked her why she was so sure that Rhynwick Williams' appearance exactly matched that of the London Monster; after all, she had described him as having light brown hair while Rhynwick did in fact have very dark brown hair, almost black. Anne Porter calmly replied that the Monster had evidently *worn his hair powdered* on these previous encounters. He then asked whether she and her sisters had had any *whisper* in the front room of the Bagnio before Coleman entered with Rhynwick Williams, but she indignantly replied 'Whisper! No, why should we? We had no occasion to whisper!' Theophilus rapidly changed the subject to that of Mr Angerstein's reward. Was it not true that she had received a part of this reward for herself? Miss Porter denied this emphatically. Well, replied Theophilus Swift, Mr Angerstein himself would be called under oath later, and then we will find out the truth about this matter. But even so, was it not true that she had 'some connection' with that dismal fishmonger John Coleman, to whom closer attention would be given later on during the trial, and that she had an *interest* in his share of the Monster rewards. Even she could not deny, under oath, that this *gentleman* had received huge sums of money for his part in the capture of the Monster? Anne Porter denied that she was engaged to marry Coleman, with the spirited words: 'Interest! Sir, I wonder how you can ask me such a question; what connection have I with Mr Coleman? Good God, Sir, No!' Theophilus replied that he had certainly heard reports to the contrary. Could she really stand up in court and deny that she had, directly or indirectly, received any part of the reward? Anne Porter drew herself up to her full height and replied that this 'was the *most infamous falsehood a malicious mind ever dared to advance!*'[9]

Anne Porter's evidence ended with this heated exchange. Judge Mainwaring wrote in his private notebook that, although the examination had been very long and trying, she had behaved 'with great decency and propriety and seemed to give her evidence with much fairness and caution'. Sarah Porter took her place in the witness box. Questioned by Mr Pigot, she gave the same evidence previously presented at the Old Bailey, concerning the events in St James's Street after the Monster had attacked them. She described Rhynwick Williams' vocabulary as 'both *threatening, indecent, prophane*, and *inhuman*'. Theophilus Swift, in his cross-examining, confronted her with the discrepancies between her present description of the Monster and that originally deposed at Bow Street. She did not deny that in her original description of the Monster she had described him as thirty years old, but added that it was not always easy to discern if a person was twenty-three, twenty-five or thirty years old, and that the Monster's powdered hair could explain the discrepancy between her original description of him and Rhynwick Williams' appearance in court. She had to admit, upon Theophilus pressing the point further, that she had never seen the prisoner with such dark hair before, and that this circumstance quite puzzled her. Judge Mainwaring, a clever man of the world, wrote in his private notebook that Rhynwick Williams had obviously put some dye in his hair for it to appear darker than its natural colour![10]

Sarah Porter vehemently denied that she had, in any way, received part of Mr Angerstein's reward. Only by asking her to repeat some of the words used by Rhynwick Williams while stalking the Misses could Theophilus Swift shake this imperturbable witness: she absolutely refused to do so, since the words were too dreadful. Pressed further by Theophilus, she reluctantly volunteered that one of his endearments had been that the next time they met, he would drown her in her own blood. Pigot and his associates again objected to this bullying of their witness, and there was an ominous murmuring among the audience. Miss Rebecca and Miss Martha Porter were the next lambs to the slaughter, but they escaped the brusque treatment that their sisters had suffered at the hands of Theophilus Swift. The eccentric Irishman was apparently looking forward to cross-examining Mrs Miel, who was next on the list of witnesses. Mr Pigot elegantly outmanoeuvred his quixotic opponent, however. At his prompting, Mrs Miel gave an account of how she had accompanied the Misses Porter to the ballroom. As they were attacked, and Sarah Porter called out in fear and pain, Mrs Miel made to turn around, but at the same moment the Monster had struck her a violent blow to the temple. Instead of witnessing Anne Porter being cut, poor Mrs Miel had seen nothing but stars, or rather, 'flashes before her eyes'. Although she had managed to keep in an upright position, it took some time before she was again capable of taking her bearings, and by then the Monster had made his escape. Theophilus appears to have been completely taken aback by this unexpected turn of events, and could only resort to his former bullying: did she or did she not consider herself a suitable guardian to *the Nuns of the Bagnio*? Fourteen-year-old John Porter, brother of the Misses, was next examined. As inflexible as Mrs Miel, he maintained that although he had opened the door to his terrified sisters on the evening of the Queen's birthday, and observed a man standing outside, he had not taken particular notice of his appearance.[11]

Surgeon Tompkins gave the same evidence as before, and steadfastly maintained that Anne Porter's wound was nine inches long, and four inches deep in the middle. There had been a considerable effusion of blood, and in fact the floor of the Bagnio was covered with it; this was due to an artery having been severed by the cut. Theophilus did not waste any of his ire on an insignificant personage like the Surgeon, but saved it for his particular 'favourite', John Coleman. The luckless fishmonger was in for many a sneering questions, and countless jibes and jeers, about his being taken for a catamite after his feeble 'gestures of offence' at the rails. After Runner Macmanus had repeated his evidence, John Julius Angerstein was called. He fully corroborated Anne Porter's story that she had refused his Monster-reward. Shortly after the Old Bailey trial he had sent for Thomas Porter and offered Anne £50, half of the reward, since she had been 'so accessory in the finding of him'. The day after, Mr Porter and Anne returned to the wealthy philanthropist's office. She thanked him for his offer, but declined, saying that she would not on any account receive even a farthing of it, and her father had commended her action. Theophilus Swift, who had previously blackguarded the female witnesses so mercilessly, was much more cautious and polite when approaching the powerful Angerstein, merely asking for confirmation that Coleman had received his £50, which Angerstein verified. Swift then hinted that when such an immense reward was offered, there were instances of people 'who have not only trumpt up evidence to obtain rewards

themselves, but to get it for others'. It may well be that Angerstein
had read Swift's slanderous (and quite possibly actionable) account
of his own part in the Monster-hunt and conveyed to him that he
would be in trouble if he tried anything similar in court.[12]

Theophilus Swift must have realised, after these further setbacks,
that he was losing the fight. As he opened the defence of
Rhynwick Williams, he depicted the prisoner as a poor, helpless,
friendless man, surrounded by gloating enemies.[13] He went on to
claim that there had been a rumour that he himself, the noble
Theophilus Swift, was an enemy of the female sex, since he had
come forward to defend the London Monster. No man would venture such an *untruth* to his face, he thundered, since it would be
treated as a matter of honour, and he was sure no woman would.
He was not defending the Monster, but a poor innocent man,
hounded by those who had profited from his downfall. If any person would suggest that he, the noble Theophilus Swift, was the
defender of the Monster, they should better keep this to themselves: 'I despise the insinuation from my soul and heart; I despise
the man who dares attempt it; I believe, I should not stoop to kick
him!' Mr Angerstein's reward was now in the hands of John
Coleman, and the testimony of this individual thus deserved no
credit at all. It was now apparent that the conspiring Porter sisters
had sworn Mrs Miel and their brother into their evil plot to *bolster
up the evidence*. He ended by quoting the case of poor Miss Zubery,
who had seven times been attacked by a Monster who said 'Oh
ho!' just like Sarah Porter's assailant; was this circumstance alone
not cause to doubt the guilt of Rhynwick Williams? Rather feebly,
he added that he would have called Miss Zubery as a witness had
she not been nursing her elderly father; he himself swore to the
truth of this story, however, and if any person chose to disbelieve
him, they were advised to keep this to themselves, since it would
otherwise be treated as a matter of honour.

After this martial and threatening remark, Theophilus called his
first witness for the defence, the mysterious Mr Smith, owner of
the house where Rhynwick Williams had given his name and

address to Coleman. Mr Smith himself probably appeared in court to scotch rumours that he was the Monster's accomplice. This was not Theophilus Swift's purpose in calling him, however: he wanted some further 'fun' at the expense of John Coleman.[14] When Smith was asked about the exact circumstances of that creature Coleman's entry into his house, he replied that Coleman had certainly not walked up to his door and demanded entry, as he had previously claimed.

'What?' asked Theophilus, feigning surprise, 'How did the dastard then gain entry?'

Smith replied that Rhynwick Williams had observed an awkward fellow skulking outside by the rails, and he had himself walked out to inquire what he wanted.

'So, Coleman *again* demonstrated his valour at the *rails*!' called out Theophilus. 'But what was then Mr Williams' purpose in calling him?'

Smith replied that his friend had thought that the poor fellow was 'deranged in his intellects'.

'Did you, Mr Smith, observe anything noteworthy about Coleman as he came into your house and observed the prisoner sitting there?'
'Yes,' said Smith, 'He was *trembling*.'

Having pulled off this further insult to 'Miss Porter's Puppy', Theophilus Swift called his friend Lady Wallace as a witness. She merrily confessed that she had wilfully presented a false testimony in the previous trial against Rhynwick Williams, and pulled Mr Pigot's leg about Amabel Mitchell's movements. Had any menial person tried anything like this, he or she would have been pulled off to Newgate by Macmanus for flagrant obstruction of justice, but Lady Wallace was let off without even a reprimand, and her actions were thought a good joke.[15]

Then it was time for the alibi witnesses to perform, goaded by Theophilus Swift. One by one, the artificial flower-makers gave their evidence, to the effect that Rhynwick Williams had been at work at their factory until well after the time when Anne and Sarah Porter had been assaulted. The maid Molly, who had contradicted her sister at the Old Bailey, was not present, nor was the workman Typhone Fournier, who had given a muddled impression on his previous examination. Either these individuals had refused to give evidence, or Theophilus may have hoped that selecting only the core witnesses would mean less danger of contradiction. If he had hoped to select the intellectual elite from the artificial flower factory, he would become sorely disappointed, however. The clever Mr Pigot had heard their testimony once before, and he had decided on a plan of attack for his cross-examination. He first went for Amabel Mitchell himself. The Frenchman was roundly abused, and accused of being the Monster's accomplice, and this apparently had the desired effect, since some of Amabel's replies were faltering and confused. He changed his story about Mrs Abingdon's gown, and stated that he had himself received the order from Jerso. Nor, he said, could he recollect whether Rhynwick Williams had actually supped at the factory that evening. No mention was made of the maid Molly and her remarks about the clock and the watchman outside, which had played such a prominent part in the alibi presented at the Old Bailey. Amabel merely said that he was able, from his long experience in the artificial flower business, to estimate the time from the amount of work done, and that he was certain that Rhynwick Williams had not left until after midnight.[16] On this point, he could not be shaken by Mr Pigot.

Mr Pigot then turned his attention to the female witnesses. After Raines Mitchell had given a somewhat guarded testimony, the forewoman Catherine Alman stalwartly repeated some of her statements from the Old Bailey. She claimed that Rhynwick Williams had been at work almost until midnight, and that he had not left the factory even for a moment. A little before midnight, the cloth was laid for supper, and Rhynwick had dined with Amabel

Mitchell before returning home. None of the workers in the artificial flower factory was the happy owner of a watch or clock, but Catherine Alman claimed, like her employer, that she could estimate the time from the amount of work done, just as precisely as if she had looked at a clock or watch. Mr Pigot vigorously pointed out that to estimate the time of day from the number of artificial flowers made is not particularly accurate. She then told a somewhat revised version of the tale of her sister and the clock: after Rhynwick had left, Molly had told her that she had heard the watchman cry out that it was half past twelve, and that she was afraid Rhynwick would not get into his lodgings that evening. Pigot bullied and provoked her as much as he could, but she declared that she was absolutely positive that Rhynwick Williams had been in the house at a quarter past eleven that evening.

The other artificial flower-makers gave a less solid impression, however. One of them admitted that a person could actually slip out of the door of the factory without being noticed by the other workers. Another workwoman said that Rhynwick Williams had in fact been out of her sight for some periods of time during that evening, but added that he must only have gone out into the yard, since it was impossible that he could have gone out through the front door. Why was that, asked Pigot. Because the door had a bell, which rang when it was opened, was the naïve reply. Mr Pigot reminded the jury that it was possible to *silence* such a bell by the simple expedients of either holding the clapper, or manoeuvring the bell out of the door's way. The workwoman, whose jaw was probably dropping at the thought of such wickedness, was very politely thanked by Mr Pigot for her valuable evidence. Theophilus Swift must have ground his teeth when his witness made a complete ass of herself, and he probably felt a potent urge to kick her backside as she shuffled past him, another worker in the flower factory taking her place. This workwoman, the aforementioned Frances Beaufils, was as obliging as her colleague when cross-examined by the polite, well-spoken Mr Pigot. Contradicting all her colleagues as to the time, she swore that she had left the factory in the evening, after having supped there, when Rhynwick Williams was still present, and arrived at her lodgings at Coventry Court, in the Haymarket, at half past eleven. Mr Pigot was quick to emphasise that this witness not only possessed a clock, which she had consulted as soon as she came home, but that she had also asked a watchman for the time on her way home. Finally, several character witnesses appeared on behalf of Rhynwick Williams, but not poor Sarah Seward, who had had enough of Monster trials after being so grossly insulted in the Old Bailey. In ringing tones, Theophilus Swift read out her affidavit that Rhynwick had once saved her life; had any one had dared to laugh, Theophilus would probably have challenged him to a duel.

In his summing up, Mr Pigot emphasised that Anne Porter's evidence was clearly not contradicted by that of Mrs Miel and John Porter, and that all the Misses Porter had pointed out Rhynwick Williams as their persecutor without any doubt. Whatever one might think of John Coleman's conduct, and his 'unnecessary stops and turnings', this gentleman was still the person directly responsible for the capture of Rhynwick Williams, and as such worthy of respect. Rather gloatingly, he pointed out the muddled testimony of some of the artificial flower-makers: was such a flimsy alibi worthy of any credence at all, he asked the jury, particularly when it had been substantially changed from the Old Bailey trial? The summing up of the prosecution had been a lengthy one, and more than one juryman wished that Theophilus Swift would keep his summing up reasonably concise, since it was now ten o'clock in the evening, and they were still hoping to have their evening meal in reasonable time. But this was not to come. For nearly an hour and a half, Theophilus bludgeoned the court with a rambling summing up, which contained all his pet theories about the Monster business. With many a pun and many a classical quotation, he spoke at length about *Tavern-Vestals*, the *Nuns of the Bagnio*, the *Amorous Captain*, *Miss Porter's Puppy*, and the adventures of the *Dastardly Fishmonger turned Catamite*, at the *rails*. When at length, his soporific audience had been entertained to an entire summary of the case, seen from his perspective, Judge Mainwaring once more recapitulated the evidence. Well aware of the popular prejudice against Rhynwick Williams, and the amount of hostile newspaper writing about his dark deeds, he spoke to the jury in ringing tones: 'For God's sake, get rid of all prejudice; let your judgement be biased by nothing but the evidence before you. One cannot help knowing how much the unnatural attacks on the fair sex have been the subject of conversation; and much I fear, that many there are who came here with a wish to hear the Defendant found Guilty. Guard your own passions; coolly and deliberately consider and weigh every part of the evidence, and then according to your own judgements find him innocent or guilty!'[17] At half past eleven in the evening, the jury finally withdrew to consider their verdict. A quarter of an hour later, they returned and found Rhynwick Williams guilty as charged, and the first day of the trial was at an end.

The next day, at eleven o'clock, the trial was resumed.[18] Five other wounded ladies were waiting to give evidence against Rhynwick Williams. Mr Fielding opened the case for the prosecution by paying a handsome compliment to the jury for their upright conduct during the long and complicated trial the day before. Rather gloatingly, he made a reference to 'a scurrilous and indecent Pamphlet that had made its appearance respecting the prisoner'. Theophilus Swift, who had previously been looking gloomy and dejected, leapt up with some warmth when his pamphlet was mentioned, and promised 'that another publication, on the subject of the last trial, would make its appearance!'

Elizabeth Davis was first called, and described her perilous encounter with the man with the artificial nosegay, in a similar manner as before. She identified Rhynwick Williams as the man responsible, adding that at Bow Street she had picked him out from among a crowd of people. In marked contrast to the evidence she had given at the time of the assault, she now described the Monster's dress as a plain grey coat, and then identified the prisoner's coat, as shown to her by Macmanus, as that of the man who had assaulted her. It is interesting to note that after she and her landlady had given evidence, the prisoner would have said something, but was stopped by Theophilus Swift, with the words 'Not a word, Mr Williams; you were prevented from speaking last night, and you shall not be permitted to speak today!' Elizabeth Davis then braced herself for an onslaught from Rhynwick Williams' formidable counsel, but Theophilus Swift merely said, rather airily, that 'they could prove a clear alibi, but would not attempt it'. The ubiquitous Mr Angerstein then appeared, to swear that he had intimate knowledge of all details of the case, which had interested him since as, although many victims had described the Monster's dress as a blue coat, Elizabeth Davis had disagreed and said it had been grey. After very brief deliberation, the prisoner was found guilty.

Miss Elizabeth and Miss Frances Baughan were next called, and described their meeting with the London Monster on Westminster Bridge, where he said, 'Blast you, is that you' into Frances Baughan's ear, and then cut both of them. They positively swore that Rhynwick Williams was the culprit. Theophilus Swift again claimed that he could prove a clear alibi, but that he would not attempt it. The prisoner was once more found guilty, and Mr Fielding made another of his gloating speeches. He pointed out that there were several other indictments against Rhynwick Williams: the assaults on Sarah Porter, Mary Forster, Ann Frost and Mrs Godfrey; the prosecution side had decided, however, that since 'the ends of public justice being answered, for which alone these prosecutions were set on foot, he would not go on with them'. He again made reference to Theophilus Swift's scandalous pamphlet, and was proud that the Porter family, who had been suffering much agony as a consequence of this vile publication, had now been vindicated. After the court had considered their final verdict, Judge Mainwaring spoke to the prisoner. For the assaults on Anne Porter, Elizabeth Davis and Elizabeth Baughan, he was to be confined in Newgate two years for each offence, each sentence to commence after the expiration of the former one. After spending these six years in Newgate, he was to provide himself bail for his good behaviour for seven years, in the sum of £200, and two sureties of £100 each. After hearing this dismal news, poor Rhynwick Williams bowed to the court and was led away to prison.

Although the Monster-mania of mid-1790 had had time to abate, the newspapers still gave considerable attention to the second trial against Rhynwick Williams.[19] The accounts of the trial suggested a sense of relief that the Monster-business was finally brought to rest, and that Rhynwick Williams had been put away for a considerable period of time. The most lengthy article, in an unnamed newspaper, maybe the *World*, was openly derisive about Theophilus Swift's shenanigans in court, particularly his scandalous and indecent cross-examination of Anne Porter.[20] About Anne Porter's refusal to accept any part of Angerstein's reward, the indignant journalist wrote: 'How must that author of a pamphlet, which has lately made its appearance, blush at the above testimony, if he has a blush left; and surely, after the publication of so infamous a composition, we may be allowed to doubt it.' Theophilus Swift's threat to bring out another pamphlet was derided with the trenchant words: 'Unless it is a more decent one than the last, we hope that it will never be any where but in the author's closet.'

The only newspaper that had actually had some sympathy for Rhynwick Williams' plight was the *Argus*. The brief summary of the second trial had spoken of him as 'this unfortunate man'.[21] In a lengthy article published just after the trial, Theophilus Swift was given an ovation for his brilliant defence of Rhynwick Williams, which the writer was certain would become part of legal history.[22] It began with the words: 'If anything could add to the reputation of Mr Swift, the stand which he made in defence of Rhynwick Williams on Monday last, must have had that effect.' Unaided by any counsel, and without even a brief in the case, the noble Theophilus had combated his four formidable opponents for the space of fifteen hours. Theophilus Swift was compared with the famous lawyer Mr Erskine, whose defence of Captain Bailey for a supposed libel on Lord Sandwich had attracted much notice; his fire and eloquence had surpassed even that of this famous barrister. Among further exaggerated braggadocio, it is claimed that 'Mr Swift's reply to Mr Pigot, which lasted more than an hour, was perhaps the most animated that had ever been made in any Court of criminal justice.' This was probably not the impression of the jury and audience at ten o'clock in the evening, after the trial had already been going on for twelve hours. In spite of all the prejudice against poor Rhynwick Williams, Mr Swift had managed to drive Mr Pigot into a situation where he had to tell the jury that the alibi story was true, and that Williams had slipped out from the flower factory for a couple of minutes and done the deed in this space of time. The jury was so impressed by his masterly defence that they went out of court for nearly half an hour before returning to find Rhynwick Williams guilty.

Having some knowledge of Theophilus Swift's character, one is not surprised to find that he was a contributor of signed editorial articles in the *Argus*. For example, he wrote a leading article about Mr Hastings and his Impeachment just a few days later.[23] It is not at all unlikely that he also wrote the unsigned article extolling his masterly defence of Rhynwick Williams! There were also rumours around town at the time (spread by whom, one may wonder!) that Theophilus Swift's brilliant defence had so impressed the jury that they had gone out of court for more than half an hour. Several jurymen had been convinced that Rhynwick Williams was innocent of assaulting Anne Porter, and he had in fact been convicted by a majority of only two! The *World* newspaper took exception to this malicious spreading of untrue rumours about the case, and wanted to 'clear the Jury from the slander that it seems the wish of *some Person* to heap on them'.[24] The journalist pointed out that the jury had been out for just fifteen minutes, and that the jurymen had been unanimous on two counts. Only one gentleman objected to finding Rhynwick Williams guilty also of 'intent to murder', but he was satisfied when the part was read over where Anne Porter deposed that Rhynwick Williams had repeatedly said that he would drown her in her own blood.

The punishment of Rhynwick Williams was a singular one. At this time, prison sentences were usually very short (six or nine months), and they were used to punish petty thieves.[25] Judge Mainwaring was probably influenced by the arguments of Mr Pigot about the serious nature of the Monster's crimes, and shared his outrage that Rhynwick Williams was not tried as a felon; the judge must also have been aware of the massive prejudice against the Monster at all levels of London society. By inflicting a lengthy prison sentence, he probably wanted to compensate for the punishment thought more suitable for this dastardly villain, and put him away in prison for a considerable period of time. In that case, it is a puzzling matter why Mr Pigot did not proceed with the other indictments against Rhynwick Williams. After all, four other wounded ladies were standing by to give evidence against him. During the first day of the trial, Mr Pigot and Mr Fielding had described Rhynwick Williams as a depraved, brutal fiend who had tried to murder several women; on the second day, they declared that justice had been met when such a man had been given a six-year prison sentence. The conduct of Theophilus Swift is also worthy of attention: during the first day, he made every exertion to save Rhynwick Williams, and bullied the prosecution witnesses mercilessly; in the second day of the trial, he mostly played the part of a spectator. It may be speculated that he had made a deal with the prosecution side, and pledged to keep quiet so that another scandalous trial could be avoided; in return, Rhynwick Williams was to be let off after Elizabeth Davis and the Misses Baughan had been called to give evidence. Perhaps Mr Pigot had nevertheless been impressed with Rhynwick Williams' alibi for the Porter assault. It may or not be significant that none of the other women pointed out as 'Nuns' or 'Tavern-Vestals' by Theophilus Swift were called to give evidence; in particular, one is surprised that Mary Forster was not called. Perhaps Mr Pigot had anticipated trouble since she had actually changed her story at Bow Street.

Just after Rhynwick Williams had been convicted for the second time, posters all over London announced that the SAVAGE MON-STER, a creature of unsurpassed ferocity, was on show to the nobility and gentry near Charing Cross. It was not Rhynwick, however, but a large bear, shaved round the face and breast, and dressed in a suit of Indian garments![26]

11

What Happened

TO

RHYNWICK WILLIAMS?

And by the heat I once felt glowing
At William's Statue's feet –
By other Williams' graving tool
And by the fame of Eton School
The muses dear retreat –
By coward Lenox' pistol ball –
And by the head of hated Hall –
By speech which Deane essay'd to read –
By embryo pamphlets in my head –
By these and by ought else I swear
'Gainst Dublin College lasting war.

Theophilus Swift, *Prison Pindarics* (1795)

After he had finally been committed to Newgate, there was very little news about Rhynwick Williams. It is apparent that it was, for a time, quite fashionable among the London swells to visit him there, perhaps to give the ladies a thrill to see the Monster in his cage. The Newgate turnkeys were well known to open the prison gates to admit any visitor who gave them a tip for

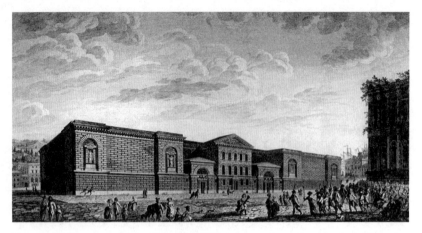

Newgate Gaol in 1790, at the time Rhynwick Williams was a prisoner there. A print by F. Bourjot.

this privilege.[1] Rhynwick himself meekly referred to the numbers of people who had come to see him out of curiosity, and to buy his artificial flowers. Apparently he was still busy at his trade, but this flower-selling was probably just used to provide a pretext for those who came to ogle him. He was something of a disappointment to some of the bloods who sauntered in expecting to see someone like the lunatics at Bedlam, or some crazed street performer; instead they saw a big-nosed little man in a worn blue coat that still showed traces of gentility, sitting peacefully on a stool making artificial flowers. More than one disgustedly called out, 'Is this the man called the *Monster*!?'; poor Rhynwick took this as evidence that they believed in his innocence.[2]

It is remarkable how quickly Londoners forgot all about the Monster and his strange crimes. Even after the first trial, which ended the proper Monster-mania, people gradually seemed to forget about him. Although the pamphlet of Theophilus Swift, and the scandalous second trial, did much to keep Rhynwick Williams and his misdeeds in the news, the whole thing was forgotten as 'yesterday's news' as soon as Williams had been permanently jailed. A large part of this was, of course, due to the fact that after the arrest of Williams there had been far fewer attacks on women on the

London streets. In 1791, Horace Walpole wrote (in a letter to Miss Mary Berry) that a certain lady acquaintance of theirs 'may be sent to Botany Bay, and be as much forgotten here as *the Monster*'.[3] The memory of the Monster was perpetuated only by Mrs Salmon's Waxworks Display in Fleet Street. Along with wax statues of some Cherokee Indians, and of Captain Anckarström stabbing King Gustaf III of Sweden, was a representation of the Monster stabbing Anne and Sarah Porter. A man who saw this display in 1793 could still remember, forty-four years later, how horrified he had been by the bloodstained figures of the King and the Misses Porter, and the Monster's bloodthirsty and threatening posture.[4] There are also shades of the Monster in a caricature print issued as late as 1802, entitled *The Little Green Man, or the Bath Bugaboo*. It concerned a certain Henry Cope, a well-known eccentric, who dressed entirely in green and had only green furniture, a green gig, and ate nothing but green vegetables etc. He was often seen in Brighton and Bath, where he made unsuccessful attempts to get acquainted with various fashionable ladies. In the caricature, Cope is seen in his green apparel, staring intensely at three comely ladies, who flee in terror when they see him, crying: 'O Lord the Monster! O dear the Monster! The Monster! The Monster!'[5]

Theophilus Swift's pamphlet *The Monster at Large* was reprinted early in 1791. A reviewer in the *Monthly Review* liked it as a literary performance, but declared himself wholly unconvinced in the question of the innocence of Mr Swift's notorious client. He also complained that the dignity of the work was let down by its 'sallies of wanton wit' and ill-placed sarcasms and *double entendres* at the expense of the female witnesses.[6] Theophilus had promised that he would write another pamphlet about the second trial, but he never did so. His own explanation was that his mind, always eager to fight injustice, had been caught up by other affairs, mainly those occurring in Ireland. Furious after his defeat at the second trial, he had written some diatribes against the people involved, but he never made any attempt to publish them. In mid-1791, these papers were turned over to Rhynwick himself. He was still a prisoner in Newgate, and felt increasingly uneasy in this rough prison. One would not imagine that the London Monster would have a high standing in the prison hierarchy; already before he was committed to Newgate, the roughs and toughs had declared their detestation of this unnatural offender in no uncertain manner.[7] Rhynwick had apparently been impressed with the partial success of Theophilus Swift's pamphlet, and the only thing he could think of that would expedite his egress from the dreaded cells of Newgate was to publish another pamphlet, to draw attention to his plight. Theophilus Swift had described Rhynwick Williams as a 'poor illiterate man', but this was as exaggerated and biased as many of his other judgements, since Rhynwick proved perfectly capable of writing a pamphlet of his own. Although his grammar and spelling sometimes fail him, his vocabulary is quite good; this certainly speaks in favour of young Rhynwick having received a decent education. In July 1792, *An Appeal to the Public by Rhynwick Williams Containing Observations and Reflections on Facts relative to his very Extraordinary and Melancholy Case* was available at the booksellers; this forty-seven-page pamphlet was printed at his own expense.

In his pamphlet, Rhynwick Williams gave a graphic picture of the two trials, some of which has already been quoted, and particularly the mortification he had felt when he was hissed and booed by the mob, when trying to speak. Mr Pigot had mocked and insulted him throughout the two trials, and 'regarded it a great effrontery of mine to try and set up an *alibi*.' Poor Amabel Mitchell had also been grossly insulted, and Mr Pigot had tried to present him as the Monster's accomplice. Rhynwick Williams' only consolation, as he sat in Newgate fretting about his misfortunes, was that the Misses Porter and John Coleman had received a proper grilling at the hands of Theophilus Swift. John Porter, Mrs Miel and even Mr Angerstein had also been give attention by Rhynwick Williams' fearless counsel, and retreated from the witness box in confusion. Nowhere does Rhynwick Williams in any way blame Theophilus for mismanaging his case; indeed, his pamphlet reflects nothing but gratitude towards his eccentric champion.[8] Their defeat at Hick's Hall was blamed on the fact that Theophilus faced no less than three opposing counsel who took turns to obstruct his cross-examining of these false hussies, the Misses Porter.

Rhynwick declared that he had known the Misses by sight since some years before the Monster-mania, 'as I believe most young men do, who have frequented the Park, Kensington Gardens, and other places devoted to Gallantry'. Rhynwick was much taken by their pretty looks, and the eldest sister, Anne Porter, was his favourite. He frequently 'solicited an acquaintance', but was treated with disdain. Once, when Anne had called him 'shop-man, and told to go my way to the shop counter, &c.' Rhynwick retorted that he certainly felt as good as a certain Captain, 'with whom you made a short excursion'! These words were, he claimed, all of the 'gross abuse' attributed to him. He also wanted his readers to believe that this uncouth reference to her elopement with Captain Crowder had inspired in Anne Porter's malicious, conniving mind, a deadly hatred, which had later inspired her to conspire with her sisters and John Coleman to denounce Rhynwick as the Monster. Although Anne Porter had, by the time of the second trial, denied upon oath, in front of the fuming Theophilus Swift, that she was engaged to marry Coleman, she actually married him shortly after that time, at St George's, Hanover Square, according to their marriage certificate dated 28 April 1791. This celebrity marriage, although involving rather yesterday's celebrities, was of course reported in the newspapers, and it was commented that 'thus Mr Coleman is rewarded for having brought the *monster* to punishment by the lady whose cause he so gallantly espoused'.[9]

This newspaper account provoked a further feeble outbreak of rage in Rhynwick Williams' breast. In his pamphlet, he called Coleman 'a cowardly impotently [*sic*] creature' and claimed that he could have knocked down a dozen such as him, with the greatest ease. Then, one must ask, why didn't he? He must have realised what was up, and still behaved like an even greater coward than the man pursuing him. If he had slapped John Coleman's face with his artificial nosegay, during their memorable debate at the rails in front of Mr Pearson's house, the timid fishmonger would probably have turned and run for his life. As things were now, with Coleman triumphant and himself a wretched convict, Rhynwick Williams could only conclude that '*Mrs Coleman* has had her revenge, and *her Husband* his reward.' Coleman had netted fifty guineas from Mr Angerstein and 135 guineas from a private subscription. Rhynwick claimed, perhaps rightly, that these huge sums were the least part of the pecuniary rewards claimed by the avaricious fishmonger.

Much of Rhynwick Williams' pamphlet is devoted to lengthy, maudlin ruminations about his present wretched state, and the prejudice against him that had resulted in his conviction. In an extremely feeble attempt to prove that the real Monster was still at large, he quoted a case from Bristol, where two women had been cut in the hip, and another instance from Watford, where a servant-girl had been cut so viciously that she had to walk on crutches afterwards. Finally, a certain Mary Clark had been attacked in Pall Mall, on 13 June 1792, by a tall man in a drab-coloured greatcoat, resembling the original description of the Monster. Rhynwick Williams suspected that this man, the proper Monster, had taken to travelling the countryside before finally returning to his old haunts in the metropolis; the authorities, unwilling to admit that Rhynwick Williams was innocent, were covering up his nefarious activities.

Rhynwick Williams had little success with his pamphlet, as could be expected from its feeble arguments, and also the general lack of interest in the Monster business after a period of more than two years had elapsed since the Monster's reign of terror in the spring of 1790. The pamphlet was neglected by the newspapers and by the reading public alike, and is today a very rare book indeed.

The Newgate Prison calendar of September 1792 lists Rhynwick, alias Renwick Williams, vulgarly called the Monster, as prisoner No.31.[10] He had been brought to Newgate on 14 June 1790. He is described as aged twenty-eight, five feet six inches tall, with grey eyes, brown hair (the dye had obviously worn off by then) and a fresh complexion. In the next calendar, dated 28 September 1794, Rhynwick Williams was listed as one of five long-time prisoners. The most famous of them was Lord George Gordon, the instigator of the London riots in 1780, who had been convicted for libels on the Queen of France. Gordon had converted to Judaism, and was a strange-looking figure with his huge beard, wide-brimmed hat and long cloak. He had bought himself into the more salubrious part of the prison, and even held dinner parties and musical concerts for his friends. It is by no means unlikely that Rhynwick Williams met him, since one of Lord George's biographers adds that he liked to walk round in other wards of the huge prison and give concerts to his fellow inmates with his bagpipes or violin, and that he sometimes joined in when some communal ball game was played.[11] Lord George Gordon died in Newgate in October 1793, however, and the prison calendar marked this with a laconic 'Dead' in the margin. Rhynwick Williams was transferred to the next ledger together with three other long-term inmates: the defrauder John Collins, the child-stealer Mary Wilson, and thirty-year-old James Carse, who had been spared a death sentence for the 'Murder of Sarah Hayes. Cut her head off'. The following year, Carse was pardoned to serve in the Royal Navy, and hauled on board a man-of-war at the Docks; Rhynwick Williams now had the dubious honour of being the veteran prisoner in Newgate.

Friends and family were allowed to visit Newgate daily, and it is to be hoped that the apothecary Thomas Williams, and perhaps also Theophilus Swift, paid Rhynwick a visit or two. The prisoners also had the right to keep animals; although dogs were forbidden in 1792, pigs and poultry were not. There was much gambling and gaming in Newgate at this time, and the Keeper's office held a

much-frequented tap room, from which the prisoners could pur-
chase beer. One would rather suppose that Rhynwick Williams was
a member of the 'Free and Easy Club', a drinking society which
prided itself in its ability to procure cheap barrels of beer and kegs
of gin from outside the prison. Indeed, the riotous noise from the
Newgate tap room was such that the neighbours complained that it
kept them awake all night. The prisoners freely urinated out of the
prison windows, or deliberately emptied their chamber-pots over
unsuspecting passers-by in the street outside. One would rather
think that elegant young ladies would have had a few surprises in
store for them, if they had dared to pass underneath the Monster's
den in Newgate. Even more interesting for Rhynwick Williams,
Newgate was at this time a favourite haunt for 'lewd women and
common strumpets'. They paid the Turnkeys a shilling and were
thus allowed to stay with the prisoners overnight. If Rhynwick
Williams' pocket money could not secure him a rendezvous with
one of these accommodating prostitutes, the rates were even
cheaper during the daytime; a visiting Member of Parliament, out
to investigate the conditions at Newgate, was outraged when he
observed 'the grossest scenes in broad daylight'.[12]

In spite of these attractions, Newgate was a veritable hell-hole.
The gaol-fever carried off numerous prisoners every year, and dis-
eases of all kinds ravaged the prison population. The vermin tor-
mented them day and night, the food was abysmally bad, and the
other thieves and villains in Newgate were unlikely to have had a
high opinion of the notorious London Monster. In September 1793,
Rhynwick Williams made a desperate attempt to get free. He had
now served three years in prison, half of the original sentence of six
years. In a letter headed 'Felon's side, Newgate, Sept 17th 1793', he
wrote to the Home Secretary, Henry Dundas, to petition for the
King's mercy, and to complain about the prejudice he had encoun-
tered at Hick's Hall.[13] In particular, he alleged that Judge William
Mainwaring had been highly biased, and that he had instructed the
jury to take much notice of the sufferings of the Misses Porter, and
to disregard the alibi witnesses from the flower factory. He declared

himself willing to again stand trial before any English jury of responsible men, and awaited the Secretary of State's reply to his letter as to the particulars of this judicial redress. No answer was forthcoming, however, to the wretched Newgate prisoner. As was the custom in cases where convicted prisoners had applied for the King's pardon, Dundas sent Rhynwick's letter on to Judge William Mainwaring to obtain his comments on the case. Someone, perhaps Dundas himself, scrawled on the envelope, 'If this case has not already, it ought to be particularly investigated'; it is likely that he remembered the two sensational trials in 1790, and was not entirely satisfied about the guilt of Rhynwick Williams. Rhynwick himself had, in a rather imprudent manner, already written to Judge Mainwaring, to complain bitterly about how he had been wrongly imprisoned upon a mass of false evidence from malicious or prejudged witnesses. Rhynwick roundly accused the judge of perjury, and claimed that his observations from the Bench, and his admonitions directed at Rhynwick and his counsel when they tried to cross-examine the Misses Porter, had been instrumental to cause his conviction. It was thus Judge Mainwaring's fault that he had been falsely imprisoned for three and a half years. In his customary overblown prose, Rhynwick declared himself ready to stand trial again, before sixteen honest gentlemen. This remarkable letter was signed:

> I am Sir, with all due obedience [*respect* written before, but heavily crossed over], and all the respect that is due, the Most injured Man Living.
>
> > R. Williams.
>
> P.S. without due attention to this letter thou are not justifiable in giving any unfavourable opinion of me unknown to me and in private.

The standard reply to any petition in favour of a prisoner was that the judge presiding at that prisoner's trial wrote a letter stating his opinion about the trial, the character of the crime, and whether the individual deserved to be pardoned. William Mainwaring's reply was not what Rhynwick Williams had hoped for, however. The judges' letters giving their opinions of prisoners were usually two or three pages long, but Mainwaring apparently feared that Rhynwick Williams would have some success with his petition, since he wrote a thirty-nine-page, closely argued summary of the trial at Hick's Hall.[14] He had been struck by the fact that the Misses Porter, although they positively identified Rhynwick as the Monster, had also observed that his hair looked particularly dark, almost black. When he had assaulted them, they described his hair as being fair or light brown in colour, Judge Mainwaring strongly suspected that Rhynwick Williams had dyed his hair black before the trial, in a futile attempt to disguise himself. He was convinced that the attacks on Anne Porter, Elizabeth Davis and the Misses Baughan had been committed by the same person, and the five witnesses involved had unanimously pointed out Rhynwick Williams as the culprit. Judge Mainwaring had looked into the transcript of the Old Bailey case, and seen that some of the alibi witnesses had changed their stories at the county sessions. He finally declared that he himself was totally convinced of Williams' guilt, and that the entire Bench of magistrates shared this feeling at the time. Rhynwick Williams was thus not a proper object of His Majesty's royal pardon, he wrote, and the authorities acted accordingly: Williams was to serve his full sentence.

In 1795, after two more years of imprisonment, Rhynwick got an unexpected companion in Newgate: his old defence counsel Theophilus Swift! After Theophilus had gone to Ireland, he had started an acrimonious dispute against the Fellows of Trinity College, Dublin. His son Deane Swift, 'the cleverest lad in all Ireland', had performed badly in his university examinations. He had failed to obtain any prize or distinction; indeed, he was at the bottom of a list of thirteen youths. Deane was a strong, beefy lad, and an expert pugilist (a former pupil of the great bruiser Daniel Mendoza). His actions were hardly those of an intellectual, but Theophilus claimed that any son of his, and any descendant of the great Jonathan Swift, must be a genius. Theophilus was present when Deane was questioned by Dr Hall, an old enemy of his:

> *Skilled in polite, and pugilistic lore,*
> *Friend to the Muses much, but to Mendoza more.*
> *Him just arrived from Eton School,*
> *Ev'n at the Academic Vestibule,*
> *Cerberus met and bay'd him for a fool.*
> *The tyrant Hall my modest youth depress'd –*
> *Twelve were preferr'd to him who must have been the best.*

Theophilus strongly objected to Dr Hall's questioning, to which poor Deane had managed few coherent answers. The fearsome Dr Burrowes then took over the questioning:

> *Nor vain my bodings! With his Gorgon look*
> *He petrified my bashful boy:*
> *Then threw him Euclid's second book,*
> *His every prospect to destroy.*

In vain, Theophilus objected that, as a result of his kinship with Jonathan Swift, Deane was a 'Mathesiphobic' just like the great Dean, and incapable of learning mathematics. Dr Burrowes and Dr Elrington, the latter the editor of Euclid, soon found this out for themselves, and Deane had to leave Trinity College in disgrace. He still had the lease of his college chambers, and these were appropriated by his father, who found it convenient to stay there when in Dublin. One day, Elrington wanted to evict this uninvited tenant, claiming that the chambers were vacant after Deane's departure. 'Vacant – and I living in them!' replied Theophilus. He immediately sent for Deane and told him about this great insult to the family. Deane armed himself with a stout cane and went out to look for Dr Elrington. He finally found him, and inflicted on the mathematician the chastisement described in another of Theophilus's deplorable stanzas:

One day Deane met Elrington in the street
And seeing that he had no stick,
Deane gave him a kick...

This outrage caused the expulsion of both the Swifts from Trinity College, which was, of course, in Theophilus's warped mind another unprovoked insult to the family, an insult that cried out for vengeance. He immediately went in for the kill, and wrote an even more scurrilous pamphlet than *The Monster at Large*, entitled *Animadversions on the Fellows of Trinity College*.[15] Theophilus accused certain Fellows of being lecherous brutes, who had broken the laws that prevented them from marrying. In Dublin College, he wrote, the Muses blushed to be seen, and the only Graces that appeared were *Silence, Stupidity* and *Sorrow*. He gloated that his strong, manly son had 'sent the punctum of his great toe in a rectilineal direction into the sphere of the Mathematician's backside'. The aforementioned Fellows – Hall, Elrington and Burrowes – were grossly insulted: 'wretched must be the condition of that country whose youths of a high and flaming spirit are enslaved by such a canter as Burrowes, such an oath-monger as Elrington, and such a coxcomb as Magee.' As a result, he was prosecuted for libel. The evidence against Theophilus was very strong, and even a spirited defence from his old friend Jonah Barrington could not prevent him joining Rhynwick Williams in Newgate for twelve months. His only consolation was that one of his adversaries, the Revd Dr Burrowes, was sentenced to six months in Newgate for perjuring *him*. The two volatile Irishmen had to share a cell, with the result that they soon became firm friends.

In December 1795, Theophilus Swift published another pamphlet while actually still languishing in Newgate; it was entitled *Prison Pindarics; or a New Year's Gift from Newgate*. It contained scurrilous reflections on the three great episodes of his quarrelsome life: the duel against Lennox, his defence of Rhynwick Williams and the libel against the Fellows of Trinity College. Colonel Lennox was again blasted as a coward, although 'He fought me on it and wounded me severely – but I never retract – anything I say must have been true'. Theophilus boasted that his timely discovery of Mr Pitt's elaborate plot to murder the entire royal family had prevented this scheme from going any further. He also prided himself on the very eloquent and ingenious defence of Rhynwick Williams, and that his pamphlet 'made as many pleasant jeux d'esprits, and double entendres on the ladies who prosecuted him, as I have on the Fellows' wives'. He complained that the jury at Rhynwick Williams' second trial had deliberately overlooked the discrepancies in the evidence made by the female witnesses: '... one lady swore to a man's stooping down, her sister swore to a man rising up, and the jury, in spite of me, would believe that it was the same man who stooped down and then rose up.'[16] The Trinity College dons were in for another torrent of abuse, often expressed in lugubrious verse:

> *Curst be your College! Curst its Constitution!*
> *Where Genious never meets regard,*
> *Where access to the Muse is barr'd*
> *Where dullness' leaden sceptre rules*
> *O'er fellow rogues and student fools...*

Theophilus Swift was let out of prison in the summer of 1796, but Rhynwick Williams had to remain in Newgate until 16 December 1796, when he was taken to the Bow Street public office and admitted to bail before the sitting magistrates, his old friends William Addington and Richard Ford. He was bound in the sum of £400, and the people who became bound for him were Mr Dawson, printer, in Fleet Street, and Mr Worship, engraver, Union Street, Southwark.[17] One would have expected that a man with Rhynwick Williams' tarnished reputation would either have changed his name or left the country, perhaps both. But this was not the case. It is recorded that on 22 February 1797, Renwich [*sic*] Williams married Elizabeth Robins in St Pancras old church. It is a fair guess that she was the Elizabeth Robins listed as the daughter of Thomas and Elizabeth Robins, born in November 1774. Remarkably, at the time of the marriage they had a young son, George Renwick Williams, conceived in Newgate and christened at St Sepulchre's church, London, on 31 May 1795.[18]

After his marriage, Rhynwick Williams completely disappeared. He may have emigrated, but this is unlikely; he may have entered the armed forces against his will; he may have decided to change his name. In 1822, Henry Wilson, who apparently had tried to trace what happened to Rhynwick Williams, wrote that 'as we cannot find any further notice of this man, we suppose his sentence entirely eradicated those diabolical propensities which so degraded the name of Rhynwick Williams. What time he paid the debt of nature is therefore uncertain.'[19] Rhynwick's brother Thomas Williams was listed in *Holden's Triennial Dictionary* of 1808 and 1811 as an apothecary practicing in Vere Street, Cavendish Square. He died in 1829, and left his worldly goods, including valuable shares in the Westminster Gas & Coke Co., to his wife Mary Williams; in his will there is no mention of Rhynwick or any other relative of his.[20]

The only lead in the search for what happened to Rhynwick Williams is an inscription on the back of one of the aforementioned Monster caricatures in my collection: 'The Monster – Rhenwick alias Henry Williams – an Artificial Flower Maker. 1831.' This inscription clearly indicates that some time after his marriage in 1797, Rhynwick changed his name to Henry, and also suggests that his occupation after his prison sentence was still that of an artificial florist; after all, this was the only trade he knew. No definite confirmation that a Henry Williams died in 1831 is available, however. Some supporting evidence comes from the 1818 Westminster Poll Book, which lists a Henry Williams, artificial florist, as residing at 9 George Street, Adelphi, Parish of St Martin.[21] No Henry Williams was in business as an artificial flower-maker with his own shop at this or any other time, so this man was probably employed by one of the larger flower factories in London. There were several of those: for example, Amabel Mitchell continued on in his old trade, and his Artificial Flower Emporium in Dover Street was a successful and lucrative establishment for many years. In *Pigot's London and Provincial Dictionary* of 1823–1824, Amabel Mitchell is prominently listed as an artificial flower-maker and court dressmaker. No Henry (or Rhynwick) Williams is mentioned in *Palmer's Index to the Times* for 1797–1850 as a serious criminal, least of all as an attacker of women; nor does this index give details of any other series of Monster-like crimes from 1797 to 1831. An odd final memento of Rhynwick Williams' strange life can be found at a small museum in the old town of Chicago, known as the House of Clocks. The collection was started by Miss Margaux Brown, a wealthy and eccentric lady, in the 1920s, and after she had amassed enough clocks to fill an entire house, it was opened to the public in the 1950s. A display known as the Rogue's Gallery of Clocks features a clock that once belonged to either Burke or Hare, and the table clock Lizzie Borden inherited from her father. This display also contains the timepiece of 'Renwick Williams, the original West End Monster'.[22]

John Coleman did not pursue a legal career, as presumed by the lying Theophilus Swift. He carried on fishmongering, and was active in his old shop as late as 1818, twenty-eight years after he had brought Rhynwick Williams to justice. He and Anne Porter had at least two children: Ann Coleman was christened in November 1792 and her brother John in August 1796. It is unknown what he did with his Monster rewards. The long and valuable life of John Julius Angerstein ended in 1824. His business ventures were successful, and he used his considerable wealth to build up a magnificent art collection, which formed the core of the National Portrait Gallery. In his obituary, it was remarked that not the least valuable of his many acts of philanthropy was his part in the detection of the London Monster thirty-four years earlier.[23]

Not unexpectedly, Theophilus Swift had a somewhat more exciting and belligerent further career. His friend Sir Jonah Barrington wrote that Theophilus 'saw every-thing whimsically, many things erroneously, and nothing like any other person.

Eternally in motion, either talking, fighting, or whatever occupation came uppermost, he never remained idle one second whilst awake'.[24] His old enemy, the Revd John Barrett DD, Vice-Provost of Trinity College, described him as a small-statured man of singular appearance, with a pale face, grey hair and bleared, distorted eyes. He always wore a large cocked hat. He was fond of reading and tolerably well-informed, but vain and crotchety.[25] In 1805, Colonel Lennox, who had nearly killed Theophilus Swift back in 1789, become Duke of Richmond, and came to Dublin as the new Lord-Lieutenant. Theophilus attended his first levee, and without ceremony said to the Duke that 'the last time he had the honour of waiting on his Grace as Colonel Lennox he had received better entertainment – for his Grace had given him a *ball!*' The startled Duke recognised his old adversary from the duel, and good-naturedly replied, 'True! And now that I am a Lord-Lieutenant, the least I can do is to give you a brace of them!' In due course he sent Theophilus invitations to two grand balls at his palace in Dublin.

In 1811, when Theophilus's estranged wife was still alive, he paid his addresses to a young Irish lady, the daughter of the Revd Joseph Dobbin DD. She seems, in a weak moment, to have promised to marry her elderly suitor, but later jilted him, which set Theophilus off on his last crusade. In a book entitled *The Touch-Stone of Truth*, he blasted Doctor Dobbin and his daughter as a pair of impostors who had basely betrayed him.[26] As a supplement, he published his collected love letters to Miss Dobbin, whom he called 'The Moon of Finglas': they certainly convey the impression that the two were closer friends than the young lady was prepared to admit. John Barrett was of another opinion: only Theophilus's overheated imagination and tremendous self-conceit had made him think he was engaged to Miss Dobbin, and he was certainly not at all the kind of person for a young female to fall in love with.

In his old age, Theophilus liked to tell stories about the dramatic episodes of his life: how he had saved the royal family by duelling against the murderous Colonel Lennox, how his brilliant advocacy had almost wrested the notorious Rhynwick Williams, accused of being the London Monster, free from his persecutors; how he had dealt the lecherous Fellows of Trinity College a crushing blow; and how he had taught the hypocritical Dr Dobbin and his faithless minx of a daughter a hard lesson. After the death of his father, Theophilus had inherited a number of manuscript papers of his famous ancestor, the Dean of St Patrick's. He also had a great store of stories about Jonathan Swift, which he communicated to the Editor of the *Swiftiana* and also to Sir Walter Scott, who gave them place in their respective publications.[27] Theophilus Swift's old enemy, the Revd John Barrett, wrote that these stories were very inconsistent with the character of that great man, and so full of the vanity and extravagance of the narrator, that any person of learning would perceive that they were Theophilus's own inventions: his ridiculous tales had transformed the great Dean into a mountebank or jester. Theophilus Swift died in September 1815. There were several articles in the *Notes and Queries* about him and his family; one of them stated that not the least of his achievements was that he had 'endeavoured with every means in his power, though fortunately with an unsuccessful result, to shelter from punishment the notorious Rhynwick Williams, who by his cowardly and unprovoked assaults upon women had earned him the designation of The Monster'.[28]

I 2

PHANTOM ATTACKERS

Could the law protect the fair,
From that Monster fell, Despair,
Scandal, still at beauty aiming,
And a thousand beyond naming –
Woman then might walk secure...

W.H., 'The Monster', from the
New Lady's Magazine, July 1790.

The London authorities of 1790 were particularly outraged by the wanton nature of the Monster's dastardly deeds: this epidemic of stabbings was a new chapter in the history of crime, as eloquently expressed by Mr Pigot. Neither in Britain or abroad had there ever been a case quite like it. The Monster's only predecessor of importance as a phantom attacker, although a rather ludicrous one, was Whipping Tom, who was active in the 1680s. After dusk, he lurked about in the alleys and courts in Fleet Street, Chancery Lane, Fetter Lane, Strand or Holborn. When chancing upon an unaccompanied woman, he grasped her, raised her dress, cried out 'Spanko!' and repeatedly slapped her buttocks, sometimes with his bare hand, sometimes with a rod. This 'Whipping Spirit' worked with such speed and skill that the popular belief attributed supernatural powers to him. In 1681, an amusing book entitled *Whipping Tom Brought to Light and Exposed to View* was written about him.[1]

A remarkable series of wanton stabbings, with a close resemblance to the Monster phenomenon, occurred in Paris in late 1819.[2] One or more stabbers or *piqueurs* were attacking women in the streets, and cutting their thighs or behinds with sharp rapiers fastened to canes or umbrellas. According to M. Froment, a historian of the early nineteenth-century French police, there was widespread popular alarm: '*La terreur se répandit dans Paris*'. It was recommended that all married ladies should be accompanied by their husbands at all times; those without husbands should instead wear cuirasses or bottom protectors. The prefect of police, M. le Comte Anglès, issued a reward for the arrest of one of the *piqueurs* caught in the act. Police agents and private *piqueur*-hunters were out in force, some of them dressed up as women to tempt the villains to attack, but they had no luck at all. The enterprising Comte Anglès then thought of a singular idea, which no one had dared to suggest during the Monster-mania in 1790. Twenty prostitutes were employed as decoys: they were to walk through the streets of Paris followed by police agents in plain clothes. They were to receive five francs a day, but had to dress respectably and behave decently, and walk with lowered eyes and modest demeanour; they were strictly forbidden to ply their trade. In spite of these bizarre *promenades piquantes*, no *piqueur* was caught. No less than 880 francs had been spent on the harlots and their wine allowance. Later, an officer named Dabasse arrested a tailor, reported to have stabbed a woman, when he was walking to the Hôtel d'Hollande to measure up a suit. One of the wounded ladies, sitting in a carriage with Dabasse as the man was walking by, could not identify him as the *piqueur* who had cut her, however, and he was released. The famous detective chief Eugène François Vidocq finally got his man, however: at least, another tailor was arrested and sentenced to six months in jail as a *piqueur*.

After this arrest had been made, the urban panic gradually abated, just as it had done in London after Rhynwick Williams had been taken as the Monster. The case against the tailor had not been a strong one, according to M. Froment.

At the same time the French *piqueurs* were terrorising Paris, the *Mädchenschneider*, or Girl-cutter, of Augsburg began his long and bloody career.[3] In 1819, several girls were cut in the arms, legs or buttocks with some sharp instrument, apparently without motive. A wine merchant apprentice named Carl Bartle was arrested after the second of these outrages, but neither victim could point him out with certainty, and he was acquitted. Next year, after this phantom attacker had performed several novel outrages, the clamour grew among the citizens of Augsburg, particularly the female ones. A company of vigilantes was set up to help the official police catch the *Mädchenschneider*, and armed men nightly patrolled the streets. In spite of these measures, the Girl-cutter continued his work, and there were outrages throughout the year 1820. Many of them were depressingly similar. A servant-girl going to fetch beer for her master or for herself, would be approached by a well-dressed, pleasant-looking man with a black beard. His manners were much superior to those of the foul-mouthed London Monster. He would politely ask her if she was married; if she said she was, he made her a bow and left her; otherwise, he carried on with his well-spoken pleasantries. He asked how old she was, and was she not afraid of the *Mädchenschneider*, going out all alone at night? When she said she was not, or made some other defiant reply, he suddenly shouted out '*Ich stech dich!*' – 'Now I stab you!' – and stabbed her with a small dagger.

Finally, late in 1820, a bank clerk named Georg Rügener was arrested after being observed to follow a woman in the street. He was imprisoned, and kept in jail for a long time, although protesting his innocence. After the real *Mädchenschneider* had struck again several times when Rügener was in jail, the authorities had to release him; for three more years to come, he kept the courts busy with his lawsuits to recover his job and the small fortune he had paid for legal assistance. But no stratagem could capture the Girl-cutter himself, who was steadily active through out the 1820s, even though the military was called in and an infantry company patrolled the streets of Augsburg in search of the *Mädchenschneider*. There was even persistent speculation that he was a devil or an evil spirit.

The Girl-cutter of Augsburg was finally caught, literally red-handed, in January 1837, after a reign of terror lasting eighteen years. He turned out to be the thirty-seven-year-old wine merchant Carl Bartle, who had been arrested in 1819 but released due to lack of evidence. According to his own confession, he had injured in all about fifty girls. He never cut a man, and preferred young, good-looking single women. He was a well-to-do man with the appearance of a prosperous merchant, but of a peculiar and morose temperament. Far from being a ladies' man, he professed aversion, and even disgust, for the female sex. In his house, a formidable collection of knives, daggers and stilettos was found. Due to the unprecedented nature of this case, a medico-legal examination of Bartle was demanded, and he was handed over to the German alienists, who took pains to determine the motive behind these wanton attacks. Bartle told them that he had always been obsessed with the sight of blood. After the first attack, when he was aged nineteen, he had seminal emission, and experienced intense pleasure. From then onwards, his sadistic impulses became stronger and stronger, until they controlled his life. He was otherwise quite impotent, and the stabbing of his victims took the place of normal sexual intercourse for him. In July 1839, when Carl Bartle had already been in prison for two and a half years, he was sentenced in Munich to another three and a half years of hard labour. His punishment thus corresponded exactly to that of the man convicted as the London Monster: for the cutting of fifty women, he had to serve six years in jail.

Rather less sinister than the formidable Girl-cutter of Augsburg was the *Mädchenstecher*, or Girl-stabber, of Bozen.[4] In 1828 and 1829, a man in the dress of a soldier had cut several women with a pen-knife. He had previously been active in Innsbruck, and after three women had been cut in Bozen in 1829, a reward of thirty ducats was proposed for the apprehension of this *Mädchenstecher*. Immediately, some soldiers reported that their corporal, a man named Xaver, had been away the evenings of these latest attacks, and this individual, when questioned, freely confessed his guilt, but without showing any shame or regret for his deeds. The German alienists diagnosed another case of perverted sexuality: in the act of stabbing, Xaver experienced the same kind of satisfaction normally produced by coitus, and this was increased by the sight of the blood dripping from his knife.

In the 1860s, a number of young women were assaulted in the streets of Leipzig by a man wrapped in a cloak, who stuck a knife into their arms, just above the elbow, and then disappeared. It was a long time before this phantom attacker could be apprehended and put on trial. The psychiatrists again found that the cause was a morbid sexual impulse: the incision with the lancet was often accompanied by seminal emission, and his entire existence had been absorbed in the alternate excitement and depression that preceded and succeeded his acts.[5] Another series of attacks took place in Strasbourg in 1880: a man in a dark cloak assaulted respectable women in the streets late in the evening, and wounded them in the breasts or genitals with a sharp instrument. After the hue and cry went up for this *Mädchenstecher*, he went to Bremen, where he carried on his dastardly campaign; when he was finally arrested, he had clocked up no less than thirty-five victims. He turned out to be a twenty-nine-year-old hairdresser named Theophil Mary. The German forensic psychiatrists considered him fully fit to stand trial; his motive was suspected to be sexual perversion coupled with hatred for women. In December 1881, he was sentenced to seven years in prison. Theophil Mary's reputation was such that he was actually suspected of being Jack the Ripper. In 1888, the Metropolitan Police contacted their colleagues in Bremen to find out more about Mary's whereabouts at the time of the Whitechapel murders; this clearly shows that they actively pursued the theory that the Ripper crimes were committed by a sadistic serial stabber of women. With regard to Mary, they drew a blank, however, since he was actually in prison throughout 1888.[6]

In their article on the London Monster, Andrew Knapp and William Baldwin, writing in the 1820s, mentioned that Rhynwick Williams did not lack pupils among the young sparks of London. It was a practice among a set of scoundrels of that time, whenever they saw a modest, well-dressed and unprotected female, to whisper the most abominable bawdry in her chaste ear, and also to pinch her in the side or behind, as to put her in both bodily and mental pain.[7] Still, none of these scoundrels came even close to the fame of their notorious predecessor. In August 1834, several London women were stabbed in Bloomsbury and Clerkenwell.[8] Charles Fenwick and William Gage, described as two ruffianly, evil-looking fellows, were taken in the act of stabbing two women in Clerkenwell; in the pocket of the former, a sharp file was found. The two men were imprisoned for two months. In February and March 1885, several women were stabbed by a young man in the streets of Northampton after nightfall.[9] He stooped, so as to hide his face, and thrust some sharp instrument into their bodies. There was much alarm in the town, as no motive could be discerned for these unprovoked attacks; the phantom attacker was still at large in mid-March. It is also of some interest that one of the suspects in the Jack the Ripper case was a Monster-type offender. In January and February 1891, a certain Mr Colicott was alleged to have attacked six women in the Kennington suburb of London and stabbed them in the behind. He was arrested, but released shortly after due to a faulty identification. In early March the same year, an escaped lunatic named Thomas Hayne Cutbush was arrested for stabbing one woman in the buttocks and attempting to stab another. This time, the identification of the culprit was rock solid, and it was of course suspected that Cutbush was responsible for the entire series of attacks. The *Sun* newspaper went one better: with characteristic boldness, it suggested that Cutbush was none other then the formidable Jack the Ripper himself. The journalist was able to prove that

Cutbush had been working at a tea factory in the East End, in the heart of Ripper country, in 1888, and that his apartment, when searched, had contained a number of extremely lewd drawings of women. The police took this suspicion very seriously, particularly as Cutbush's uncle was Superintendent Charles Henry Cutbush, of Scotland Yard. Sir Melville Macnaghten, Assistant Chief Constable of the CID at Scotland Yard, wrote a memorandum describing the Cutbush case, and giving the reasons why this girl-cutter could not be the Ripper. His knife could not have been used in the 1888 killings, and it was unreasonable to believe that the frenzied disem-boweller of 1888 could remain dormant and in hiding for two years after his last awful glut in Miller's Court, and then merely stab a few girls in the bottom. Cutbush was turned over to the asylum system, and he died in Broadmoor.[10]

In July 1895, a French youth was arrested in Paris for cutting a large number of young girls in the buttocks in broad daylight. He was caught in the act and submitted for a psychiatric examination, which was performed by the leading alienist Dr Paul Garnier, chief physician of the military psychiatric hospital in Paris. The nine-teen-year-old Philippe-Joseph V. was described as a short-statured, pasty-faced, beardless youth, unmanly-looking and with a timid, embarrassed manner. He apparently hid nothing from his clever interrogator, and described how he had, ever since the age of fif-teen, felt a high degree of excitement whenever he saw a woman's buttocks. This craving for female posteriors was soon coupled with an overpowering desire to cut, pinch or slap this part of the female anatomy. It took him an almost superhuman effort to master this morbid craving: he continuously trembled, had prolonged feelings of anxiety, and sweated profusely. With time, the impulse to cut became irresistible: he approached an unaccompanied woman in the street, and at the moment his knife stabbed her buttocks, ejacu-lation took place, and he felt much relieved in both body and mind. He was otherwise quite impotent, and incapable of normal sexual intercourse. This candour on the part of young Philippe-Joseph might well be something he later had occasion to regret, since Dr Garnier's diagnosis was that he was a dangerous criminal lunatic, the victim of mental degeneration and a perverted sexual mind, and that he should be locked up in a mental asylum for an indefinite period of time.[11]

Another German *Mädchenstecher* was at large from 1898 until 1901, attacking young women and cutting them in the buttocks or genitals. He was caught in 1901 and turned out to be a twenty-four-year-old railway worker. He was not an imbecile, although not particularly gifted mentally. Unlike the majority of his fellow perverts, he was not impotent; indeed, he was engaged to be married at the time of his arrest, and was the father of a child. He was sentenced to nine years' imprisonment. In 1902, another *Mädchenstecher* was arrested, and made the subject of a psychiatric inquiry to find out the motive for his actions; although he was considered to be an individual of low intellect and perverted mind, he was considered fit to stand trial, and imprisoned for nine years. Two years later, in Hamburg, a third German pervert was jailed for fourteen years for a series of dangerous stabbings.[12]

At the turn of the century, these phantom attackers made their first appearance in the United States. In the 1890s, a maniac was at large in Brooklyn: he specialised in grabbing well-dressed ladies who were walking in the street, and cutting their calves or feet. In Chicago, the manhunt was on for 'Jack the Cutter', who had stabbed the shoulders and buttocks of several unwary pedestrians with a sharp knife. In February 1906, it was reported that he had cut seven females in just one day, and that the Chicago police were flabbergasted: they had no clue whatsoever to his identity, except that he must be a lunatic at large.[13] In the same year, another maniac, called 'Jack the Stabber', ran amok in central St Louis and cut several women's buttocks. He was caught red-handed and proved to be a twenty-two-year-old man named James Lawrence Brady, who worked as a checker in a restaurant. He confessed that he had, for some time, been in the habit of stabbing women in the streets with a pen-knife. The wounds were slight, and none of his victims were seriously hurt. Brady seems to have led a vicious life:

The 'Brooklyn Monster' claims another victim. A drawing from an unknown newspaper showing a maniac cutting the lower leg of one of the several women he assaulted.

he often visited prostitutes, and once drank twenty-six glasses of beer just before one of his attacks. His father was a man of a violent temper, who had often been in trouble for attacking people with a poker or a butcher's knife. He used to thrash poor James with a large bullwhip, and often chased him away from home. There was considerable debate among the American psychiatrists as to whether Brady was legally insane or not, and several articles were written on this subject: the outcome was, however, that despite the brutal treatment from his father, he was sane and fit to stand trial for his crimes.[14]

In 1925, the hunt was on for another American phantom attacker, the 'Connecticut Jabber' of Bridgeport, Connecticut. He worked with almost clockwork regularity: every few months he stabbed a sharp-pointed instrument into the breast or buttock of a well-dressed woman and made off with alacrity. There was a widespread hue and cry for this dastardly Jabber, but he was still at large as late as 1928, having at that time clocked up no less than twenty-six victims. The attacks took place both at night and in daytime; some of them in the streets, others in public places, like department stores, churches and libraries. The descriptions of the Jabber given by the victims varied greatly. The death of Superintendent Patrick Flanagan was blamed on the strain of hunting this elusive Jabber, who was, like Jack the Cutter in Chicago twenty years earlier, apparently never caught.[15]

In 1926 and 1927, there were a series of attacks on women in Halifax, Yorkshire: in various public places, a man had cut or slashed their clothes, and on some occasions the skin beneath, with a sharp instrument. Once, he had cut the Sunday finery of a woman named Annie Inman, who afterwards pointed him out to a policeman; the cutter rapidly made himself scarce, however. On 28 January, two young ladies named Louise Hartley and Mary Whelan were sitting in a theatre, when a man suddenly thrust his face between their heads and grinned at them; they could hear a fabric-ripping sound behind, and their dresses were badly cut up. On 12 February, these same girls led a policeman directly to the man who had cut their clothes: he was a smart-looking young labourer named James Francis Leonard, of no fixed address. Like Rhynwick Williams, he had a rather peculiarly-shaped nose, and this made him easy to identify; furthermore, several razor blades were found on his person. He was sentenced to two months in prison for each of the three cases found against him. Similar dress-cutters or snippers had operated in Birmingham in 1926, in Portsmouth in 1923, and on the upper decks of London buses in 1910.[16]

The Halifax Slasher scare of 1938 had an even more striking resemblance to the Monster-mania of 1790.[17] In November and December 1938, there were a baffling series of attacks on both men and women in the same city terrorised by James Leonard eleven years earlier. After three women and a man had been slashed on 25 November, the local newspapers were filled with the activities of this mystery assailant. The Slasher was described as a clean-shaven man of about thirty years old, wearing a dirty grey mackintosh and shoes with rubber soles that enabled him to sneak up on his victims unnoticed. After a much publicised series of slashings in late November, the streets of Halifax were deserted after dark, and the cinemas and fish and chip shops lost much money, which was instead spent on knuckle-dusters, cudgels and stout walking sticks for use as protection against the Slasher. Gangs of vigilantes patrolled the streets, and sometimes beat up innocent people by mistake. The women took an active part in the vigilante action, and carried around pokers wrapped in newspapers, or lengths of hose-pipe filled with lead shot; the less belligerent females preferred to carry bottles of red paint to throw over the Slasher. At the height of the hysteria, the manhunt for the Halifax Slasher was likened to that for Jack the Ripper: no less than 122 policemen were working on the case. A troop of 150 scouts were used as an auxiliary anti-Slasher force, but the attacks still spread outside Halifax, and the entire area was in an uproar. The British Legion was mobilised, and a considerable part of the adult population of Halifax enrolled in various vigilante societies.

The local police were as baffled by this elusive Slasher as their 1790 counterparts had been by the London Monster. In spite of their massive efforts to catch him, their only leads were a few discarded razor blades, presumed left behind by the Slasher. The local force had to call in Scotland Yard, and Detective Chief Inspector William Salisbury and Detective Sergeant Harry Stoddard got to work scrutinising the 200 police reports about the Slasher. When these experienced officers re-interrogated some of the Slasher victims, they noticed several contradictions in their accounts of the incidents. One silly girl had two separate cuts in her arm, but there was only one cut in the mackintosh she had been wearing at the time; it did not require the skill of a Sherlock Holmes to figure out that just like the enterprising Miss Barrs in London 148 years earlier, she had faked her injuries to gain compassion. She herself later freely admitted that this was the case. One person after the other, when pressed by the police, confessed that they had cut themselves and made up the stories of the attacks to gain sympathy and recognition; they included a feeble, nervous man, several hysterical women and a couple of silly boys. To read their tales does not inspire confidence in the intellectual gifts of the inhabitants of this region: one is not surprised that the police, disgusted with this mixture of 'nerves', mischief-making and plain stupidity, charged and convicted all of them for wasting police time. The police officers in charge considered the Halifax Slasher scare as a formidable mass hysteria: there had never been a Slasher, and the whole thing was a typical example of how an urban community could react in an erratic and inexplicable way to an elusive outside threat against its safety.

According to the media, at least, these phantom attackers are still with us, although the more elaborate ones, like the London Monster, the *Piqueurs* of Paris, and the Augsburg Girl-Cutter, fortunately still remain unsurpassed. Although hair fetishists cutting long hair off women, and clothes-snippers removing the backsides of skirts, are still common, serial sadists purposely cutting women are getting rarer. In 1977, 'Jack the Snipper' – or the

'Phantom Skirt-slasher of Piccadilly' – was active on the London Underground. Before the London Transport Police put an end to his fun in July 1977, he had cut seventeen skirts from behind and exposed their wearers' backsides to all viewers. He specialised in young, well-dressed women. He turned out to be a certain Graham Carter, a neat, twenty-three-year-old schools career officer who had kept a meticulous diary of all his dastardly offences. One girl had, to his great satisfaction (and, one might presume, that of other pedestrians!), walked the entire length of Oxford Street before anyone told her that her backside was exposed to view.[18] In Paris, during the same period of time, a perverted individual cornered women in lifts and thrust fish-hooks into their breasts. In 1978, this individual, or another one, was still at large, although using hypodermic needles instead of fish-hooks. Another pervert, in Malaya, was active at the same time, and used exactly the same *modus operandi*. In 1984, according to the *News of the World*, a very short and stunted man had attacked nine women in Birmingham, stabbing them in the buttocks. In 1985, this 'pint-sized pervert' was still at large. In China, a certain Wang Jinhou was sentenced to death for slashing twenty-five women on the buttocks and breasts with a fruit knife in 1986.[19] This harsh sentence seems to have brought an end not only to this perverted Chinaman, but also to the sadistic serial stabber community at large. At least, no convincing case of similar 'monstrosities' has since been reported, in the newspaper press or elsewhere.

The psychiatrists and writers on abnormal sexual behaviour of the early twentieth century had no difficulty in diagnosing and classifying the *piqueurs* and *Mädchenstecher*: they were examples of a variant of sexual sadism. Today's idea of a sadist is the standardised and ridiculous one of some middle-aged 'consenting adults' applying various instruments of torture in their cosy 'dungeon', or of a fat, bald-headed 'slave' being flogged by a shapely dominatrix. But, as we have seen, the depraved male sadists of the nineteenth century often sought unwilling 'partners' in the streets. The early psychiatrists identified several sub-types of this abnormal behaviour.[20] The most common were the *frotteurs* and bottom-pinchers that infested the Paris omnibuses. Other, more elaborate sadists were stalking women through the streets, and slapped their faces or whipped their posteriors when they were alone together; some found gratification in throwing dung, urine or other unappetising and foul-smelling substances onto the clothes of well-dressed ladies. Others were hair fetishists who got satisfaction from cutting strands from women with long and beautiful hair. One hair despoiler, active in the early years of the 1900s, was a student in Hamburg and a leading member of a moral rearmament society. He was quite impotent, and his major purpose in life was to cut hair off beautiful women; for this purpose, he travelled extensively within Germany, and also visited London and Stockholm. When the police arrested him and searched his apartment, they found thirty-one long pigtails of female hair, all adorned with coloured ribbons and labelled with the date and hour he had cut them off.[21]

The sadistic stabbers were a fifth, well-recognised category: they achieved their sadistic pleasure from the feeling of the knife entering the woman's warm body, from the sight of her blood, and from her pain and terror. Some authors on legal medicine even subdivided the sadistic serial stabbers further: some stabbed or slashed the hand of their victim to see her blood flowing from the wound; others preferred to stab the feet, genitals or upper arms; the majority were buttock or thigh-stabbers.[22] There is no example of a female serial stabber. A learned review on this subject emphasises that the typical sadistic serial stabber of women is a man whose early experiences has left him with a depraved mind and an overactive libido; he is usually impotent and incapable of normal sexual relations, and the act of stabbing his object of lust, and the sight of her blood, is often accompanied with ejaculation, and takes the place of normal sexual intercourse for him.[23] It is interesting that although most writers on the London Monster professed ignorance as to the motive of this 'previously unknown' crime, the Editor of the *Rambler's Magazine*, a lewd publication for libertines and men about town, had a theory that was ignored at the time. He ridiculed Mr Pigot for his talk in court about the Monster's 'unaccountable' crime, and asked what 'motive impels him who, in his amours, imitates the canine howl, and gnaws the dirty bones rejected by his fair one?' To attack beautiful and innocent women, pour indelicacies into their ear and stab their buttocks, was that not as likely to provoke a perverted pleasure as the aforementioned practice, which was very common and fashionable among the London debauchees?[24]

As we have seen, serial stabbers of women were by no means rare in the nineteenth century; in some German articles around the turn of the century, they were even described as a serious threat to decent society. But although other kinds of depraved crimes have become more frequent during the twentieth century, the sadistic stabbers have declined in number. The modern perverts cutting dresses or wounding people with needles or fish-hooks cannot be compared with their great historical counterparts: the London Monster, the French *piqueurs*, and the Girl-Cutter of Augsburg. Nor are there any recent articles in forensic or psychiatric journals about sadistic serial stabbers of women, and the subject is only briefly mentioned in recent reviews on paraphilias and sex offenders.[25]

13

THE MONSTER,
Epidemic Hysteria
AND
Moral Panics

Out hideous Monster; in thy name
Blacknesse and furie dwell:
Home to thy Native Hell,
Whose foule Complexion is ye same,

The same with thee; both Hell & Thee
Proud furious DISCONTENT
At once begat, & sent
DARKNESSE your Monstrous Nurse to bee.

John Beaumont, 'Melancholie'.

Conversion hysteria is a psychiatric term for the presentation of symptoms suggestive of organic illness, but for which there is no identifiable physical basis. Mass hysteria, or epidemic hysteria, is also known as mass psychogenic illness; it is defined as the collective occurrence of hysterical conversion symptoms in a more or less well-defined group of people, who share a belief relating to those symptoms. In the Middle Ages, epidemics of hysterical dancing, convulsions and seizures have been described as early examples of mass hysteria; these symptoms are becoming increasingly rare in

Western society. Instead, the prevailing form of epidemic hysteria has symptoms of anxiety: abdominal pain, dizziness, nausea, fainting and hyperventilation. A typical example is an 'epidemic' of fainting pupils in a girls' school, or the female workers in a factory for canned fish complaining of nausea, sore throats and headaches which are blamed on a mysterious gas that is supposed to emanate from the cooling system of the plant. These episodes are often triggered by some external stimulus: one of the girls in the school is taken seriously ill just before the fainting fits begin, and the factory workers are told that many of them will soon be made redundant. A reviewer listed seventy-eight outbreaks of epidemic hysteria from 1872 until 1972.[1] It was concluded that the typical outbreak involved a segregated group of young females; it appeared, spread and subsided rapidly, and was easily controlled by the dismemberment of the group in question. The number of people involved was generally around ten to fifteen, but in nineteen cases, more than thirty people were affected. The affected individuals usually have no history of mental illness. The hysterical reaction is brought on by some imagined or real threat to the group, but is supported by deeper underlying anxieties.[2]

In most instances, an outbreak of epidemic hysteria is a reaction to an impersonal, unseen threat, and encompasses a definite population. An exception to this rule were two outbreaks of suspected gas poisoning in the United States, which both involved mystery stalkers, and affected entire communities. The first of them occurred in Botecourt County, Virginia, from December 1933 until February 1934.[3] On the evening of 22 December, a farmer's wife felt nauseated and smelt a gassy odour. The Sheriff was called, but just after he had left, the odour returned, and all seven family members felt ill. It was suspected that some person had pumped poisonous gas into the house, but no one had been seen near the house and no tracks or footsteps could be detected. The Mad Gasser, as this mysterious assailant was named by the press, struck twice on 27 December: people felt ill and detected a strange odour. In January, the attacks became more numerous and the press coverage more intensive: timorous old ladies stuffed their keyholes to thwart the Gasser, vigilante farmers patrolled the streets with loaded shotguns, and a $500 reward was posted for the arrest of the elusive criminal. In February, the police took pains to investigate the increasing numbers of complaints about mystery gas. One day, they investigated nine calls and found a natural explanation for the smell in each case: a passing automobile, coal fumes from a stove, or burning rubber. In several cases, only one member of the household was affected by the 'gas' while others were perfectly well. In mid-February, the police announced their conviction that the Mad Gasser was a figment of overwrought imaginations, and the local newspaper echoed that view. There were no further complaints.

A similar outbreak of alleged gassing took place in September 1944, in Mattoon, Illinois, when a woman reported to the police that someone had opened her bedroom window and sprayed her with a sweet-smelling gas that partially paralysed her legs and made her feel nauseated. There were many similar attacks, nearly all on younger women, and the press had a field-day: The Mad Anaesthetist and his 'deadly nerve gas' were headline news in the entire district. The Mattoon citizens armed themselves, and sat up all night with loaded shotguns, waiting for the Anaesthetist to appear, or hear him pumping his spray-gun. Gangs of vigilantes patrolled the area, hoping to take a shot at the Mad Anaesthetist. Nevertheless, there were more gassings, and the state police was called in. They discovered that no one had actually seen the Anaesthetist, that police patrols responding very quickly to calls of distress had seen no signs of untoward activity, and that four people taken to hospital after being 'gassed' had all been diagnosed as hysterics. Gradually, the epidemic died down, and a psychiatrist helped the police to calm people down, even getting the co-operation of the press. In a later investigation of the Anaesthetist of Mattoon, a psychiatrist found that 93% of the total fifty-two individuals 'gassed' were women, most aged between twenty and twenty-nine, and of a low educational and economic level. They were not mentally ill in themselves, although many had a history of minor nervous complaints. The newspaper press, and the rumour mill of the local community, had played a major role in the spread of this epidemic hysteria. The deeper, underlying reason for these two gassing hysterias has been presumed to be anxiety about the use of nerve gases and other chemical weapons in wartime, a topic that was discussed a good deal in America in the 1930s and 1940s.[4]

The definition of epidemic hysteria requires that the individuals must have illness symptoms reminiscent of anxiety and hysterical conversion reactions. There are, however, quite a few reports of community-wide 'mass hysterias' that do not involve illness or conversion symptoms. These are categorised as 'collective delusions', and follow much the same mechanisms of spreading as epidemic hysteria. Examples include the bizarre reaction to the *War of the Worlds* broadcast; an epidemic of windshield pitting near Seattle, Washington; cattle mutilation scares; mass appearances of the Virgin Mary; head-hunter rumour panics in Borneo; and the sightings of unidentified flying objects over the state of Illinois in 1897 and in Sweden in the late 1940s.[5] A similar mode of explanation has recently been applied to the American 'epidemics' of recovered memories, satanic ritual abuse and alien abductions.[6] These epidemics of aberrant behaviour have spread to parts of Europe, but without finding the same fertile subculture as in their country of origin.

Two other examples in the literature on collective delusions have closer relevance to the London Monster. In early twentieth-century Paris, there were a series of complaints from people claiming that they had been pricked by a long hat-pin or a similar instrument. There was a good deal of media interest, and a suspect was arrested and brought to court, but released due to a complete lack of evidence. The psychiatrists explained the whole thing as a collective delusion.[7] In April and May 1956, a remarkable series of alleged razor slashings occurred in the city of Taipei, in Taiwan. A number of people of both sexes, many of them children, had suffered various degrees of injury; most were slight wounds to the hands or head, although it was alleged that one victim was castrated and killed. There were various theories as to the motive of this phantom slasher: sexual sadism; to facilitate theft by drawing away the attention of potential victims; or a blood ritual. There was a local superstition that the drawing of blood from a number of small children brought good luck. The police were out in force, and several arrests were made; in one instance, a mob gathered outside the police station and threatened to lynch the woman who had been taken into custody. Vigilantes roamed the streets, and parents kept their children at home in fear of the Slasher. Faced with a situation not dissimilar to the Monster-mania of 1790, the Chief Prosecutor of Taiwan ordered an extensive investigation of the numerous cutting or slashing episodes. The police soon reported that out of twenty-one recent slashings, twelve were either fakes or complete lies, and the others were still being investigated. In one much-publicised case, a boy had sustained a cut on his elbow from a broken bottle; he had made up a story about being attacked by the Slasher rather than face his mother's reproaches for carelessness. The Phantom Slasher of Taipei did not strike again, and there was no further newspaper interest in this business. A sociologist found that the slasher 'victims' were drawn from those elements in the local society considered to be the most easily suggestible: women and children in families with low income and low education. The vernacular Chinese press played an important part in spreading the Slasher delusion through a series of sensational reports, and the local rumour mill was even more instrumental in heightening the suggestibility. As with the Monster-mania of 1790, or the Halifax Slasher scare of 1938, some individuals deliberately faked their 'Slasher' injuries for various motives, mainly the desire for personal publicity. Two deeper, underlying reasons for the Phantom Slasher delusion were the political unrest in the area (Taipei was the nominal seat of the Chiang Kai-Shek's government-in-exile), and also some pre-existing local Chinese traditions about blood-letting from children and physical mutilation.[8]

After studying the available literature on epidemic hysterias and collective delusions involving phantom gassers and slashers, it is possible to reinterpret some important aspects of the Monster-mania. Firstly, there is one major difference. While the Mad Gasser of Botecourt, the Halifax Slasher, the Mad Anesthetist of Mattoon and the Phantom Slasher of Taipei were ghost-like figures who did very little actual damage, there was definitely something sinister afoot in London in 1789 and 1790. Quite a few women, perhaps as many as ten or fifteen, were wantonly stabbed by an unknown man who made no attempt to rob her, and who was unlikely to have aimed for her pocket. Many of the attacks took place before the Monster-mania began in earnest. There is no question of these attacks being part of the steady undercurrent of crime; at this time, it was quite uncommon for a woman to be stabbed by an unknown person in the street.[9] These attacks were probably the work of a serial sadistic slasher. Whether this individual remained active throughout the Monster-mania in April and May, or if he stood aside to watch the mayhem that ensued, is uncertain; during that period of time, the descriptions of the Monster varied greatly in almost every particular. The role of the London newspaper press in spreading the Monster-mania is not negligible, but the newspapers of the 1790s did not reach the lower strata of society, many of whom were either illiterate or unlikely to spend money on reading material. Instead, the role of Mr Angerstein's campaign cannot be overestimated: his large posters, pasted up on house walls all over London, proclaiming that a bloodthirsty monster was ravaging London's women, was what really started the alarm in all social strata of London's female world. There was no shortage of easily suggestible presumptive Monster victims among the nervous, swooning females of 1790, and the number of dubious Monster attacks increased accordingly, just days after Angerstein had started his anti-Monster campaign. Some attacks were faked to achieve compassion and publicity, a phenomenon well recognised in the twentieth-century outbreaks. Angerstein's offer of a large reward similarly set the scene for violent vigilante action, which was much more brutal and extensive than in any of the twentieth-century phantom attacker hysterias, and nearly cost several people their lives.

Was there any deeper, unconscious factor that made the Londoners of 1790 susceptible to a collective delusion? In this context, it is impossible to overlook the almost concurrent outbreak of the French Revolution, which changed people's outlook on life to a considerable degree. The fall of the Bastille in 1789 was a momentous event, even more so than the sacking of Newgate during the Gordon riots, and there was much unrest regarding what it might portend for Britain's future. The conservative rulers were already conscious of a world changing under the influence of revolutionary ideas, and the reformers were confronted by reaction. It was in 1790, the year of the Monster, that Edmund Burke published his reactionary *Reflections on the Revolution in France*. There was an increased sense of insecurity, a state of mind conducive to increased suggestibility and collective delusions. But the Monster-mania also functioned as a release for hidden social pressures that are less easy to define. The threat of the Monster led to an increase in community spirit: the Londoners stood united against this detestable enemy, and the vigilantes and amateur detectives enjoyed posing as the protectors of the Monster's helpless, swooning victims. Another factor that should be taken into account is the double morals of the time, and the male-dominated sexual relations. The married woman should obey her husband, stay indoors and be industrious with her needlework; the young unmarried woman should be chaste, sensible and modest. At the sight of a mouse, not to say a man, she was expected to show off her delicate, refined nerves. Yet at the same time, the predatory male gallants stalked the streets, and expected a maidservant or waitress – or for that matter a 'Tavern-Vestal in St James's Street' – to be easy prey. In a way, the Monster-mania can be seen as a paradoxical reaction to this situation: an outburst of *show* respectability and sensibility against the sexual threat of the man-monsters surrounding womankind. The Monster-mania also had elements of a last line of defence for the culture of sentimentality against the new social and political ideals threatening it. The Monster phenomenon identified sexual liberty with bloody violence; his sexual deviancy could be linked to political anarchy. In the act of catching a Monster, and putting him away in jail, the authorities demonstrated their ability to control even aberrant sexual urges, thus re-establishing the sentimental definition of human relationships that many people feared was under threat from the French revolutionaries.

A variant of collective delusions is the so-called moral panic, a concept first defined in a study of adolescent deviance among working-class youth in Britain, but which has later been applied to situations of greater social and historical significance.[10] The creation of a moral panic requires an initial deviance of some kind, which can be used as an excuse for the focusing of the attention of the press and other media on phenomena which may have been long in existence. The media recapitulation of the scare contains elements of distortion and exaggeration, as when a few cut pockets and frightened ladies became 'novel sanguinary outrages'. Greater notice is taken of any new instances of the deviance in question, and there is a reclassification of events: when a woman is pushed over in the street, or frightened by someone who shouts 'Buh!', the newspapers report it as the actions of the Monster. These factors result in an over-estimation of the deviance, and a 'moral entrepreneur' like Mr Angerstein can then impose a 'control culture': women are kept indoors, bands of armed men patrol the streets, and the regular police force is criticised in the newspapers by outraged citizens.

It is instructive to compare the Monster-mania of 1790 with some other instances of moral panics in London, triggered by crimes that were considered just as 'new' and threatening as the Monster's wanton assaults. In early 1712, rumours began to circulate in London that the members of a club of wealthy rakes, who called themselves the Mohock Club in emulation of a tribe of violent 'savages' in America, were roaming the streets of the capital at night, blackguarding, assaulting and beating innocent passers-by. It was said that they slit people's noses, tumbled old women down hills in barrels, and overturned carriages using long weighted poles. They stuck fish-hooks through people's cheeks and dragged them about using fishing lines; and tied ropes to the feet of women, suspended them upside down, and did them unspeakable mischief. The elderly, defenceless watchmen who patrolled London's streets were favourite victims of the Mohocks. There were many broadsides, pamphlets and bloodthirsty newspaper accounts about the Mohock outrages, and John Gay's play *The Mohocks* was as successful as the play *The Monster* would become in 1790. People feared to venture out after dark, and women in particular were warned to stay indoors, as many Mohock victims were said to have been women. Just like during the Monster-mania in 1790, there were ribald suggestions that the scare had been concocted by some jealous married men who wanted to prevent their wives from straying outdoors in the evenings! In March, the Privy Council met to discuss the disturbances, and it was concluded that although many people had been assaulted and wounded, not a single Mohock had been arrested. The large reward of £100 was offered to any person who brought to justice one of the offenders who had stabbed or wounded people in the streets. It is by no means unlikely that there really was a Mohock Club, and it is a fact that six 'gentlemen', including Viscount Hinchingbrooke and Sir Mark Cole, were later prosecuted for assaulting a watchman. Hinchingbrooke was acquitted, probably through the good offices of his father, the influential Earl of Sandwich; the others were released after paying a fine of just three shillings and four pence each. Yet the number of attacks was exaggerated in number and gravity, and the panic lead to more vigorous law enforcement that discovered a fictitious 'crime wave' that largely consisted of the steady undercurrent of street violence. The Mohock scare died out as quickly it had begun, and the dangerous rakes who had made all London walk in fear were soon forgotten.[11]

The London garrotting scares of 1856 and 1862 also bear more than a passing resemblance to the Monster phenomenon. This time the victims were almost all male, since no respectable female walked the streets of London after dark in Victorian times. In 1856, there were a number of newspaper reports of a 'new' crime, that struck the Londoners as just as inhuman and disgusting as the Mohock atrocities and the Monster's wanton attacks: several respectable citizens had been robbed by gangs of criminals who used a novel technique of subduing their victims. One ruffian grabbed the unwary Victorian from behind and brought his forearm across the Adam's apple to apply a choke-hold: his companion in crime could then empty the wretched man's pockets, before they released their semi-unconscious victim, who was in no state to raise the alarm or attempt a pursuit. During the winter months of 1856, *The Times* published seven editorials and thirty-one letters on the subject of garrotters and how they should be punished. There were calls for the death penalty, or at least transportation, and two men were actually transported for life after a street assault. The number of reports in the newspapers then diminished, and the panic gradually subsided. But on 17 July 1862, Mr Hugh Pilkington MP was garrotted and relieved of his watch by two ruffians as he was walking from the House of Commons to the Reform Club. Such an outrage against a leading citizen was of course widely publicised, and the panic was reborn with a vengeance. The outcry against the garrotters was taken up by every London paper, and diffused into the provincial press. 'Garrotter' was an epithet almost as powerful as 'Monster' had been in 1790, and the criminal 'roughs' of 1862 were considered as a sub-human species. Those Victorians who were intrepid enough to venture out after dark armed themselves with cudgels and revolvers; this sometimes led to both dangerous and farcical situations when they mistook each others for garrotters in the dark. For those less belligerent, there was a metal anti-garotting collar for sale, aimed to protect the throat just as the armoured petticoats had protected the backsides of the ladies in 1790. Later research showed that the garrotting scare was largely fictional: in the first half of 1862 there was just fifteen robberies with violence, about the same number as in 1860 and 1861, again reflecting the steady undercurrent of street violence. But just like during the Monster-mania of 1790, the number of reported street robberies rose dramatically when the scare was established, and events were taken greater notice of and reclassified to fit the current mood.

The underlying reason for the garrotting scares was fear of working-class indiscipline and social insubordination, and a widespread concern that the convicted prisoners were treated too leniently. Transportation had virtually ended in 1852, since the Australian colonies were reluctant to accept any more convicts. The overcrowding of the prisons that resulted, and the liberal prison reforms of the 1830s, led to many convicts receiving a ticket of leave for good behaviour when a year or two remained of their prison sentence. During the panic of 1862 there were calls for hanging or transportation of convicted garrotters, or that they should be employed in chain gangs to scour the London streets, or at least that they should be fed a very 'low' diet while in custody to avoid their emerging from prison strong and ready for novel outrages. The lasting results of the garrotter scare, as it gradually died out in 1863, was that the opinion in favour of prison reform had suffered a considerable decline, and that a number of London 'roughs' caught for offences that had any resemblance of a garrotting had been extremely harshly punished. There is good evidence that the judges and magistrates of this time were affected by the scare, and the conservative politicians who wanted to appear as crimefighters and advocates of longer prison sentences played along with the scare unashamedly. Indeed, the garrotting panic of 1862-1863 played a part in establishing the concept of a 'criminal class' of sub-human, amoral brutes: a criminal sewage that polluted the streets of London, and that could no longer be deodorised by hanging, or floated out towards the Antipodes on the convict ships.[12]

After these demonstrations of moral panics striking London in 1712, 1790 and 1862, it is tempting to extend the analysis to the sensational events of 1888, when the elusive Jack the Ripper stalked his victims in the streets of Whitechapel. There are several similarities between reactions to the activities of the London Monster in 1790, and those to the Whitechapel Monster (as he was really called) in 1888. The mood in Whitechapel in 1888 was very similar to that in London in 1790. It was hardly possible to see a woman walking alone at the height of the terror, and the respectable married women did their shopping in couples before darkness descended. All women, particularly prostitutes, were on guard against male attackers. Posters were pasted up all over Whitechapel, not by Ripper-hunters, but by the newspaper bill-stickers, who wanted to advertise their gory and salacious accounts of the latest murder. A reward of £1,200 was posted for the apprehension of the Whitechapel Monster, by private subscription, and vigilantes and amateur detectives were out in force.[13] The police presence also made itself felt; in addition to the uniformed officers patrolling their beats, there were hundreds of plain-clothes detectives. Much police time was wasted by people accusing others of being the Ripper, either out of malice or out of a genuine belief that they knew the killer, and by drunks and madmen themselves falsely confessing to the crimes.[14] The respectable newspapers were full of letters with suggestions on how to catch the Ripper, and the popular press, headed by the *Illustrated Police News*, had a field-day selling illustrated supplements about the Ripper crimes. A dangerous and excited mob could set on any individual at the slightest excuse, and any man pointed out as 'Jack the Ripper' in the streets was in danger of his life. For example, a seaman was rescued by the police from a vicious mob near Ratcliffe Highway; the reason they had singled him out was that his clothes were stained with paint, which was mistaken for blood. When the seaman was taken into a police station for his own protection, the angry mob swelled outside, and it took considerable time before the police deemed it safe to let him go.[15] At least one London newspaper reminded its readers of the Monster's reign of terror when discussing the Ripper crimes. The *St James's Budget* of 6 October 1888, compared the two series of attacks, commenting that Rhynwick Williams was a maniac who in ordinary life was mild and inoffensive. Just like the Ripper, he had preyed on women, and the newspaper writer speculated that he might have attempted to mutilate his victims. This is somewhat beside the point, however, since as we know, the Monster does not appear to have seriously injured any of his victims: the link between the Monster and the Ripper, made already in 1888 and elaborated by some later writers, is not as strong as it might seem.[16]

Viewed in the terms of a moral panic, the initial deviance was the terrible mutilation of the Ripper's first victim, Polly Nicholls; this was a 'new' crime just like the garrottings, and it gave rise to considerable revulsion and fear. This led to intense media interest and a reclassification of events. The murders of Emma Smith, in April 1888, and Martha Tabram, in August 1888, were also considered as the handiwork of the Whitechapel Monster. But Emma Smith had been robbed by three roughs who had bludgeoned her about the head and thrust a blunt instrument up her genitals. She herself lived long enough to give a crude description of one of them, who had looked like a youth of nineteen. Martha Tabram was stabbed (or probably rather bayoneted) thirty-nine times by two different weapons; it was suspected at the time that two soldiers from the Coldstream Guards might have been involved. Few serious students today consider the murders of these two women as crimes committed by the Ripper. The death of Rose Mylett, in December 1888, was also considered as one of the Ripper's crimes, but not only was she neither 'ripped' or mutilated in any way, but the authorities at the time were undecided as to whether she had been murdered at all or had choked to death while drunk. Sir Robert Anderson wrote that, in his opinion, she had died a natural death, and had it not been for the 'Ripper' scare, no one would have even considered the possibility of a homicide.[17] There were also some events of falsification: for example, the alleged first Ripper victim of all, a prostitute called 'Fairy Fay', is unlikely to

have existed at all. On the evening of 20 November 1888, a prostitute named Annie Farmer was heard to scream, and a man came
racing out of the lodging-house to which he had taken her, shouting 'What a – cow!' as he disappeared. Annie Farmer claimed that
the man had attacked her, and the police found that her throat was
lightly cut by a blunt blade, but in a manner very unlike the proper
Ripper killings. But they also discovered that she was hiding
money in her mouth; their interpretation was that she had robbed
her client, and to protect herself after being discovered, devised the
ingenious protection of injuring herself and accusing the man of
being Jack the Ripper.[18]

Already in 1888, it was clear to some American alienists that the
killer must have been a sexually insane sadist, and this was accepted
also by one of the policemen in charge.[19] But the authorities on the
Ripper crimes remain undecided exactly how many victims Jack
disposed of: was it five, six, or as many as eleven, and did he remain
active into 1889 and 1890? The view of Sir Melville Macnaghten, Sir
Robert Anderson and Chief Inspector Swanson, who all took a
leading part in the hunt for the Ripper, was that the Whitechapel
murderer had five victims and five victims only: Polly Nicholls,
Annie Chapman, Catherine Eddowes, Elizabeth Stride and Mary
Jane Kelly. This is accepted by the majority of serious researchers,
and supported by medical evidence concerning the mutilations, as
well as by today's knowledge about serial killers.[20] But not all
Ripperologists agree: for example, it has been suggested that
Elizabeth Stride was murdered by her violent, drunken boyfriend
Michael Kidney, who had no motive to perform any of the other
murders, and that Mary Jane Kelly was murdered by her jilted, jealous ex-lover Joseph Barnett.[21] It has also been noted that the four
trustworthy descriptions of the Ripper are as dissimilar as those of
the London Monster at the height of the Monster-mania. One witness described the companion of Annie Chapman as a shabby-gen-
teel, foreign-looking, dark-complexioned, short man who was
more than forty years old; a policeman and two other witnesses saw
Elizabeth Stride with a twenty-eight-year-old, tidy-looking man

with a small dark moustache just before she was murdered; Catherine Eddowes was seen with a rough, shabby-looking character like a sailor, who was thirty years old and had a fair complexion and a fair moustache; finally Mary Jane Kelly was observed with a thirty-five-year-old, Jewish-looking gentleman, with dark hair and an elegantly curled moustache, who was expensively dressed and wore a thick gold watch-chain.[22] Although it has been suggested that the Ripper was adept at disguises, just like the Monster was supposed to have been in 1790, these descriptions cast further doubt on the presumption that the murders were committed by the same person.[23] Only one author has gone as far as to suggest that there never was a Jack the Ripper and that the crimes were all unrelated, parts of a 'murder epidemic' induced by the Ripper scare.[24] The publication of the details of one murder led to their repetition in another 'copycat' murder. In the autumn of 1888, no less than seventeen murders took place, involving the use of a knife and some degree of mutilation. A 'copycat' Ripper mutilation took place as far away as in Co. Durham, Northern Ireland. Detective Chief Inspector Walter Dew, who knew the Ripper business well, wrote in his memoirs that people in 1888 had 'what may be described as a Jack the Ripper complex. Immediately a murder and mutilation was reported, whether in Whitechapel or in any other part of the country, they jumped to the conclusion that he was the culprit.'[25]

But if the Mohocks, the London Monster and the Phantom Garrotters are forgotten today, the Jack the Ripper mass hysteria has never quite died out. The Ripper crimes have inspired a spate of worthless, cynical books, in which some of the highest in the land, including King Edward VII, the Duke of Clarence, Prime Minister William Gladstone and Lord Randolph Churchill, have been falsely accused of the most loathsome crimes. The groundless denigration of Sir William Gull, a most reputable physician, as a Ripper suspect, is a similarly distasteful phenomenon. The elusive Ripper, who quite possibly never existed at all, is also one of the proudest upholders of the pseudo-history that is presented to London tourists and visitors. The exhibitions in his honour at

Madame Tussaud's and the London Dungeon never lack visitors, nor do the Ripper Memorial Walks through the sterile East End landscape, which has changed completely since 1888.

After surveying the primitive and irrational response of the Londoners of 1790 when they faced the Monster threat, the reader's immediate reaction must be that nothing even remotely similar could happen today. But in April and May 2001, strange things were afoot in New Delhi and its environs: a mysterious 'Monkey-Man' was attacking people as they slept on the roofs of their houses in the extremely hot weather. The electricity was turned off during night time in New Delhi's crowded concrete jungles, and torches were the only source of light: the descriptions of the phantom attacker only stated that he was short, dark and hairy, with a monkey-like face. By mid-May, there had been sixty-five attacks: the Monkey-Man climbed up the houses and scratched sleeping people on the hands and face. He was able to bound off tall buildings with almost superhuman agility. The panic spread, and the descriptions of this strange attacker became increasingly fanciful: he had dark glasses, red shiny eyes, hands with metallic claws, a mask and a helmet. But was he a sadistic maniac who dressed in a gorilla costume, a mutant monkey escaped from a zoo, or an extra-terrestrial being with supernatural powers? People did not dare to sleep on the roofs without sentinels watching over them with torches and bludgeons. One pregnant woman was awoken by the shout 'The Monkey-Man is coming!' and tried to run down stairs, but fell and broke her neck. Another man was so terrified by the same outcry that he jumped headlong off the roof of his house and was killed.

By late May, there had been around 350 sightings of the Monkey-Man, and people lived in fear. Armed vigilantes roamed the streets, on the lookout for anything suspicious. A mechanic wearing black overalls was beaten and arrested, and a man wearing a monkey-mask lynched by a furious mob. The latter individual was one of several thieves who relied on the Monkey-Man's deterrent powers to facilitate nocturnal burglaries; there were also examples of people dressing up as the Monkey-Man to settle old scores by frightening old adversaries, and putting them to headlong flight. A doctor painted a pair of inflated surgical gloves black, and gave the fingers a claw-like appearance; he then dropped them from his surgery window, straight onto a man riding a motorcycle. The man nearly died of fright, and there was a riot resulting in the arrest of the mischievous medic. A large police force was busy investigating the Monkey-Man mystery, but they had their hands full calming people down and preventing full-scale riots. They made it clear that the Monkey-Man was really a man, not an animal or an extraterrestrial being, and offered a reward of 50,000 rupees for his arrest. Nine out of ten sightings turned out to be completely bogus, and many people had faked their injuries to gain compassion and newspaper interest. The police seem to have kept an open mind on whether some of the early attacks may have been the work of a prankster in a gorilla costume with a sick sense of humour, but the psychiatrists were inclining towards the whole thing being just another mass hysteria. They speculated that the scare might have originated as a ruse intended to secure power supply throughout the night, since many people were adamant that bright light scared the Monkey-Man away. On 22 June it was officially declared that there was not, and never had been, a Monkey-Man, and this seems to have had the desired effect to end the scare just as suddenly as it had begun.[26]

In July and August 2002 there was another, even more ludicrous, scare in the town of Biswan, in the province of Uttar Pradesh in northern India. A 'Crawling Ghost' was attacking unaccompanied women, pinching and scratching their buttocks. The victims invariably lost consciousness during these attacks, and later woke up feeling dizzy and suffering scratch marks from the Ghost's claws. Just as during the Monster-mania, many women took to wearing padded posteriors as protection from the Ghost. There were at least twenty registered complaints, most of the attacks occurring at night, but two in broad daylight in the premises of the local hospital. People demonstrated in front of the police station, demanding an end to the bottom-pinching Ghost's reign of terror. The police chief responded that his force could only arrest men, not ghosts, but the local magistrate boldly declared that the incidents were definitely real. Things had reached a point where Biswan had become a town of insomniacs: men, women and children spent the nights on the terraces of their homes, torches in hand to ward off the Ghost. A team of skilled police detectives and forensic experts were dispatched there to investigate the mystery, and they apparently managed to calm things down; at least, there were no further reports in the press about the Ghost's activities.[27]

I4

Who *WAS* the
MONSTER?

The frightened Ladies tremble, run and shreek;
But Ah! in vain they fly! in vain protection seek!
For he can run so swift, such diff'rent forms assume;
In vain to take him, must the Men presume.
This Monster then, who treats you so uncivil,
This Cutting Monster, Ladies, is the Devil!

Verses from *The Monster Detected*,
a satirical print issued on 29 May 1790.

The Londoners of 1790 were particularly outraged by the wanton nature of the Monster's crimes: this epidemic of stabbings was a new chapter in the history of crime, as eloquently expressed by Mr Pigot. Neither in Britain or abroad had there ever been a similar case. In the early stages of his dastardly career, the Monster was content with insulting his victims with his foul-mouthed innuendo, and cutting her clothes or giving her a slight wound. But in 1790, his lust for blood had increased, and a series of increasingly violent attacks took place. The Monster was apparently something of an inventor of cutting and stabbing implements, and used quite a variety of diabolical instruments during the attacks. Firstly, there was the 'Wangee-cane' with its hidden knife inside; he also had some kind of clasp-knife, carried in his waistcoat pocket. Then there was the nosegay with its sharp stiletto waiting for the unsuspecting nose, the iron claw with several sharp prongs, and the sharp instruments attached to his knees, for use when kicking women from behind, as in the assault on Mrs Payne.

London society of 1790 gradually responded to the threat posed by the Monster's actions. The police force, as we have seen, was singularly ill-equipped to cope with a threat of this kind. The parish constables lacked organisation and the watchmen were too feeble, both mentally and physically, to be up to the task of tracking down one or more serial offenders operating under the cover of darkness, particularly since there was no co-operation between parishes. The bumbling eighteenth-century watchmen have been ridiculed by criminologists and historians, and they certainly come very badly out of the Monster-hunt: once, one of them lost the Monster's trail through the most abject stupidity. The Bow Street Runners were the only detective police in London at the time, and they were kept continuously busy with other cases; furthermore, several of the Runners had private employment as securitymen or bodyguards. At no time was there a magistrate or police officer in sole charge of co-ordinating the monster-hunt. Even more seriously, there is no evidence that the Runners tried to liaise with the parish police organisation in the monster-hunt. After Mr Angerstein had announced his reward, every pretence of co-operation disappeared, and it was every (police)man for himself in the monster-hunt. The Bow Street magistrates and Runners were overwhelmed by enthusiastic and avaricious monster-hunters, who wasted their time with false accusations, and even made citizen's arrests of innocent people who were dragged before the magistrates. Indeed, some of the most praiseworthy efforts of the Bow Street police force were to save the lives of several falsely accused persons from the mob threatening to kill them.

In April 1790, Sir Sampson Wright announced that a special 'Foot Patrol', consisting of young, able-bodied, armed men, had been established at Bow Street; it has been presumed that they were intended to bring the well-organised and tough London footpads to justice, but Sir Sampson may well have had the Monster in mind. The monster-hunt must have come as a further reminder to the London judges and magistrates of the woefully insufficient police organisation. There were gradual improvements: in 1792, a 'Horse Patrol' was established, to pursue highwaymen and other serious criminals on the main routes into London. Later the same year, the police reform outlined seven years earlier finally became reality. Seven public offices, each with three fully paid magistrates and six full-time constables, with its organisation shaped in the image of Bow Street, were built up in various parts of London, thus providing a great increase in the number of full-time, capable police officers in the metropolis. It is unknown exactly what part the Monster phenomenon played in this police rearmament, but it remains a fact that William Mainwaring, the judge in the second trial against Rhynwick Williams, who had been a stern opponent of police reform in 1785, made a complete about-face and strongly supported the new system.[1]

A rather enigmatic figure in the Monster-hunt is that of John Julius Angerstein. In no other instance, either before or after the Monster-mania of 1790, did this worthy gentleman play the role of a crimefighter. What exactly prompted him to do so in 1790 is unclear. He was a respectable family man with two teenage daughters, whose house in Pall Mall was in darkest Monster territory, and it may be that he was concerned for the safety of his own family. A less charitable view is that at least initially, one of his prime objectives was to sympathise with the wounded beauties, and to obtain a good excuse to visit them repeatedly to discuss new leads and descriptions of the culprit. Angerstein's actions were directly responsible for the Monster phenomenon's mushrooming from a mere nuisance to almost a national concern. The pasting of 'Monster' posters all over London, and the offer of an immense reward, was the perfect recipe to build up a mass hysteria. But Angerstein's actions did not end there. It is clear that by mid-May, he, and not Sir Sampson Wright, was the leader of the official Monster-hunt. By this time, he had established what was almost a second police office at his house in Pall Mall, where he received callers and sifted through the evidence against various Monster suspects.[2] His knowledge of the most minute details of the Monster assaults was impressive, and he was even called to give an expert opinion on the Elizabeth Davis case during the second trial. It is clear that he had a register of Monster victims, detailing descriptions of the culprit; this register was used in his advertisements, and later also in his handbook for prospective Monster-hunters. The Angerstein reward was justly criticised for opening the door to irresponsible and violent vigilante action, frauds by fake Monster victims, and giving rise to avarice, or even deliberate false arrests by the official police force. But did it also pervert the course of justice? Angerstein had invested a good deal of his personal prestige in the Monster-hunt, and it was vital for him that a Monster was found and convicted. Had Rhynwick Williams been acquitted, Angerstein would have looked like a complete fool. The newspapers and satirists would have poured scorn on his obsession with the Monster, something that had actually begun to happen in late May, just before the arrest of Williams. His great friends the wounded ladies would probably have been depicted in a large caricature print, standing in a row with their skirts above their heads, waiting for their darling Monster to show them some attention again. It is a fact that the original legal counsel of Rhynwick Williams left the day before the trial at the Old Bailey; Theophilus Swift's accusation that Angerstein had threatened Mr Chatham and forced him to withdraw may well have had some foundation.

The appellation 'Monster' for a criminal was a novel one in 1790, and thus suited these previously unheard-of outrages. The word itself was used for strange and hideous creatures in its old derivation from the Latin *monstrum natura*: something noteworthy 'shown up' by nature. It could be a prodigy or marvel; it could be a misshapen animal or plant, or a deformed human being. Chaucer, in *Ariadne*, wrote that 'Minus hath a monstre, a wikked beste', and Caxton, in *Eneydos*, described 'a monstre fulle terrible, that hath as many eyen in her hede ... as she hathe fedders upon her'. The use of 'monster' as a derogatory term starts to appear in early sixteenth-century English; it then signified an individual with extreme physical ugliness and/or moral perversion. Ben Jonson, in *Every Man out of his Humour*, wrote of some person who would 'turne monster of ingratitude, and strike his lawfull hoste', and Purchas, in his *Pilgrimage*, mentions 'that Monster of Irreligion, Mahomet'. An ungrateful slave trader is spoken of, in Raynal's *West Indies*, with the bitter words: 'They were no sooner landed at Barbadoes, but the monster sold her who had saved his life.' It is interesting that the London Monster appears to have made a small contribution to the etymology of the English language, since the term 'monster' for a criminal was, at least for some years after 1790, particularly used for cowardly attackers of women. In 1814, the Hammersmith Monsters assaulted two women in an indecent manner; their trial and conviction was described in a contemporary illustrated pamphlet.[3] Later, 'monster' became more commonly used for particularly dastardly and bloodthirsty criminals, and is still used in this meaning. In 1842, Elizabeth Eccles, the Female Monster, poisoned her three children and ten other people; in 1850, Jane Crosby, another Female Monster, burned her little daughter alive. A famous twentieth-century example is Peter Kürten, the Düsseldorf Monster, one of the most sadistic mass murderers ever recorded.[4]

If one should assume the role of Mr Pigot and build up a case for the prosecution of Rhynwick Williams, the mainstay of the evidence against him is that he was identified as the London Monster, under oath, by no less than seven women: Anne and Sarah Porter, Elizabeth and Frances Baughan, Elizabeth Davis, Mary Forster and Sarah Godfrey. In addition, Martha and Rebecca Porter, Mrs Franklin, Kitty Wheeler and Ann Frost, who had been insulted or whose clothes had been cut by the Monster, swore that Rhynwick Williams was the man responsible. Three more Monster victims: Miss Toussaint, Mrs Payne and the unnamed servant-girl in the Strand, could not swear as to Rhynwick Williams being the culprit, although they thought he resembled the man. Looking back into Mr Angerstein's chronicle of the Monster's assaults, it is clear that some of the other victims, like Mrs Chippingdale, Mrs Drummond and Jane Hurd, gave descriptions of their assailant that fitted Rhynwick Williams reasonably well.[5]

Other circumstantial evidence against Williams includes the fact that he himself admitted that previously, on two independent occasions, he had been taken as the Monster by vigilantes, but released. He also voluntarily admitted to being present when Charlotte Payne was assaulted. Another victim, Mrs Gordon, was assaulted with exactly the same *modus operandi* as Mrs Payne. In at least three other instances, the culprit was carrying an artificial nosegay, just as during the stabbing of the maidservant in the Strand and the assault on Elizabeth Davis, where Rhynwick Williams was again implicated. It was not common for a man, at this time, to carry an artificial nosegay about, and it is certainly a suspicious circumstance that artificial flowers occur in no less than six of the Monster outrages. Rhynwick Williams may well have been proud of his handiwork, and it could have been part of his dastardly plan that the woman was to believe that the flowers were genuine, in order for the 'surprise' hidden in the nosegay to have the maximum effect. In particular, it should be noted that when Elizabeth Davis resolutely refused to smell his nosegay, and said that it looked artificial, the Monster became infuriated and slashed her with one of his other cutting implements. Another argument against him is that after Rhynwick Williams had been arrested, the typical Monster attacks ceased. The two assaults discussed by Theophilus Swift were quite different: one of the women had probably been cut by a pickpocket, and the other probably knew her assailant, since he had cut her no less than five times.[6] Yet more circumstantial evidence is provided by the discovery that in early

1797, shortly after Williams had been released from Newgate, there were again reports of women being wantonly stabbed in the streets of London.[7]

In addition, a geographical study of London in 1790 provides some food for thought. If the Monster attacks are plotted, it is seen that a cluster occurs near the flower factory in Dover Street and Rhynwick Williams' lodgings in Duke's Court (and also his later lodgings at the George public house in nearby Bury Street). On 18 January 1790, he could easily have made a dash down Dover Street just after eleven o'clock, cutting Miss Felton on his way down to St James's Street, where Mrs Harlow, the Misses Porter, Miss Toussaint and Mrs Burney were accounted for, before he ran back to his lodgings at Duke's Court. This dismal rookery is not on the London map of today, but by perusal of some late eighteenth-century maps, it can be ascertained to have been some kind of yard accessed from Duke Street, on the block surrounded by the Bury, Jermyn, Great Ryder and Duke Streets, by a narrow passage.[8] A photograph of the back of some old houses on the west side of Duke Street depicts a warren of dirty, blackened buildings, added at different times; it may well be the best likeness of what Duke's Court must have looked like at that time.[9] Such a place would have been an excellent hideout for the London Monster, just like the George public house in Bury Street nearby. It can be seen that no less than thirty of the Monster attacks took place near the flower factory and the Bury Street/Duke Street hideouts, and that twenty of them happened in their immediate vicinity.

Rhynwick Williams was desperately poor after Sir John Gallini had thrown him out, and although he was of better than average breeding, it appears as if he was not highly regarded by the ladies. Anne Porter was probably not the only supercilious young miss to call this penniless, impudent upstart a 'shop-man' and tell him to go back to his shop counter. His odd occupation as an artificial flower-maker did not suggest the possession of either wealth, social standing or a superior intellect. According to Theophilus Swift, Rhynwick had, for some years, been in the habit of pursuing good-looking women through the streets, and making them indecent proposals. Rhynwick's kinsman Joshua Williams added that he was in the habit of damning and blasting them if they did not take him to bed with them. There is no question that he was a well-known bugbear, who frequently pestered good-looking women, as evidenced by several women who had been abused by his foul language and unwelcome attentions in 1788 and 1789: Mary Forster, Anne Porter, Frances Baughan, Mrs Franklin and Kitty Wheeler. It is also clear that Rhynwick's habits of life were dissolute, and that he often frequented the haunts of prostitutes. Ludicrously, even the character witnesses who gave such unequivocal evidence concerning Rhynwick's attachment to the female sex were actually women of the streets.

If one would, after this review of the evidence against Rhynwick Williams, instead assume the role of his defence counsel, there would be no lack of arguments in his favour. Firstly, he was clearly not *the* Monster: many victims either said that he was not the man, or described culprits of vastly differing appearance. Some attacks are likely to have been the work of bungling pickpockets; others unconnected instances of brutality towards women; there may well have been one or more 'copycat' Monsters at work; finally, quite a few of the alleged attacks in May and June 1790 are likely to have been fakes.

In both the trials against Rhynwick Williams, the Porter case was selected as the strongest one by the prosecution, but this does not mean that it is rock solid. When surveying the available evidence, it is a great pity that there is no record of the exact wording of the description of the Monster who attacked Anne Porter, as lodged at Bow Street by her father. According to Theophilus Swift, this description was quite unlike Rhynwick Williams: it depicted a tall man aged about thirty. Theophilus Swift is an unreliable source, but it should be noted that according to Judge Mainwaring's notes, Sarah Porter did not contest that Theophilus's quotations from the Bow Street deposition were correct.[10] Nor did she contest that she had once told Nicholas Bond that she was absolutely unable to describe the Monster. According to Theophilus Swift, both Anne and Sarah Porter had said that they were unable to describe the culprit, although they would recognise him the moment they saw him. It also arouses some suspicion that the sisters' early descriptions of the Monster in various newspaper reports are often very brief, and that they never mentioned the very important fact that the Monster had previously stalked them on many occasions. According to Theophilus Swift, Anne Porter had instead said that she presumed her attacker to be a clumsy pickpocket who had meant to cut open her pocket.[11]

If one would for a moment assume that Anne and Sarah Porter had been led astray by Angerstein's offer of a reward, what kind of man would they be likely to falsely accuse as the London Monster? Clearly not a respectable tradesman like William Tuffing, or a man of some social standing like Lieutenant Hill. That pathetic little bugbear Rhynwick Williams, who used to follow them around the streets, would come in very handy, though. He was clearly an individual of low intellect, weird habits and perverted sexuality; his position in society was a generally despised one, and he would command little sympathy if he were to be taken as the Monster. Anne's stolid, dense boyfriend John Coleman could be relied on as the dupe who 'caught' him, particularly if Anne herself pointed him out in a dramatic manner, after first having brought up the subject of the Monster-hunt in conversation. The presence of several hundred pounds in Coleman's strong-box would definitely make the fishy smell of this persistent suitor much more palatable even to a delicate, pretty young lady like Anne Porter. It was also hinted, by none more strongly than Theophilus Swift, that neither Anne Porter nor John Coleman were wholly sincere about their own relation, and she may well have perjured herself at Hick's Hall when she denied any relationship with him. It was proven at the second trial that although the Porter family took no share of the reward, Coleman certainly did; in all probability, the fishmonger managed to lay his hands on both Angerstein's £100 and some other private rewards. It is another fact that John Coleman and Anne Porter were married in April 1791.[12]

Another argument in favour of the innocence of Rhynwick Williams is that his actions when taken were certainly not those of a guilty man. If, as Anne Porter and Coleman claimed, he had seen how she pointed him out, why, if he was the Monster – the man for whose capture an immense reward had been posted – did he not run away at once? When he was followed by Coleman, he even passed the Bagnio twice when walking up and down St James's Street, although he must have known that this was the home of the Misses Porter. Later, when cornered by Coleman in Mr Smith's house, he made no attempt to escape, and meekly gave the fishmonger his name and address. Nor did he resist when Coleman brought him back to the Bagnio. Even considering the 'sensitive' female ideals of the time, the great fainting scene in the front room seems just a bit exaggerated and theatrical. One of Theophilus Swift's many mistakes during the second trial was that he did not raise the matter of the brown coat, which Anne Porter had identified, with dead certainty, as the garment worn by the Monster, on top of another coat, when he attacked her. It later turned out that this coat was very close-bodied, and certainly not the type worn as a surtout. In addition, Rhynwick himself claimed that he could prove that he had bought this coat in April 1790, long after the Porter attack.[13]

Several proponents of the innocence of Rhynwick Williams have pointed out that, at the Old Bailey, his alibi appeared quite impressive: there were no less than seven alibi witnesses, and the contradictions among them were relatively minor. There is every reason to believe that Amabel Mitchell and his workforce came forward to give evidence on their own accord, and that they were not influenced by any bribe or threat. After all, Rhynwick Williams was destitute and had no influence whatsoever; he was not even currently employed at the flower factory. In the second trial, Amabel Mitchell still firmly believed that he was telling the truth, and his testimony was reasonably solid, as was that of the forewoman Catherine Alman. Some of the other alibi witnesses did not shine, however: Mr Pigot gave them a proper grilling and exposed that they appeared to know less about Rhynwick's whereabouts on the evening of the Queen's birthday than they had claimed at the Old Bailey. In particular, it is a damning circumstance that none of them had a watch or clock, and that Mr Pigot could demonstrate that their assessment of the passage of time seems to have been quite muddled. It should be taken into account, however, that several of the alibi witnesses could not speak English, and that some of them were clearly not particularly clever. Their evidence had to be given through the court interpreter, and they were unable to correct any mistakes or misconceptions; this made it even easier for a skilled prosecuting attorney to make them appear confused and unreliable.

It is clear that in spite of their informants, and the Angerstein campaign, the Bow Street police never suspected Rhynwick Williams in any way before he was taken by Coleman. There are some intriguing hints that, even after the first trial, some of them were still unconvinced of his guilt.[14] Runner Macmanus, who had actually been Rhynwick's neighbour, was as surprised as any when he was taken as the Monster. As evidenced by an article in *The Times*, Rhynwick Williams was well known about town, many people recognised this odd, rather unsavoury little man, who was obsessed with sex and sometimes chased women about the streets, but they had never linked him with the Monster's crimes.[15] Mr Angerstein, when at the Bow Street examination of Rhynwick Williams, also heard many people say that they had seen him before, but never suspected him.[16] It should also be appreciated that with his reward, Angerstein had created a culture of Monsterism: at any cost, a culprit had to be found. The public hysteria, huge reward, and the great power of suggestion induced by this extraordinary case formulated a potent mix for injustice.

If sufficient doubt is cast on the veracity of the Misses Porter, the other Monster cases fall like a house of cards. The identification made by Ann Frost was ludicrous, and Mary Forster changed her story twice at Bow Street. The Misses Baughan showed some reluctance to identify Williams as the Monster, as did Mrs Godfrey; a good barrister would have been able to shake the testimony of all these ladies considerably. Mrs Godfrey had originally described her assailant as gentlemanly-looking and about thirty years old, and her recognition of Rhynwick Williams at Bow Street was somewhat faltering. Even more remarkably, Elizabeth Davis, who had originally described the Monster as tall, stout and very elegantly dressed, later identified the scrawny little Rhynwick Williams in his threadbare blue coat as the man who had cut her. There might well be some truth in Williams' own story that she had been 'coached' beforehand by the Runners; this raises a whole set of unpleasant questions about how the other witness confrontations had been arranged.

If, finally, one would assume the gown and wig of the judge in the case against Rhynwick Williams, it cannot be denied that several women identified him as the culprit, and that there is considerable circumstantial evidence against him. It is certain that he abused and insulted several women, and probable that he cut their clothes, and sometimes the flesh underneath, of some early Monster victims. It is by no means unlikely that his actions set off the Monster hysteria, which then mushroomed out of proportion. But was there really sufficient evidence to convict him in a court of law? We will never know, since both trials against him were deeply flawed, due to the massive prejudice against Rhynwick Williams; furthermore, in both trials, his defence was seriously mismanaged.

In the Old Bailey trial, the feeble exertions of Mr Knowlys on Rhynwick Williams' behalf left the field open for Mr Pigot to show off the injured, veiled Misses Porters as witnesses for the prosecution; from the transcripts of the trial, it almost appears as if Knowlys himself was convinced of Williams' guilt. Nor did he take full advantage of the alibi witnesses, and it appears to have been a surprise to him as well as to the rest of the court that the alibi was as strong as it really was. Judge Buller exaggerated the contradictions from the alibi witnesses in his summing-up, and contrasted the candour of the fair sufferers with that observed on Amabel Mitchell's unprepossessing, swarthy countenance. Even more remarkably, he directly challenged the jury to choose whom to believe: the flower-makers, whose testimony he had just discredited, or the heroines who had been so barbarously treated by the Monster. The outcome could only be one. It would have been more natural for a judge to emphasise that no less than seven people had sworn that Rhynwick Williams was elsewhere when the Misses Porter were cut, and to ask the jury to consider whether this cast any reasonable doubt on the identification of him as the Monster who had cut Anne Porter. In that case, they should acquit him. It is questionable, in view of the reigning hysteria in London, whether even this measure would have altered the outcome; it was not a man the jury convicted, it was a Monster, and London had to be cleansed of this abomination of mankind.

At the time of the second trial, the anti-monster hysteria had had time to abate, and there was less prejudice against Rhynwick Williams. What the wretched man would now have needed was a clever, experienced lawyer, who could expose the flaws in the case against him, and knock the Misses Porter down from the pedestal onto which Angerstein and the popular feeling had put them. But if he had hoped for a doughty knight-errant to defend him, poor Rhynwick instead got a champion who resembled the ridiculous knights in Monty Python's *Holy Grail*; Theophilus Swift was egocentric, vain and irresponsible, and mishandled his defence in an almost incredible manner. Theophilus was certainly right when he accused Coleman of being a coward, but this is insubstantial and does not affect the fact the fishmonger's testimony was rock solid, and that Swift only replied to it by insults. Theophilus's main argument – that the Misses Porter were ladies of low morality – cannot be given any credence. It is clear, from the contemporary sources, that the Porter family was a respectable one, and although Theophilus may well have been telling the truth about Anne Porter's previous elopement with 'Captain' Crowder, this does not make her and her sisters into prostitutes, or have any bearing on the

Monster business. At this time, a male chauvinist like Theophilus Swift defined every young unmarried woman who was not a virgin as a 'whore'.[17] Theophilus Swift's invention of the ribald jokes about the 'Nuns of the Bagnio' and their way of entertaining the young men about town deserves nothing but contempt. It must also be remembered that the word 'Bagnio' was, at this time, almost synonymous with 'brothel'. Although certain London bagnios, like the Royal Bagnio in Bath Street, the Duke's Bagnio in Long Acre, and Pero's Bagnio itself, were respectable and legitimate enterprises, the 'bagnios' near Covent Garden were little more than concealed brothels.[18] Theophilus, who may well have been a frequenter of this latter form of 'bagnio', probably believed that Pero's Bagnio was an establishment of a similar kind. His scandalous behaviour in court was equally counter-productive, and damaged rather than aided the case for Rhynwick Williams' innocence. It shines through that Theophilus must have been enjoying himself when he harried the female witnesses and ridiculed the wretched Coleman, who was a sitting duck to all his heavy-handed jibes and jeers. To see the rude, unattractive Theophilus Swift, the Monster's Champion, blast and bully the beautiful Porter sisters must have arisen powerful protective feelings in the breasts of Judge Mainwaring and the jurymen; this cannot have predisposed them in favour of the Irish adventurer and his already notorious client.

It is not the action of an innocent man to dye his hair to confuse the female witnesses as to his appearance, as Rhynwick Williams did in the second trial; Judge Mainwaring, who saw through this trick, thought that it added further evidence for Williams' guilt. If any reader still, after the exposure of all his caddish lies and cunning schemes, would consider Theophilus Swift as a sincere and upright person, it is sad but true that Theophilus was apparently a party to this dastardly plan, since he described the hair of Rhynwick Williams as being 'as black as Coleman's conscience'. It is likely that the hair-dying was in fact Theophilus's idea, since he had the effrontery to write in his disgraceful pamphlet, on the subject of Rhynwick's hair colour, that 'Black takes no dye; we cannot alter nature; we cannot change into a light brown those locks which nature had formed as dark as the Raven's wing!'[19] Theophilus Swift was a supporter of lost causes and desperate actions, and an unmitigated liar and scoundrel. He probably appeared as the champion of Rhynwick Williams for self-seeking motives, to get into the public eye, just as he had challenged Colonel Lennox the year before. For someone who is capable of accusing the Prime Minister of planning to assassinate the entire royal family, it is a mere trifle to act as the defence counsel for some wretched little man just for the fun of it, and to blast the honour of the Monster's female victims.

Had a fictitious third trial of Rhynwick Williams taken place today, the outcome might well have been a different one. Unlike the situation in 1790, the court would have assessed the evidence calmly and with circumspection, without the emotional overtones of the Monster-mania. It would have spoken in Rhynwick Williams' favour that he had stubbornly denied any guilt, and made every effort to get his case retried. There was no forensic evidence whatsoever against him: no bloodstains on his clothes, no signs that a sharp knife had been carried in his pocket, no sharp cutting implement found in his possession. When his artificial flower-making tools were produced at Bow Street, the magistrates were convinced that they could not have been used for cutting or stabbing people. The histrionics of the Porter sisters would have been to little avail when the barrister of Rhynwick Williams raised the subject of the discrepancy between their original description of the Monster and the appearance of Williams: clearly, there was quite some difference between a six-foot tall, thirty-year-old Monster, and a twenty-three-year-old man of just five feet six inches. These swooning, irrational creatures would no longer have been regarded as defective males (the prevailing female ideal): once knocked down from the pedestal onto which the 'sensitive' ideals of 1790, and their status as Monster victims, had put them, they would have some other hard questions to answer. No one could deny that the prevalent atmosphere in London was highly conducive to falsehood and perjury, and that Angerstein's immense reward had previously led to many false accusations. The Misses Porter's statements that they could not describe the Monster, but that they certainly would recognise him if they saw him, would be interpreted that they were plotting to accuse someone. Their readiness to (falsely) identify Rhynwick Williams' brown coat as the one worn by the Monster over another coat would also be viewed with suspicion.

The evidence given by Mrs Miel and John Porter, the brother, at the second trial, appears solid at first sight; at least, it seems to have completely floored Theophilus Swift, who made no attempt to cross-examine them, except with insults. It should be pointed out, however, that none of the accounts of the attack on the Misses Porter, some of them very detailed indeed, mentions any blow to the head of Mrs Miel. Young John Porter's assertion that he could recall nothing about the Monster is similarly suspect; would it not have been natural for this alert teenager to take particular notice of a man who he had clearly observed, and who moments later turned out to have wounded his sister? The barrister of Rhynwick Williams could have done nothing to improve the linguistic and intellectual level of the alibi witnesses, but unlike Theophilus Swift, he could at least have seen to it that they all appeared in court, and were relatively well aware of what was expected of them. Had the alibi been anything as solid as at the Old Bailey, and the arguments throwing doubt on the Misses Porter quoted above been taken into account, it is quite possible that Rhynwick Williams would have been acquitted.

If the Porter case had resulted in an acquittal, the others are likely to have ended in the same way. None of the other ladies had identified Rhynwick Williams with the same certainty. For two of the cases (Baughan and Davis), Rhynwick claimed to have an alibi, for whatever it was worth.[20] Both Ann Frost and Mary Forster had behaved somewhat oddly at the confrontation, and a clever barrister could have made much of their errors and histrionic behaviour. Similarly, Mrs Godfrey and Elizabeth Davis had previously given descriptions of the Monster that did not fit Rhynwick Williams.

As discussed earlier, the Monster-mania was a typical moral panic, in which people in an urban community reacted to an elusive outside threat in a neurotic and erratic way. Had no Monster been caught, the Monster-mania from April until June 1790 would have been regarded as a schoolbook example of a collective delusion. It would have been claimed that there had never been a Monster, and that the attacks had been either invented or exaggerated, and the Monster-mania would have been compared with escapades of the Mad Gasser of Botecourt, the Halifax Slasher and the Phantom Slasher of Taipei. But as we know, there were at least ten or fifteen bona fide stabbings of women, some of them in 1788 and 1789 before the onset of the Monster-mania. These attacks, and probably a proportion of those occurring in 1790, are likely to have been the work of a sadistic serial stabber of women. It is rather questionable whether Rhynwick Williams fits the psychological profile of such a sadistic stabber. There is some evidence that he used to stalk good-looking women through the streets, making them indecent proposals. The step from stalking unaccompanied women and abusing them verbally, to actually cutting and assaulting them, would not have been a great one for him. It is typical for a sadist not to run away after the assault, but to remain to gloat over the sight of the blood and the terror and confusion of his victim, just like the Monster did on several occasions. On the other hand, the early psychiatrists that specialised in this area agreed that the typical sadistic stabber was impotent and incapable of normal sexual relations. This was clearly not the case with Rhynwick Williams, who appears to have been a young man with very active sexual desires. He had no girlfriend or steady female companion, but was a steady client of various low-class prostitutes, some of whom even testified in court about his sexual prowess.

In 1790, many considered that the punishment of Rhynwick Williams had been ridiculously lenient, at least compared with the wholesale hanging of petty thieves and bandits. It was clearly out of touch with the prevailing mood in London at the time, which demanded pillory, transportation or even hanging. As we know, it was at this time a capital offence to steal a sheep or to pickpocket more than a shilling. In 1777, a destitute woman with starving children took a piece of raw linen from a shop counter, but put it back when the shopkeeper observed her. She was arrested, tried and executed.[21] Even many years later, the biographer of John Julius Angerstein marvelled at what he called the benignity and mercy of the English laws, which had sentenced this degraded Monster to only six years in prison, for crimes that in many other countries would have been punishable with death.[22] Had Rhynwick Williams been found guilty in a court of law today, he might well have been committed to a mental hospital rather than sent to prison.

Central London has changed very much since 1790, but the broad outline of the streets is still basically the same, and it is possible to identify some of Rhynwick Williams' old haunts. The old rookery in Duke's Court is no more. Not even the court itself exists today, but at the site is a modern house with an underground garage. I managed to gain an entry to the inner court of this building, but there was no single trace of Rhynwick's old hideout. Nor are there any ale-houses, disreputable or otherwise, in Bury Street. Although the Dover Street flower factory is no more, the house next to it, an upmarket shop for antiques and gentleman's effects, looks Georgian in character and the shop has been there since 1812, when Amabel Mitchell (and perhaps Rhynwick, alias Henry, Williams) was still active next door.

It is also possible to re-enact the Monster Memorial Walk, the exact route Rhynwick Williams was pursued by Coleman on 13 June 1790. St James's Park is as busy as it was on the afternoon that the Misses Porter took their afternoon stroll with Coleman, but there are no longer any narrow passages near the Admiralty leading to Spring Gardens. In Pall Mall, where Rhynwick Williams was closely pursued by Coleman, there are a few older houses which must have been there in 1790, and St James's Palace at the bottom of St James's Street is of course unchanged. At the corner of Pall Mall and St James's Street, formerly the site of the china shop where Rhynwick tried to gain entry, are the offices of the Dunhill tobacco company. Some of the houses on the east side of St James's Street, like Berry Bros wine merchants at No.3 and Lock & Co. Hatters at No.6, must have been there in 1790. It is of particular interest that No.62 St James's Street, near whose bow windows Anne and Sarah Porter faced the Monster, is still in existence. That it is the same house seen in the engravings of St James's Street from 1750 and 1800 is apparent from its characteristic bay windows and tall five-funnelled chimney. Pero's Bagnio at No.63 was purchased by Francis Fenton in 1800, and he had the old building pulled down in 1824 and a new hotel erected in its place. The elegant office building that today is at No.63 was constructed in 1886-88, after Fenton's second hotel had been pulled down, and bears no resemblance to the old Bagnio formerly occupying this site. The 'Stable Yard', through which the Misses Porter once escaped their dastardly stalker to gain entrance through the Bagnio's back door, is the Blue Ball Lane, in which there is now a restaurant and a mews development.

Although there are some remaining older houses in Bolton Street, its character must have changed beyond recognition since 1790, and if Rhynwick Williams were to search this sterile area of forbidding-looking office buildings for a *fille-de-joie* willing to give him a five-minute rendezvous, he would have had to return unsuccessful. Although there are some older houses in Old Bond Street, it is difficult to find one with rails, since these have mostly been taken away to give room to pedestrians. New Bond Street has changed even more; nor would John Coleman and Rhynwick Williams have found any familiar landmarks in South Moulton Street.

As we know, there are some indications that Rhynwick, alias Henry, Williams lived in London in 1818, and perhaps even until his presumed death in 1831. He had at least one child: a son, George Renwick Williams, born in 1795. It is unknown whether George Renwick (son of the Monster) had any little monsters of his own, and indeed whether any descendants of Rhynwick Williams are today walking the streets of the metropolis. If one of them set his mind to carry on the work of his infamous ancestor, who was imprisoned as the London Monster, the Underground would provide a perfect setting. It is true that the policing of the London Underground is far more efficient than the London nightwatchmen of 1790, but this does not make it impossible to evade capture in these warren-like underground structures. After all, the notorious 'Jack the Snipper', the perverted young man who cut young women's skirts behind and exposed their backsides to all viewers, managed to dodge the London Transport Police for five months in 1977. He turned out to be a school careers officer, not a profession known to attract criminal masterminds. The presence of closed circuit television equipment in the Underground and railway stations, and in many London streets, would certainly impede the career of the twenty-first-century Monster. He would have to become even more adept at disguise than the Monster of 1790, and to carry not only a cloak ready to be discarded, but also several jackets and baseball caps in different colours, and a false beard and moustache. Another more formidable threat is that his victims would be unlikely to just scream and swoon like the sensitive females of 1790; the growing knowledge of oriental martial arts among the female sex could provide the Monster with some unpleasant surprises, as could the presence of teargas and pepper spray in their handbags.

Once the attacks got underway, it would not take a lot of media hype to build up the figure of an insane, bloodthirsty attacker prowling the streets of London, attacking unaccompanied women, and specialising in seeking out his victims late at night on the Underground. As clearly demonstrated by the Halifax Slasher hysteria in 1938, a serial attacker of this kind has a particular fascination. The popular newspapers have advanced very little since 1790 with regard to their credulity and sensationalism, and would seize upon a sensational scare in which an elusive maniac slashes women in the Underground with gusto. The articles in these dismal tabloids would probably be much less amusing than the 1790 newspaper debate concerning the Monster's existence; the ribald eighteenth-century caricatures would probably be replaced with a pair of exposed buttocks, decorated with a tastefully inserted artificial nosegay, on Page Three. If the attacks persisted, there would be increasing fear and criticism of the police, and perhaps vigilante action with volunteers patrolling the Underground and arresting innocent people. If there were no attacks for some time, the previous outrages would be blamed on a 'phantom' and the whole thing considered a hoax or a mass hysteria. It would thus not, even today, be difficult to make a sad, pathetic little man with an unfortunate sexual perversion into a formidable Monster with a syringe and needle, perhaps containing HIV-contaminated blood, hidden in his artificial nosegay. Perhaps he is waiting for you?

NOTES

Dates of newspapers are 1790 unless otherwise stated. The reference is first to the newspaper's name, then the date, then the page and the column. 'The Times 2 May 3b' thus refers to the second column on the third page of The Times of 2 May 1790.

Newspaper clippings from Miss Banks' Monster scrapbook are referred to by newspaper name and the page number on which they are pasted, except in the case of those newspaper clippings pasted directly onto folio 53. Other material from this scrapbook is referred to by folio number.

Four recurring key titles: John Julius Angerstein, *An Authentic Account of the Barbarities lately practised by the Monsters* (London 1790); E. Hodgson, *The Trial at Large of Rhynwick Williams* (London, 1790); Theophilus Swift, *The Monster at Large; or, the Innocence of Rhynwick Williams Vindicated* (London 1790); and Rhynwick Williams, *An Appeal to the Public by Rhynwick Williams, Containing Observations and Reflections on Facts relative to his very Extraordinary and Melancholy Case* (London 1792) are referred to by short title only after they are first mentioned in a footnote. The notes of Judge William Mainwaring, in the Public Record Office, are also referred to by short title.

CHAPTER I – THE COMING OF THE MONSTER
1. J.M. Bulloch, 'The Monster', *Notes & Queries* 173 (1937): pp. 44-5.
2. P.D. James and T.A. Critchley, *The Maul and the Pear Tree* (London 1987).
3. Donald Rumbelow, *The Complete Jack the Ripper* (London 1987); Martin Fido, *The Crimes, Detection and Death of Jack the Ripper* (London 1987);

Colin Wilson and Robin Odell: *Jack the Ripper* (London, 1991), Paul Begg, *Jack the Ripper: the Uncensored Facts* (London, 1988); Melvin Harris, *The True Face of Jack the Ripper* (London, 1994); Philip Sugden, *The Complete History of Jack the Ripper* (London 1994) and Paul Begg *et al.*, *The Jack the Ripper A-Z* (London, 1996) are some of the superior books on this mystery.

4. Henry Wilson and James Caulfield, *The Book of Wonderful Characters* (London 1869), pp. 265-66. See also the curious article 'An Old Story Retold: Renwick Williams, the Monster' in Charles Dickens' *All the Year Round* NS 26 (1881): pp. 324-29.

5. Andrew Knapp and William Baldwin, *The New Newgate Calendar* (London 1826), Vol. III, pp. 511-18.

6. Phantom attackers are discussed by Michael Goss in *The Halifax Slasher* (*Fortean Times* occ. paper 3; London 1987); on Sawney Bean, see Ronald Holmes, *The Legend of Sawney Bean* (London 1975); on Spring-heeled Jack, see Peter Haining, *The Legend and Strange Crimes of Spring-heeled Jack* (London 1977) and the article by Mike Dash, 'Spring Heeled Jack: To Victorian Bugabo from Suburban Ghost', *Fortean Studies* 3 (1996): pp. 7-125); on Sweeney Todd, see Peter Haining, *Sweeney Todd. The Real Story of the Demon Barber of Fleet Street* (London 1993).

7. British Library shelfmark L.R. 301.h.3-11. Sarah Sophia Banks' Monster Scrapbook was bound into Vol. h3 when the volumes were restored. Under the heading 'The Monster' are five folios, numbered 44-48, of handbills and letters, followed by mounted pages from the original scrapbook containing clippings from newspapers, numbered 1-20. There follows a mounted copy of L. Williams' pamphlet on the Monster trial, an extract from the *New Lady's Magazine* on the same subject, and finally five more folios numbered 52-57.

8. Both are bound into a volume labelled 'Account of Rynwick Williams', donated to the Library by Mr John Ashhurst III (Librarian, 1916-32).

Chapter 2 – A Melancholy Occurrence in St James's Street

1. On Charles Burney's newspaper collection, see Arundell Esdaile, *The British Museum Library* (London 1946), pp. 208-10.

2. *World*, 17 May 3b.

3. *Public Advertiser*, 15 April 3a.

4. *Public Advertiser*, 5 Feb. 3c.

5. *World*, 15 March 3a.

6. On the Gordon riots, see John Paul De Castro, *The Gordon Riots* (London 1926) and Christopher Hibbert, *King Mob* (New York 1989).

7. For general accounts of crime and punishment in the eighteenth century,

see Peter Linebaugh, *The London Hanged* (London 1991); J.M. Beattie, *Crime and the Courts of England* 1660-1800 (Oxford 1986) pp. 582-637; Donald A. Low, *Thieves' Kitchen: The Regency Underworld* (London 1982) pp. 13-62; Frank McLynn, *Crime & Punishment in Eighteenth Century England* (Oxford 1991) and David Taylor, *Crime, Policing and Punishment in England* 1750-1918 (New York 1998).

8. *The Times*, 11 Dec. 1789 4a.

9. On women as victims of crime in the late eighteenth century, see Anna Clark, *Women's Silence, Men's Violence* (London 1987), and McLynn, *Crime & Punishment*, pp. 96-115.

10. Skitch's plight is detailed in *The Times* of 14 April 1789 3d, and the hangings in *The Times* of 12 May 1789 3b.

11. This anonymous article was in the *Gentleman's Magazine* 60 (1790): 1185.

12. *British Mercury* 14 (1790): pp.336-37.

13. On eighteenth-century London debating societies in general, see Donna T. Andrew: *London Debating Societies* 1776-1799 (London 1994). The debate on whether women had souls was announced in *The Times* of 18 Nov. 1789 1b.

14. On the debates, see *The Times* 29 Oct. 1789 and 26 March 1789 3c. On eighteenth-century female 'sensibility', see G.J. Barker-Benfield, *The Culture of Sensibility* (Chicago 1992) and Claudia L. Johnson, *Equivocal Beings: Politics, Gender, and Sentimentality in the 1790s* (Chicago 1995).

15. See the article by Jennie Gray, 'Hags and heroines of the 1790s', *The Goth* 8 (1992): pp. 3-6.

16. On the role of women in late eighteenth-century London society, see Roy Porter, *English Society in the Eighteenth Century* (London 1991), pp. 22-34. On late eighteenth-century sexual mores, see Roy Porter, 'Mixed feelings: The Enlightenment and sexuality in eighteenth-century Britain' in P.G. Boucé (ed.), *Sexuality in Eighteenth-Century Britain*, (Manchester 1982), pp. 1-27, and Porter, *English Society*, pp. 260-65; also Anthony E. Sampson, 'Vulnerability and the age of female consent', in G.S. Rousseau and Roy Porter (eds), *Sexual Underworlds of the Enlightenment* (Manchester 1987), pp. 181-205.

17. McLynn, *Crime & Punishment*, p. 99. One can only speculate what the proportion would have been today.

18. *British Mercury* 14 (1790): 282.

19. For contemporary accounts of the sport of 'ratting', see an anonymous article in the *Annals of Sporting* 2 (1822): 265, and Henry Mayhew, *Mayhew's London* (ed. Peter Quennell, London n.d.), pp. 401-14. A later analysis is that by E.S. Turner, *All Heaven in a Rage* (London 1964), pp. 151-6.

20. Probably from intestinal obstruction; see *World*, 11 March 3c.

21. *World*, 9 Jan. 1790; quoted from Lyson's *Collecteana* (C 103 K.11.), f. 159, in the British Library.

22. *Public Advertiser*, 3 Feb. 4b.

23. *World*, 13 Jan. 3c.

24. On the festivities on the Queen's birthday, see the *World*, 19 January 2a-b; *Public Advertiser*, 19 January 2b.

25. About Pero's Bagnio, see F.H.W. Sheppard (ed.), *Survey of London* (London 1960), Vol. 30, pp. 459-60; Edward Walford, *Old and New London* (London 1873), Vol. 4, pp. 167-69; Edwin Beresford Chancellor, *Pleasure Haunts of London during Four Centuries* (London 1925), pp. 181-85; Bryant Lillywhite, *London Coffee-Houses* (London 1963), p. 407; and E.J. Burford, *Royal St James's* (London 1988). The first of these sources places Pero's Bagnio at No.19, the others at No.63 St James's Street. The *Survey of London* states, on what authority is not known, that there were two bagnios in St James's Street: one at No.63 and one at No.19 on the other side of the street; the latter, active in the early eighteenth century, was Pero's Bagnio. What definitely settles this question is that Anne Porter said that she had once escaped from the Monster who stalked her, through the 'stable yard' leading to the rear of the Bagnio; there was such a yard next to No.63, but not in the vicinity of No.19. Pero's Bagnio had originally been based in the northernmost of three narrow houses built on the site of No.63 in 1699, but in 1733 the Bagnio took over the middle house, and also used a substantial building behind the street houses. In 1748, a man named Will Stevens was listed as keeper, and his wife kept the Bagnio until 1757, when it was taken over by a certain Edward Wilson, who kept it until 1780; it is not unlikely that Mr Porter purchased Pero's Bagnio in that year.

26. See Ben Weinreb and Christopher Hibbert (eds.), *The London Encyclopaedia* (London 1992), pp. 742-43 and Roy Porter, *London: A Social History* (Cambridge, Mass. 1998), pp. 171-72; also E.J. Burford, *Royal St James's* (London 1988). There was only one regular brothel in St James's Street at this time, Miss Fawkland's Temple of Love, an elegant upper-class establishment that boasted that it never lacked 'fresh goods'.

27. The assault on the Misses Porter was reported by John Julius Angerstein, *An Authentic Account of the Barbarities lately practised by the Monsters* (London 1790), pp. 37-41; the *World*, 15 June 3a-b and 9 July 3b-c; the *Oracle*, 9 July (from Banks p.12); the *London Chronicle* (68 [1790]: 33-4); the *New Lady's Magazine* (5 [1790]: 372-77); and by E. Hodgson, *The Trial at Large of Rhynwick Williams* (London 1790), pp. 9-17.

28. Theophilus Swift, *The Monster at Large; or, the Innocence of Rhynwick Williams Vindicated* (London 1790), pp. 98-100; also referred to by Judge

Mainwaring in his handwritten notes (Public Record Office, HO 47/17), ff. 9-10.

29. Judge Mainwaring's notes (Public Record Office, HO 47/17), ff. 13-14 and *Diary*, 1 May, from Banks p.5.

30. The London police of the 1790s have been described by Gilbert Armitage, *The History of the Bow Street Runners* 1729-1829 (London 1932), pp. 101-43; Anthony Babington, *A House in Bow Street* (London 1969), pp. 164-209 and McLynn, *Crime & Punishment*, pp. 17-35.

31. For an account of the mid-eighteenth-century night watchmen, see Beattie, *Crime and the Courts of England*, pp. 67-72; for an acrid criticism of the watch of 1797, see Patrick Colquhoun, *A Treatise on the Police of the Metropolis* (London 1797); for a no less critical account of the Watch in 1811, see P.D. James and T.A. Critchley, *The Maul and the Pear Tree* (London 1987), pp. 18-24.

32. David Philips, '"A new engine of power and authority": The institutionalization of law-enforcement in England 1780-1830' in V.A.C. Gatrell *et al.* (eds), *Crime and the Law* (London 1980), pp. 155-89.

33. The role of the Bow Street public office has been described by Percy Fitzgerald, *Chronicles of the Bow Street Police Office* Vol. 1-2 (London 1888); Armitage, *The History of the Bow Street Runners*, pp. 101-43; Joan Lock, *Tales from Bow Street* (London 1982), pp. 43-58, and particularly Babington, *A House in Bow Street*, pp. 164-96.

34. These three assaults were described by Angerstein, pp. 34-37; see also the second edition of John Julius Angerstein's *Authentic Account of the Barbarities lately practised by the Monsters* (London 1790), which contains a supplement of additional Monster attacks, including that on Mrs. Harlow, which is detailed on p.169. Mr. Stephen Z. Nonack, Head of Reference at the Boston Athenæum Library, which owns what is probably the only extant copy of Angerstein's second edition, is thanked for sending relevant copies and information.

35. *World*, 28 April (from Banks, p.5).

CHAPTER 3 – A MONSTER ON THE PROWL

1. For the assault on Mrs Smyth, see Angerstein, pp. 9-13, and the *Diary* of 1 May 1790 (Banks p.5). Angerstein adds that, since this cruel assault was so inexplicable (he made no attempt whatsoever to rob her), Mrs Smyth's friends advised her not to report it to the Bow Street magistrates unless she heard of similar attempts made upon others. There are actually two even earlier examples of a Monster-type assault. One was very briefly described in *The Times* of 7 March 1788 3d. The other, concerning a certain Mrs Wright

who was stabbed in Bow Lane, Cheapside, by a man 'of a shabby appearance, much like a hair-dresser' in March 1788, is described in the second edition of John Julius Angerstein's *Authentic Account of the Barbarities lately practised by the Monsters* (London 1790), pp. 167-69.

2. Angerstein, pp. 17-21.

3. Angerstein, pp. 17-19; *Morning Herald*, 12 April 1790 (Banks p.1).

4. Angerstein, pp. 22-25; *Public Advertiser*, 17 June 3d-4a.

5. The Frost, Morley and Dodson assaults are described by Angerstein, pp. 25-31.

6. The Baughan case was discussed by Angerstein, pp. 31-3; in the *Lawyer's and Magistrate's Magazine* 2 (1790-91): 345-60; and by Judge Mainwaring (Public Record Office (HO 47/17)).

7. Angerstein, pp. 42-5.

8. Angerstein, pp. 41-2.

9. Angerstein, pp. 45-8; *Public Advertiser*, 1 May 4b; *Public Advertiser*, 17 June 3d-4a; *British Mercury* 13 (1790): 272.

10. Notice from unstated newspaper, Banks p.4; Angerstein, pp. 51-2.

11. See Banks p.1 for several examples of imaginative newspaper articles. Andrew Franklin may have been the poet and playwright by that name, with eleven works to his name in the British Library. His letter was published in the *Morning Herald*, 20 April (from Banks p.4), and it gives reference to earlier letters from him about the Monster business.

12. *Morning Herald*, 8 April (from Banks p. 1); *World*, 14 April 3b.

13. *Morning Chronicle*, 3 April 1790, quoted by Angerstein, pp. 72-5.

14. *World*, 20 April 3d; *Morning Herald*, 20 April (Banks p.3); *Diary*, 1 May (Banks p.5); Angerstein, pp. 82-9.

15. *The Times*, 20 April 3b; Angerstein, p.87.

16. This critical account was in the *Oracle*, 20 April (Banks p.3).

17. *British Mercury* 13 (1790): 216-17.

CHAPTER 4 – THE ANGERSTEIN REWARD

1. John Julius Angerstein's biography was told in *Public Characters* 6 (1804): 385-404; in the *Annual Biography and Obituary* 8 (1824): 275-298; by William Jerdan in Vol. 1 of the *National Portrait Gallery* (London 1835) and later by Charles Wright and Charles Ernest Fayle, *A History of Lloyds* (London 1928), pp. 114-15 *et seq.* The controversial account of his birth is by Cyril Fry, 'The Angersteins of Woodlands', in *John Julius Angerstein and Woodlands 1774-1974* (Woodlands Art Gallery, London 1974), pp. 1-9.

2. Angerstein's descriptions of the Monster victims are often very detailed indeed, and sometimes have ribald elements; those of Miss Toussaint and

the Porter sisters are to be found on pp. 35 and 38 in his pamphlet.

3. See Miss Banks' Monster scrapbook, pp. 2-3 and 6 for many press cuttings of Angerstein's advertisement, which appear to have been published in almost every newspaper. The actual Angerstein handbills are today quite rare: the only examples I know of are in Miss Banks' Monster scrapbook, ff. 44-5.

4. *Gazetteer*, 17 May 3a; *The Times*, 15 May 3a.

5. *The Times*, 21 April 3c-d.

6. Angerstein, pp. 52-3. The second attack on Mrs Harlow is described in the second edition of John Julius Angerstein's *Authentic Account of the Barbarities lately practised by the Monsters* (London 1790), pp. 169-70.

7. Angerstein, pp. 53-4.

8. Angerstein, pp. 54-6 and the *World*, 29 April 3b.

9. *The Times*, 4 May 3c.

10. Angerstein, pp. 56-8 and *Public Advertiser*, 1 May 4b.

11. *Gazetteer*, 6 May 3b.

12. The assault on Elizabeth Davis was described by Angerstein, pp. 59-61; further details were added by the *World* newspaper of 8 May 3b and 17 June 3d, the *Gazetteer* of 8 May 3c, and the *Oracle* of 11 May quoted from Banks p.6. Yet more details appear in the *Lawyer's and Magistrate's Magazine* (2 [1790-1]: 345-60).

13. *World*, 8 May 3b, and *Court Chronicle* of 15 May, quoted from Banks (p.7).

14. *Oracle*, 12 May, from Banks p.7.

15. *Gazetteer*, 10 May 2d; *World*, 10 May 3a; *The Times*, 10 May 2d. Walter Hill, alias Walter Hill Coyney, had become a Lieutenant in 1785 but resigned his commission in 1795, according to David Syrett and R.L. DiNardo (eds), *The Commissioned Sea Officers of the Royal Navy 1660-1815* (Aldershot 1994).

16. *World*, 10 May 3a.

17. *Morning Herald*, 10 May, from Banks p.6.

18. *World*, 14 May 3a.

19. Angerstein, pp. 13-16, 28-31.

20. Angerstein, pp. 61-4.

21. For these attacks, see Angerstein, pp. 58-59, 65 and Angerstein's poster of 7 May in the Banks scrapbook, f. 45.

22. *The Times*, 8 May 3a.

23. From Angerstein's poster of 7 May in the Banks scrapbook, f. 45.

24. This poster, and even the handwritten protocol of the meeting, are in the Banks scrapbook at the British Library, ff. 46-47.

CHAPTER 5 – MONSTER-MANIA

1. *Oracle*, 15 May, quoted from Banks (p.7). Anna Clark, *Women's Silence, Men's Violence* (New York 1987), pp. 110-27, mentions the Monster briefly in a discussion on whether the streets of London were safe for women in the eighteenth century, but misdates the Monster-mania by one year, placing it in 1791.

2. Lady Newdigate-Newdegate: *The Cheverels of Cheverel Manor* (London 1898), p.99.

3. Angerstein, pp. 98-9.

4. Georg Forster, *Werke Vol. 12. (Tagebücher)* (Berlin 1973), pp. 297-98. Translated by J.B.

5. *British Mercury* 13 (1790): 212.

6. The references to the Prince and the Knights are in the *British Mercury* 13 (1790): 212, 371-2.

7. M. Dorothy George, *Catalogue of Political and Personal Satires* (London 1938), Vol. 6, pp. 725-26; *The Times*, 19 May 3a.

8. M. Dorothy George, *Catalogue of Political and Personal Satires* (London 1935), Vol. 5, p.242, mentions that cork-rumps, a support which extended the dress at the back, were all the rage among fashionable females in the 1770s and 1780s.

9. *The Times*, 4 May 3b and *Gazetteer*, 4 May 1790, quoted from Banks p.6.

10. *World*, 11 May 3b.

11. *Diary*, 14 May, quoted from Banks p.7; *World*, 14 May 3b and *Gazetteer*, 14 May 3a.

12. *Oracle*, 17 May, quoted from Banks p.8.

13. *St James's Gazette*, 15-18 May 2b.

14. On Astley's popular play, see *World*, 15 May 1c; *Public Advertiser*, 12 May 3c; *St James's Gazette* 6-8 May 3a; *The Times*, 30 April 3c; *Morning Herald*, 27 April (from Banks p.4).

15. *British Mercury* 13 (1790): 320.

16. Charles Beecher Hogan (ed.), *The London Stage* (Carbondale IL 1968), Vol. 5, pp. 1252-253.

17. *World*, 5 May 2d; *British Mercury* 13 (1790): 270.

18. *World*, 14 May 3b; *The Times*, 15 May 3a and 19 May 3c.

19. *World*, 14 May 3b.

20. *The Times*, 15 May 3a.

21. *Ibid.*, 21 May 3d.

22. *St James's Gazette*, 13-15 May 4d.

23. Extract from unnamed newspaper, Banks p.5.

24. Angerstein, pp. 66-7.

25. *Ibid.*, pp. 67-9.

26. *British Mercury* 13 (1790): 240-41.

27. Angerstein, p. 106.

28. *St James's Gazette*, 13-15 May 4d.

29. Quoted from Angerstein, pp. 100-2.

30. Georg Forster, *Werke Vol.* 12. *(Tagebücher)* (Berlin 1973), pp. 297-98. Translated by J.B.

31. Angerstein, pp. 102-5.

32. *Gazetteer*, 17 May 3a.

33. See Hester Lynch Piozzi, *Thraliana: Diary of Mrs Hester Lynch Thrale, later Mrs Piozzi,* 1776-1809, Katherine C. Balderson (ed.) Vol. 2 (Oxford 1942), p.770. Like some others, Mrs Thrale was of the opinion that the Monster was a member of an unnatural society of homosexuals, who held women in abhorrence. See also the article by Darryl Jones, 'Frekes, Monsters and the Ladies: Attitudes to Female Sexuality in the 1790s', *Literature & History* 4(2) (1995), 1-24, although this author wrongly accuses the Monster of vaginal mutilation and compares his ferocious assaults with those of the Yorkshire Ripper.

34. Angerstein, p. 105-6.

35. *The Times*, 31 May 3a.

36. *British Mercury* 13 (1790): 307.

37. *Oracle*, 10 June (Banks p.8).

38. *Diary*, 31 May (Banks p.18).

39. On Lady Wallace, see the *Dictionary of National Biography*. Her supposed encounter with the Monster was detailed in *The Times* of 27 May, 2d.

40. The amusing story of 'Fat Phillis' and his perilous encounter with the two timid young gentlemen is in the *British Mercury* (13 [1790]:343-4), under the heading 'A Shocking Charge!'

41. On eighteenth-century caricatures in general, see Vols 5-8 of M. Dorothy George's *Catalogue of Political and Personal Satires* (London 1935-1947) and Mark Hallett, *The Spectacle of Difference: Graphic Satire in the Age of Hogarth* (New Haven, Conn. 1999). J.A. Sharpe, *Crime and the Law in English Satirical Prints 1600-1832* (Cambridge 1986) is a valuable source on crime and criminals in eighteenth-century satire, and mentions the Monster briefly on pp. 184-85. See also J.M. Bulloch, 'The Monster', *Notes & Queries* 173 (1937): 44-5 and Anon., 'The Monster', *Notes & Queries* 173 (1937): 106.

42. On Philip Thicknesse, see Philip Gosse, *Dr Viper* (London 1952), in particular pp. 273-76 for his quarrel with Captain Crookshanks. For some of Thicknesse's own comments, see the *World*, 15 June 2c. The poster is in Banks' scrapbook f. 48 and the caricature is f. 57.

43. M. Dorothy George, *Catalogue of Political and Personal Satires* (London 1938), Vol. 6, p.729, discusses this caricature, but is unable to identify the person pilloried. Nor does B.M. Benedict, 'Making a Monster' in *Defects* (H. Deutsch and F. Nussbaum (eds); Ann Arbor 2000), pp. 127-53, have a correct perception of the campaign against Captain Crookshanks. The same author also misinterprets Gillray's *Swearing to the Cutting Monster* as a caricature of Rhynwick Williams at Bow Street.

CHAPTER 6 – THE ARREST OF RHYNWICK WILLIAMS

1. Accounts of these dramatic events are in the *World*, 15 June 3a-b and 9 July 3b-c; *Oracle*, 9 July (Banks p.12); *London Chronicle* (68 [1790]: 33-4); E. Hodgson, *The Trial at Large of Rhynwick Williams* (London 1790), pp. 19-22.
2. L. Williams, *The Trial of Renwick Williams* (London 1790), p.8.
3. Theophilus Swift, *The Monster at Large* (London 1790), pp. 168-70.

CHAPTER 7 – RHYNWICK WILLIAMS AT BOW STREET

1. *Diary*, 15 June (Banks p.8); *Morning Herald*, 15 June (Banks p.8); *World*, 15 June 3a-b.
2. *The Times*, 15 June 3c.
3. *World*, 17 July (Banks p.16); *World*, 12 July 2d.
4. Sir John Gallini is in the *Dictionary of National Biography*, but a better account of his life and career in London is in Philip H. Highfill Jr *et al.* (eds), *Biographical Dictionary of Actors &c. in London 1660-1800* (Carbondale IL 1978), Vol. 5, pp. 444-49.
5. *World*, 17 July (Banks p.16).
6. See Highfill Jr *et al.*, *Biographical Dictionary of Actors*, Vol. 16, p.113.
7. Angerstein, p.125.
8. Public Record Office; will of Thomas Williams dated 9 June 1785, PROB 11/1131/346.
9. List of Members of the Society of Apothecaries. Guildhall Library Archives, Ms. 8206/2-3.
10. *World*, 17 July (Banks p.16).
11. Highfill Jr *et al.*, *Biographical Dictionary of Actors*, Vol. 5, pp. 447-48.
12. Rhynwick Williams, *An Appeal to the Public by Rhynwick Williams, Containing Observations and Reflections on Facts relative to his very Extraordinary and Melancholy Case* (London 1792), p.13.
13. On 4 June, the King's Birthday, according to Amabel himself, giving evidence at the Old Bailey; see Hodgson, p.30.
14. *World*, 15 June 3a-b; *General Magazine* 4 (1790): 282-3 and particularly the *British Mercury* 14 (1790): 49-50.

15. The first examination of Rhynwick Williams is described in the *World*, 15 June 3a-b and *the St James's Gazette*, 12-15 June 4d.

16. Although these alleged previous observations of the Monster were alluded to by Angerstein, pp. 38, 41 and Hodgson, pp. 10-1, 14-5, by far the most complete account is that by Judge Mainwaring in his handwritten notes (Public Record Office, HO 47/17), ff. 4-7.

17. *World*, 15 June 3a-b.

18. Swift, *Monster at Large*, p.204.

19. *World*, 15 June 3a-b.

20. Angerstein, pp. 24-5.

21. *Oracle*, 10 June (Banks p.8).

22. *World*, 15 June 3a-b; Swift, *Monster at Large*, p.212.

23. The second examination of Rhynwick Williams at Bow Street is covered by the *Morning Herald*, 17 June (Banks pp. 9-10); *World*, 17 June 3d; *Public Advertiser*, 17 June 3d-4a; *Diary*, 18 June (Banks p.10). The quotations are from the *World*, 18 June 3c and the *Morning Herald*, 17 June (Banks pp. 9-10).

24. *The General Magazine* 4 (1790): 282-3; *Public Advertiser*, 17 June 3d-4a.

25. For these conflicting views see Williams, *Appeal to the Public*, p.41, and *World*, 18 June 3c.

26. *The General Magazine* 4 (1790): 282-3.

27. Williams, *Appeal to the Public*, pp. 40-1; Swift, *Monster at Large*, pp. 154-5, 203.

28. *Morning Herald*, 17 June (Banks pp. 9-10); *World*, 17 June 3d.

29. *Public Advertiser*, 17 June 3d-4a and *Morning Herald*, 17 June (Banks pp. 9-10).

30. Extract from an unnamed newspaper, Banks f. 54.

31. The third and final examination of Rhynwick Williams at Bow Street was covered by the *World*, 19 June 3c and the *Diary*, 21 June (Banks p.12).

32. *The General Magazine* 4 (1790): 282-3; *World*, 19 June 3c. The identity of this unwise and imprudent Joshua Williams remains obscure; it is unlikely that he was Rhynwick's brother. There was a tea broker in London by that name.

33. For a discussion of the difference between a felony and a misdemeanour in the eighteenth century see McLynn, *Crime & Punishment*, pp. x-xi.

34. *World*, 8 July 3d.

35. *Gazetteer*, 19 June 3b; *The Times*, 6 July 2c; *World*, 3 July 3c; *Diary*, 23 June (Banks p.12).

36. See *British Mercury* 14 (1790): 105-6, *Morning Herald*, 19 June (Banks p.11), *The Times*, 17 June 3a and *World*, 22 June 3c.

37. Quoted from Angerstein, pp. 127-29.

CHAPTER 8 – THE FIRST TRIAL

1. The trial of Rhynwick Williams was headline news all over Britain. It was reported in many newspapers, among them the *World*, 9 July 3b-c; *The Times*, 9 July 3a-c; *London Chronicle*, 68 (1790): 33-4; *Oracle*, 9 July (Banks pp. 12-14). It was also reported in the magazines, among them the *New Lady's Magazine* 5 (1790): 372-7; the *Lady's Magazine* 21 (1790): 369-73; the *Annual Register* 32 (1790): 264-7 and the *Gentleman's Magazine* 60(2) (1790): 660-2. It even penetrated to the European continent, most particularly in the *Annalen der Brittischen Geschichte* 5 (1791): 175-83.

2. See Swift, *Monster at Large*, pp. 128-29.

3. *World*, 3 July 3c; *Diary*, 27 July (Banks pp. 16-7).

4. On Judge Buller, see the *Dictionary of National Biography* and in particular William Charles Townsend, *Lives of Twelve Eminent Judges* (London 1846), Vol. 1, pp. 1-32.

5. Williams, *Appeal to the Public*, pp. 36-7. Neither Hodgson nor any of the other transcripts of the trial mention any witnesses of this description.

6. Swift, *Monster at Large*, pp. 192-94.

7. Hodgson, p. 6.

8. See the *London Chronicle* 68 (1790): 33-4; *Oracle*, 9 July (Banks pp. 12-4); *New Lady's Magazine* 5 (1790): 372-7.

9. Hodgson, pp. 9-12.

10. Williams, *Appeal to the Public*, pp. 16-7.

11. Coleman's evidence is in Hodgson, pp. 19-22.

12. Hodgson, pp. 22-3. Contemporary maps show that No. 52 Jermyn Street was really at the corner of Duke Street and Jermyn Street.

13. L. Williams, *The Trial of Renwick Williams* (London 1790), p. 10. Rhynwick's speech is in Hodgson, pp. 25-6.

14. Mitchell's evidence is in Hodgson, pp. 26-32.

15. The questions and answers are from Hodgson, pp. 31-2; the explanation from Swift, *Monster at Large*, pp. 192-94.

16. Her evidence is in Hodgson, pp. 32-5.

17. She was quite a famous Irish actress, active in London at this time; see Anon., *The Life of Mrs Abington* (London 1888).

18. The evidence of the Alman sisters, Frances Beaufils and Typhone Fournier is in Hodgson, pp. 35-47.

19. Hodgson, pp. 48-9.

20. Williams, *Appeal to the Public*, pp. 19-21.

21. L. Williams, *The Trial of Renwick Williams* (London 1790), p. 15; Nathaniel Jenkins, *A Full Account of the Trial of Renwick Williams* (London 1790), pp. 26-7.

22. *Oracle*, 9 July (Banks pp. 12-14).

23. Judge Buller's summing-up is in Hodgson, pp. 49-55.

24. *World*, 9 July (Banks p.15); this advertisement did not mention the trial of Rhynwick Williams. The evidence in favour of Angerstein as the author of the *Authentic Account* is that the book was advertised under his name in the newspapers, that it was clearly written as a handbook for Monster-hunters, and that it contains information available only to Angerstein or a member of his close circle. It would have been a logical thing to do for Angerstein to compile such a book; nor would it have been illogical for him to publish it anonymously, as he was already being ridiculed by some for his obsessive anti-Monster activities. It may be objected that Angerstein is not otherwise recorded as writing as much as a pamphlet, and that he was busy with an issue of annuities in 1789 and 1790; the advertisement of the book under his name might have been to give it some spurious authenticity. There is no evidence of Angerstein disclaiming authorship, however, and many libraries catalogue the book under his name.

25. An example of these posters is in Banks scrapbook, f. 52; the scrapbook also contains several advertisements for this pamphlet, one of them marked *World*, 13 July, on p.16.

26. See the NUC catalogue under R. Williams; it also lists a US edition of Hodgson's pamphlet published in 1791, held by the Library of the Historical Society for Pennsylvania.

27. Angerstein, pp. 159-60 and *The Rambler's Magazine* 8 (1790): 285-6.

CHAPTER 9 – THE MONSTER'S CHAMPION

1. John Nichols, *Literary Anecdotes* (London 1812), Vol. 3, p.181. The basic facts of the life of Theophilus Swift are in the *Dictionary of National Biography*.

2. Theophilus Swift, *The Female Parliament* (London 1789).

3. Theophilus Swift, *A Letter to the King; In which the Conduct of Mr Lenox, and the Minister, in the Affair with his Royal Highness the Duke of York is fully considered* (London 1789).

4. *Annual Register* 31 (1789): 215-6.

5. Theophilus Swift, *A Letter to Sir William Augustus Brown, Bart., on a Late Affair of Honor with Mr Lennox* (London 1789). See also Theophilus Swift, *Prison Pindarics* (Dublin 1795), p.22.

6. *The Times*, 7 July 1789 2c, 14 July 1789 1c, 3 August 1789 3a.

7. Anon., 'The late Edmund Lenthall Swifte, Esq.' *Notes and Queries* 5s. 5 (1876): 60.

8. Swift, *Prison Pindarics*, p.9. But Theophilus himself asserts, in his *Monster at Large* p.194, that he did not know Rhynwick or any member of his family, at the time of his arrest as the Monster! He was such a liar that one does not

know which version to believe.

9. Swift, *Prison Pindarics*, p.7.

10. Swift, *Monster at Large*, p.212.

11. *Ibid.*, pp. 81-3. It is quite true that No.62 St James's Street, on one side of the Bagnio, had (and still has) a large bow window. On the other side of the Bagnio was a stable yard, however, and no contemporary map or illustration shows a house with a bow window even on the other side of this yard.

12. *Ibid.*, pp. 95-7.

13. *Ibid.*, pp. 37-9.

14. The pursuit of Rhynwick Williams is detailed in *ibid.*, pp. 119-32.

15. *Ibid.*, pp. 112-14.

16. *Ibid.*, pp. 128-29.

17. *Ibid.*, pp. 65-6, 103-5.

18. *Ibid.*, pp. 49-50.

19. These pleasant jokes are in *ibid.*, p.150 and p.66. The truth would appear to be that there were two entrances to Pero's Bagnio, one descending and the other with two or three steps up to the main front door.

20. *Ibid.*, p.156.

21. *Ibid.*, p.184.

22. *Ibid.*, pp. 43-4.

23. *New Lady's Magazine* 5 (1790): 438.

24. *The Times*, 12 July 1b.

25. *Diary*, 27 July; *Oracle*, 9 August; *Morning Herald*, 12 November; *Diary*, 13 November, all from Banks, pp. 17-8; also *World*, 17 October 3d.

26. On the Monster's Ball, see R. Thuston Hopkins, *Life and Death at the Old Bailey* (London 1935), pp. 82-3, and a contemporary account in the *Oracle* of 20 August, quoted from Banks, p.18.

27. *British Mercury* 14 (1790): 398-9.

28. *The Times*, 23 August 2b.

29. These two quotations are from Swift, *Monster at Large*, p.200 and p.89.

30. The meeting of the judges is described in the *Oracle*, 12 November; *Morning Herald*, 12 November; *Court Chronicle*, 20 November; Banks pp. 18-9.

31. The proceedings at the Old Bailey were described, and Rhynwick's pathetic speech quoted, in the *Diary* of 9 December, from Banks pp. 19-20.

32. *Argus*, 9 December 3c.

CHAPTER 10 – THE SECOND TRIAL

1. The first day of the second trial of Rhynwick Williams was extensively covered by the *Lawyer's and Magistrate's Magazine* (2 [1790-1]: 345-60), by a large extract from an unnamed newspaper in the Banks scrapbook f. 53; and

by a report by E. Hodgson in Reel 18 of the *Old Bailey Proceedings*, Part 1, 1714-93, and by the notes of Judge Mainwaring, PRO (HO 47/17).

2. Anthony Babington, *A House in Bow Street* (London 1969), pp. 170-71.

3. *Lawyer's and Magistrate's Magazine* 2 (1790-1): 345-60.

4. *Lawyer's and Magistrate's Magazine* 2 (1790-1): 345-60; Banks f. 53.

5. Williams, *Appeal to the Public*, p.21.

6. Mainwaring, ff. 3-4.

7. Banks f. 53; Mainwaring, f. 10.

8. Banks f. 53 and Williams, *Appeal to the Public*, pp. 20-2, graphically describes these dramatic moments.

9. E. Hodgson in Reel 18 of the *Old Bailey Proceedings*, Part 1, 1714-93, p.98 and Banks f. 53.

10. Mainwaring ff. 10, 17.

11. Banks f. 53; Mainwaring ff. 17-8, E. Hodgson in Reel 18 of the *Old Bailey Proceedings*, Part 1, 1714-93, p.99.

12. Mainwaring, f. 23.

13. *Lawyer's and Magistrate's Magazine* 2 (1790-1): 345-60 and E. Hodgson in Reel 18 of the *Old Bailey Proceedings*, Part 1, 1714-93, pp. 99-100.

14. Williams, *Appeal to the Public*, p.31.

15. Lady Wallace's part in the trial was described in *The Times* of 22 December 3b.

16. The evidence of the artificial flower-makers is in Mainwaring ff. 26-7, with a few additions in Banks f. 53.

17. *Lawyer's and Magistrate's Magazine* 2 (1790-1): 345-60.

18. The second day of the trial was covered by the *Lawyer's and Magistrate's Magazine* 2 (1790-1): 345-60 by Miss Banks' scrapbook f. 53, by the notes of Judge Mainwaring, PRO (HO 47/17), and by E. Hodgson in Reel 18 of the *Old Bailey Proceedings*, Part 1, 1714-93, pp. 104-108.

19. See, for example, the *World*, 14 December 3d; *Public Advertiser*, 16 December 4c; *Argus*, 15 December 3d

20. Banks, f. 53.

21. *Argus*, 14 December 4d.

22. *Ibid.*, 15 December 3d.

23. *Ibid.*, 21 December 3c.

24. *World*, 17 December 3d.

25. See Beattie, *Crime and the Courts of England*, pp. 582-93 and McLynn, *Crime & Punishment*, pp. 294-98.

26. *British Mercury* 15 [1790]: 400.

CHAPTER 11 – WHAT HAPPENED TO RHYNWICK WILLIAMS?

1. See Arthur Griffiths, *Chronicles of Newgate* (London 1987), pp. 186-87 and

elsewhere for instances of various notorious prisoners being put on show by the warders; for example, the turnkeys earned no less than £200 by exhibiting Jack Sheppard.

2. Williams, *Appeal to the Public*, p.29.

3. Paget Toynbee (ed.), *The Letters of Horace Walpole* (Oxford 1905), Vol. 14, p.381.

4. Richard D. Altick, *The Shows of London* (Cambridge, Mass. 1978), p.53.

5. See M. Dorothy George, *Catalogue of Political and Personal Satires* (London 1947), Vol. 8, pp. 116-17. Cope committed suicide in 1806 by jumping from a precipice in Brighton, according to the *Annual Register* (48 [1806], 451-2).

6. Anon., *Monthly Review* N.S. 4 (1791): 81-2.

7. See *World*, 22 June 3c. According to the *British Mercury* 14 (1790): 281, even the felons in Newgate shunned the Monster's company.

8. Williams, *Appeal to the Public*, pp. 16,17,28 *et seq.*

9. From an unknown newspaper, quoted by Anon., 'Mr John Coleman', *Notes and Queries* 2s. 8 (1859): 229.

10. This prison calendar (HO 26/56), and those for 1793-96 (HO 26/3-5), are held at the Public Record Office.

11. See Robert Watson, *The Life of Lord George Gordon* (London 1795), pp. 107-9 and Christopher Hibbert, *King Mob* (New York 1989), pp. 167-172.

12. W.J. Sheenan, 'Finding solace in 18th century Newgate', in *Crime in England*, (J.S. Cockburn (ed.) London 1977), pp. 229-45.

13. This letter (and its envelope) is kept at the Public Record Office (HO 47/17)

14. This report, as well as the letters of Rhynwick Williams, are held at the Public Record Office (HO 47/17).

15. Theophilus Swift, *Animadversions on the Fellows of Trinity College* (Dublin, 1794), p.10 *et seq.*

16. Theophilus Swift, *Prison Pindarics; or a New Year's Gift from Newgate* (Dublin 1795), pp. 9, 18.

17. See the *Oracle* of 16 December 1796 3d.

18. Both the marriage and the christening are verified in the International Genealogical Index (on CD-ROM).

19. Henry Wilson, *Wonderful Characters* (Vol. III, London 1822), pp. 42-52.

20. See the Quarterage Book of the Society of Apothecaries, Vol. 4-5. Guildhall Library Archives, Ms. 8208/4-5. His will is at the Public Record Office, (Thomas Williams, July 1829, PROB 11/1759/460).

21. *Westminster Poll Book of* 1818. Reprinted (Exeter 1996), p.131.

22. G. Wolfe and N. Garman, *A Walking Tour of the Shambles* (Chicago 2001).

23. *Annual Biography and Obituary* 8 (1824): 275-98.

24. Sir Jonah Barrington, *Personal Sketches of his Own Time* (New York 1854), chapter 22.

25. John Barrett, manuscript annotations to Theophilus Swift, *The Touch-Stone of Truth* (Dublin 1811) in the British Library.

26. Theophilus Swift, *The Touch-Stone of Truth* (Dublin 1811). Miss Emma Dobbin married her father's curate, Thomas Philip Le Fanu, and became the mother of J. Sheridan Le Fanu, the celebrated novelist. The Le Fanu family have of course had little good to say about Theophilus Swift. See W.J. McCormack, *Sheridan Le Fanu and Victorian Ireland* (Dublin 1991), p.4.

27. John Nichols, *Illustrations of the Literary History of the Eighteenth Century* (London 1828), Vol. 5, pp. 374-97. On Theophilus Swift's eccentric actions as his great ancestor's literary executor, see the article by George Mayhew, 'Swift's "On the Day of Judgment" and Theophilus Swift', *Philological Quarterly* 54 (1975): 213-21.

28. Anon., 'Theophilus Swift', *Notes and Queries* 5s. 5 (1876): 60, 153, and also the articles by E. Solly, 'Theophilus Swift', *Notes and Queries* 5s. 5 (1876): 434-5 and W.F. Prideaux, 'Miss Trefusis', *Notes and Queries* 9s. 6 (1900): 281-3.

CHAPTER 12 – PHANTOM ATTACKERS

1. Whipping Tom is described by Magnus Hirchfeld, *Sexual Anomalies and Perversions* (London 1939), pp. 393-94. Several contemporary pamphlets and poems celebrated his bizarre exploits; some of them are still kept at the British Library.

2. M. Froment, *La police dévoilée depuis la revolution* (Vol. 1, Paris 1829), pp. 236-40; Francis Wharton, *A Treatise on Mental Unsoundness* (Philadelphia 1873), §573, and Dr Cormier, 'Le "Piqueur" de Londres', *Aesculape* 37 (1955): 20-3.

3. Wilhelm Ludwig Demme, *Das Buch der Verbrechen* (Leipzig 1852), NF 1, pp. 281-329; Richard von Krafft-Ebing, *Psychopathia Sexualis* (London 1906), pp. 109-10; Hirchfeld, *Sexual Anomalies and Perversions*, pp. 392-93.

4. Wilhelm Ludwig Demme, *Das Buch der Verbrechen* (Leipzig 1851) Vol. 2, pp. 341-54; Krafft-Ebing, *Psychopathia Sexualis*, pp. 108-9; Hirchfeld, *Sexual Anomalies and Perversions*, p.392.

5. Francis Wharton, *A Treatise on Mental Unsoundness* (Philadelphia 1873), §621.

6. D. Travers, 'Mädchenstecher', *Archiv für Kriminal-Anthropologie und Kriminalistik* 15 [1904]: 396-7 and J. Bondeson in *Ripperologist* 37 (2001): 16.

7. Andrew Knapp and William Baldwin, *The New Newgate Calendar* (London 1826), Vol. 3, pp. 511–18.

8. *The Times*, 28 August 1834 4d.

9. *Ibid.*, 13 March 1885 8d.

10. Paul Begg *et al*, *The Jack the Ripper A-Z* (London 1996), pp. 85, 96-7.

11. Paul Garnier, 'Le Sadi-fétichisme', *Annales d'Hygiène Publique et de Médecine Légale* Ser. 3 43 (1900): 97-121.

12. On these three cases, see Dr Doerr, 'Mädchenstecher', *Archiv für Kriminal-Anthropologie und Kriminalistik* 15 (1904): 280-1, Dr Paffrath, 'Ein sogenannter Mädchenstecher (Piqueur) und die Begutachtung seines Geisteszustandes vor Gericht', *Aerzliche Sachverständigen-Zeitung* 9 (1903): 301-8 and D. Travers, 'Mädchenstecher', *Archiv für Kriminal-Anthropologie und Kriminalistik* 15 (1904): 396-7. Erich Wulffen, *Encyclopädie der modernen Kriminalistik VIII: Der Sexualverbrecher* (Berlin 1910), pp. 334-36, also briefly discusses cases from Metz (23 victims), Berlin and Copenhagen.

13. Charles Fort, *Complete Books* (New York 1974), pp. 896-97; Paul Sieveking (ed.), *Man Bites Man* (London 1980), p.23; Michael Goss, *The Halifax Slasher* (*Fortean Times* occ. Paper 3, London 1987), pp. 42-3.

14. Sidney I. Schwab, 'A critical analysis of the expert testimony in the "Jack the Stabber" case', *Interstate Medical Journal* 13 (1906): 927-938 and D.S. Booth, *Medical Fortnightly* 31 (1907): 75-9.

15. Goss, *The Halifax Slasher*, p.43.

16. Goss, *The Halifax Slasher*, pp. 6-7, and Anon., 'Compulsions', *Fortean Times* 28 (1979): 12.

17. Goss, *The Halifax Slasher*, is the great authority on this business. He later added some further material in his article 'The Halifax Slasher and other "Urban Maniac" tales' in Gillian Bennett and Paul Smith (eds), *A Nest of Vipers. Perspectives on Contemporary Legend V.* (Sheffield 1990), pp. 89-111.

18. Goss, *The Halifax Slasher*, p.36; Anon., *Fortean Times* 28 (1979): 12.

19. These three cases are reported by Bob Rickard, 'Compulsions', *Fortean Times* 39 (1983): 19-21, and Anon., 'A festival of fetishism', *Fortean Times* 46 (1986): 12-4.

20. Léon Henri Thoinot, *Attentats aux mœurs et perversions du sens génital* (Paris 1898), pp. 449-54 and Paul Garnier, 'Le Sadi-fétichisme', *Annales d'Hygiène Publique et de Médecine Légale* Ser. 3 43 (1900): 97-121.

21. On hair despoilers, see an anonymous case report in the *Revue de l'Hypnotisme et de la Psychologie Physiologique* (4 [1889-90]: 247-50); Krafft-Ebing, *Psychopathia Sexualis*, pp. 241-45, and Wulffen, *Encyclopädie VIII: Der Sexualverbrecher*, pp. 535-42. The Hamburg case is reported by Hirchfeld, *Sexual Anomalies and Perversions*, pp. 543-49. The original documents concerning a persistent London hair despoiler are kept in the Public Record Office (MEPO 3/347).

22. Paul Garnier, 'Le Sadi-fétichisme', *Annales d'Hygiène Publique et de Médecine Légale* Ser. 3 43 (1900): 97-121, 210-47. Garnier's work on sadism is

discussed by Vernon A. Rosario, *The Erotic Imagination: French Histories of Perversity* (Oxford 1997), pp. 145-51, but without any new insights about the serial stabbers.

23. Krafft-Ebing, *Psychopathia Sexualis*, pp. 105-11 and Wulffen, *Encyclopädie VIII: Der Sexualverbrecher*, pp. 334-36.

24. *The Rambler's Magazine* 8 (1790): 285-86.

25. See M.J. MacCulloch *et al.*, 'Sadistic fantasy, sadistic behaviour and offending', *British Journal of Psychiatry* 143 (1983): 20-9; P.E. Dietz *et al.*, 'The sexually sadistic criminal and his offenses', *Bulletin of the American Academy of Psychiatry and the Law* 18 (1990): 163-78; T. Gratzer and J.M.W. Bradford, 'Offender and offense characteristics of sexual sadists', *Journal of Forensic Sciences* 40, 450-5, 1995; A. Rose, 'Verhaltenstherapie bei Frotteurismus – ein Fallbericht', *Verhaltenstherapie* 5 (1995): 154-60.

CHAPTER 13. THE MONSTER, EPIDEMIC HYSTERIA AND MORAL PANICS

1. François Sirois, 'Epidemic Hysteria', *Acta Psychiatrica Scandinavica* Suppl. 252, 1974.

2. See the papers by Sidney M. Stahl and Morty Lebedun, 'Mystery gas: an analysis of mass hysteria', *Journal of Health and Social Behavior* 15 (1974): 44-50; Simon Wessely, 'Mass hysteria: two syndromes?', *Psychological Medicine* 17 (1987): 109-20 and Robert E. Bartholomew, 'Ethnocentricity and the social construction of mass hysteria', *Culture, Medicine and Psychiatry* 14 (1990): 455-94; and 'Tarantism, dancing mania and demonopathy: the anthropological aspects of "mass psychogenic illness"', *Psychological Medicine* 24 (1994): 281-306. The book *Mass Psychogenic Illness: A Social Psychological Analysis* (Michael J. Colligan *et al.* (eds), Hillsdale NJ 1982) gives an extensive overview of the field; the chapter by Alan C. Kerckhoff about 'A social psychological view of mass psychogenic illness' on pp. 199-236 was particularly pertinent to this study. The review by Leslie P. Boss, 'Epidemic hysteria: a review of the published literature', *Epidemiologic Reviews* 19 (1997): 233-43, added 70 further outbreaks of epidemic hysteria between 1973 and 1993. There were two major demographic changes, more males were involved in the modern material, and more people were affected in each episode. Interestingly, there has lately been attempts to redefine epidemic hysteria to encompass much more extensive epidemics of poly-symptomatic reactions presumed to be caused by external factors. An example is the 'epidemic' of oral galvanism that raged in Scandinavia in the 1970s and '80s: thousands of people complained of various diffuse symptoms, which they were firmly convinced were caused by the amalgam fillings in their teeth. The same model of explanation has been applied to

other outbreaks of diffuse symptoms thought to be caused by the external environment, like the arsenic poisoning scare in Sweden and Germany in the 1910s and '20s, theories of low grade carbon monoxide poisoning in the 1940s, and the current spread of an unexplained disorder that has been blamed on computer screens and allergy against electricity. See the paper by C.J. Göthe *et al.*, 'The environmental somatization syndrome', *Psychosomatics* 36 (1995): 1-11. A similar mode of explanation has recently been applied to the recent 'epidemics' of chronic fatigue syndrome and Gulf War Syndrome, but with less impressive evidence; see Elaine Schowalter, *Hystories: Hysterical Epidemics and Modern Culture* (London 1998), pp. 144-58.

3. Robert Bartholomew and Simon Wessely, 'Epidemic hysteria in Virginia', *Southern Medical Journal* 92 (1999): 762-69.

4. Donald M. Johnson, 'The "Phantom Anesthetist" of Mattoon: a field study of mass hysteria', *Journal of Abnormal Social Psychology* 40 (1945): 175-86.

5. See the papers by David L. Miller *et al.*, 'A critical examination of the social contagion image of collective behavior', *Sociological Quarterly* 19 (1978): 129-40; Robert E. Bartholomew, 'Redefining epidemic hysteria: an example from Sweden', *Acta Psychiatrica Scandinavica* 88 (1993): 178-82 and 'Collective delusions: a skeptic's guide', *Skeptical Inquirer* 21(3) (1997): 29-33.

6. Elaine Schowalter, *Hystories: Hysterical Epidemics and Modern Culture* (London 1998), pp. 171-201.

7. Robert Bartholomew and Simon Wessely, 'Epidemic hysteria in Virginia', *Southern Medical Journal* 92 (1999): 762-9, giving reference to W.H. Burnham, *The Normal Mind* (New York 1925), pp. 337-38.

8. Norman Jacobs, 'The phantom slasher of Taipei: mass hysteria in a non-Western society', *Social Problems* 12 (1965): 318-28.

9. A survey of reports of non-Monster stabbings of women in *The Times* newspaper in 1785-1789 turns up eight instances. A man cut his wife (11 August 1786 3d); a journeyman comb-maker cut his wife's throat (24 November 1787 3d); a hairdresser cut a prostitute's arm after a quarrel at an ale-house (28 November 1788 2d); an old woman was stabbed with a bayonet after being mistaken for a thief (29 April 1789 2d); a man stabbed his wife to death (13 July 1789 3b); a ship-builder stabbed his wife and then himself (25 November 1789 3c) and a butcher cut a woman's throat and married her after she had recovered (27 November 1789 2d). The only odd one out is the 'Uncommon and melancholy circumstance' reported on 12 October 1789 (3d). A young servant-girl was familiarly addressed by a young man on the steps of Old Boswell Court. She replied that, 'she was not the person he wanted', i.e. that she was not a prostitute. The man then

laid hold of her and stabbed her in the body. The woman was carried off to hospital 'without hope of recovery' and the man was arrested.

10. Stanley Cohen, *Folk Devils and Moral Panics: The Creation of the Mods and Rockers* (London 1972). A modern overview is given by Erich Goode and Nachman Ben-Yehuda, *Moral Panics. The Social Construction of Deviance* (Oxford 1994).

11. See the articles by Daniel Statt, 'The case of the Mohocks: rake violence in Augustan London', *Victorian Studies* 20 (1995): 179-99, and Neil Guthrie, '"No truth or very little in the whole story?" – a reassessment of the Mohock scare of 1712', *Eighteenth-Century Life* NS 20(2) (1996): 33-56.

12. On the London garrotting panics, see Rob Sindall, *Street Violence in the Nineteenth Century* (Leicester 1990), and the articles by Jennifer Davis, 'The London garrotting panic of 1862' in *Crime and the Law* (V.A.C. Gatrell *et al.* (eds); London 1980), pp. 190-213, and Rob Sindall, 'The London garrotting panics of 1856 and 1862', *Social History* 12 (1987): 351-8. Boston had a garrotting scare in 1865, which was described by Jeffrey S. Adler, 'The making of a moral panic in 19th century America: the Boston garroting hysteria of 1865', *Deviant Behavior* 17 (1996): 259-78.

13. Peter Turnbull, *The Killer who Never Was* (Hull 1996), p.252, and Paul Begg *et al.*, *The Jack the Ripper A-Z* (London 1996), pp. 464-65.

14. A number of letters denouncing various people as the Ripper have been reproduced by Stephen Knight: *Jack the Ripper: The Final Solution* (London 1977), pp. 225-35. On confessions, see Turnbull, *The Killer who Never Was*, pp. 244, 256.

15. Turnbull, *The Killer who Never Was*, pp. 249-50.

16. Alan Moore and Eddie Campbell: *From Hell* (London 2000), appendix p.41.

17. Begg *et al.*, *The Jack the Ripper A-Z*, pp. 309-11.

18. *Ibid.*, p.131.

19. See the articles by Jas. G. Kiernan, 'Sexual perversion, and the Whitechapel murders', *Medical Standard* 4 (1888): 129-30, 170-2, and E.C. Spitzka, 'The Whitechapel murders: their medico-legal and historical aspects', *Journal of Nervous and Mental Disease* 13 (1888): 765-78; also Stewart Evans and Paul Ganey: *The Lodger* (London 1995), pp. 180-81 and Martin Fido, *The Crimes, Detection and Death of Jack the Ripper* (London 1987), pp. 177-84.

20. For examples of serious Ripper books, see the works of Donald Rumbelow, *The Complete Jack the Ripper* (London 1987); Martin Fido, *The Crimes, Detection and Death of Jack the Ripper* (London 1987); Colin Wilson and Robin Odell: *Jack the Ripper* (London 1991); Paul Begg, *Jack the Ripper: the Uncensored Facts* (London 1988); Melvin Harris, *The True Face of Jack the*

Ripper (London 1994) and Philip Sugden, *The Complete History of Jack the Ripper* (London 1994) On forensic projects, see the articles by William G. Eckert, 'The Whitechapel murders', *American Journal of Forensic Medicine and Pathology* 2 (1981): 53-60, and 'The Ripper project: modern science solving mysteries of history', *American Journal of Forensic Medicine and Pathology* 10 (1989): 164-71.

21. A.P. Wolf, *Jack the Myth: A New Look at the Ripper* (London 1993), pp. 33-46, Begg *et al.*; *The Jack the Ripper A-Z*, pp. 35-6, 192, 222-3, and Bruce Paley, *Jack the Ripper: The Simple Truth* (London 1996).

22. An analysis of these descriptions can be found in Sugden, *The Complete History of Jack the Ripper*, pp. 95-6, 113-7, 200-8, 220-4, 333-8, and in Begg *et al.*, *The Jack the Ripper A-Z*, pp. 195-96.

23. William G. Eckert, 'The Ripper project: modern science solving mysteries of history', *American Journal of Forensic Medicine and Pathology* 10 (1989): 164-71, and Sugden, *The Complete History of Jack the Ripper*, pp. 366-67.

24. Turnbull, *The Killer who Never Was*.

25. Walter Dew, *I Caught Crippen: Memoirs* (London 1938), p.156.

26. Original accounts of the Monkey-Man scare are in the online *Hindustan Times* of 17, 18 and 21 May and 21 June 2001. Further commentary is in the *Fortean Times* 148 (2001): 8-9 and 149 (2001): 7, and in an article by D. Chapman in *Strange Magazine* online 2001.

27. *Hindustan Times*, 1 August 2002.

CHAPTER 14 – WHO WAS THE MONSTER?

1. Anthony Babington, *A House in Bow Street* (London 1969), pp. 169-75. Mainwaring's involvement is described by David Philips, '"A new engine of power and authority": The institutionalisation of law-enforcement in England 1780-1830' in *Crime and the Law* (V.A.C. Gatrell *et al.* (eds), London 1980), pp. 155-89.

2. Angerstein's posters and advertisements (see Banks ff. 44-45 and pp. 2-3) told the Monster victims and witnesses to report what they knew directly to his house in Pall Mall, or to the Bow Street public office. On his expert testimony in the Elizabeth Davis case, see E. Hodgson in Reel 18 of the *Old Bailey Proceedings*, Part 1, 1714-93, pp. 104-108.

3. Anon., *The Trial of the Hammersmith Monsters* (London 1814).

4. On the Düsseldorf Monster, see Theodor Lessing and Karl Berg, *The Monsters of Weimar* (London 1993), pp. 161-289.

5. Angerstein, pp. 9-13, 13-5, 44-5 and 54-6, respectively.

6. Swift, *Monster at Large*, pp. 95-6.

7. *True Briton*, 22 February 1797 3d.

8. Horwood's *Plan of London, Westminster, Southwark, & Parts Adjoining,* 1792-9. London Topographical Society Publ. 109, London 1966. Duke's Court was called Grey's Yard in 1746; it still existed in 1818 according to a later edition of Horwood's map book, but was gone in 1894 according to the Ordnance Survey Map of that year.

9. Reproduced in F.H.W. Sheppard (ed.), *Survey of London* (London 1960), Vol. 29, p. 309.

10. Swift, *Monster at Large*, pp. 98-100 and Mainwaring, f. 10, 17.

11. *Ibid.*, p. 143.

12. Their marriage certificate is in the Guildhall Library Archives.

13. Williams, *Appeal to the Public*, p. x.

14. See Swift, *Monster at Large*, p. 162.

15. *The Times*, 15 June 3c.

16. Angerstein, p. 125. B.M. Benedict, 'Making a Monster' in *Defects*, (H. Deutsch and F. Nussbaum (eds); Ann Arbor 2000), pp. 127-53 is wrong to claim that Williams was charged under the Coventry Act, and also mistakenly states that his arrest was a result of him again approaching Anne Porter with his usual improper behaviour, as she was walking with Coleman in Green Park. Benedict expresses doubt concerning the guilt of Rhynwick Williams, and doubts the motives of the individuals who received parts of the Monster reward. It is going too far, however, to claim that the arrest of Williams was a direct result of his 'sociability and innocuousness', and his gentleness and conformity to the sentimental social rules of the time. His weird habit of pursuing women through the streets, and damning and blasting them if they rejected his advances, was in fact considered wholly aberrant by both men and women at the time.

17. Anna Clark, 'Whores and gossips: sexual reputations in London 1770-1825' in Arina Angerman *et al.* (eds) *Current Issues in Women's History* (London 1989), pp. 231-48.

18. Edwin Beresford Chancellor, *Pleasure Haunts of London during Four Centuries* (London 1925), pp. 181-85. For an amusing account of the notorious Haddock's Bagnio in Covent Garden, and others of that ilk, see E.J. Burford, *Wits, Wenches and Wantons* (London 1986), pp. 65-75. It should be noted that although most of the contemporary accounts from 1790 agreed that Pero's Bagnio was a respectable establishment, the Bagnio in St James's Street (probably Pero's Bagnio) had a resident prostitute in 1764 according to E.J. Burford, *Royal St James's* (London 1988), pp. 144-46, quoting Jack Harris's *List of Cyprians* for that year. There is also a popular tradition that No. 63, St James's Street had once been the site of a house of ill-repute, and that a murder had been committed there (Westminster

Library Archives, Enquiries No.6857).

19. Swift, *Monster at Large*, p.99.

20. With regard to Rhynwick Williams' other alibis, he claimed that he was at work in the flower factory when Elizabeth Davis was attacked. When the Misses Baughan were attacked, more than a year before, he had been at his lodgings, something that he claimed could be proven by two people who remembered this particular day with unerring clarity. See Williams, *Appeal to the Public*, p.10.

21. McLynn, *Crime & Punishment*, pp. x, 125.

22. *Annual Biography and Obituary* 8 (1824): 275-98.

Appendix

ALLEGED VICTIMS
of the
LONDON MONSTER

NAME	PLACE	DATE	INCIDENT
Unnamed woman		Mar. 1788	Cut
Mrs Wright	Bow Lane	Mar. 1788	Cut
Mrs Maria Smyth, wife of Dr Smyth	Johnson's Court	May 1788	Abused and cut
Mrs Chippingdale	St James's Place	May 1788	Abused and cut
Servant of Mr Collins	Jermyn Street	May 1788	Abused and beaten
Mrs Sarah Godfrey	Leicester Street	May 1789	Abused and cut
Miss Kitty Wheeler	Bennet Street	Summer 1789	Insulted
Servant-girl	New Boswell Court	Summer 1789	Cut in thigh
Miss Mary Forster	Dean Street	Sept. 1789	Abused and cut
Miss Ann Frost	Jermyn Street	9 Nov. 1789	Abused and cut
Miss Ann Morley	Whitehall	Oct. 1789	Thrice cut
Miss Eleanor Dodson	St Martin's Lane	Nov. 1789	Abused and cut

Name	Place	Date	Incident
Frances and Elizabeth Baughan	Bridge Street	7 Dec. 1789	Abused and cut
Anne Porter	St James's Street	18 Jan. 1790	Abused and cut
Sarah Porter	St James's Street	18 Jan. 1790	Knocked on the head
Miss Felton	Dover Street	18 Jan. 1790	Clothes cut
Miss Toussaint	St James's Street	18 Jan. 1790	Clothes cut
Mrs Burney	St James's Street	18 Jan. 1790	Clothes cut
Mrs Harlow	St James's Street	18 Jan. 1790	Clothes cut
Mrs Allan	Piccadilly	Late Jan. 1790	Clothes cut
Maidservant		Late Jan. 1790	Kicked and cut
Mrs Drummond	Theatre	Early Feb. 1790	Clothes cut
Mrs Charlotte Payne	Grafton Street	Mid-Mar. 1790	Kicked and cut
Mrs Blaney	Bury Street	28 Mar. 1790	Stabbed
Unnamed maidservant	Holborn	Late Mar. 1790	Clothes cut
Unnamed servant-girl	Holborn	Early Apr. 1790	Stabbed in the nose
Mrs Harlow	Pall Mall	Early Apr. 1790	Pushed and clothes cut
Servant-girl	Strand	Apr. 1790	Stabbed in the face
Mrs Susannah Thompson	Princess Street	Apr. 1790	Abused and cut
Rebecca Lohr	St Martin's Lane	19 Apr. 1790	Arms scratched
Jane Hurd	Edgware Row	26 Apr. 1790	Cut across breast
Servant-girl	Greville Street	Late Apr. 1790	Clothes cut
Mrs Green	Coventry Street	27 Apr. 1790	Knocked down

NAME	PLACE	DATE	INCIDENT
Two unnamed women	Bishopsgate Street	29 Apr. 1790	One pushed, one cut
Unnamed woman	Leadenhall Street	29 Apr. 1790	Shoulder cut
Unnamed woman	Vigo Lane	30 Apr. 1790	Abused and cut
Unnamed woman	Salisbury Square	30 Apr. 1790	Face cut
Mary Carter	Conduit Street	1 May 1790	Abused and cut
Miss Barrs	Marylebone Street	2 May 1790	Twice cut?
Servant to Mr Sullivan	Arlington Street	4 May 1790	Abused and threatened
Unnamed woman	Marybone Street	4 May 1790	Wounded
Mrs Elizabeth Davis	Holborn	5 May 1790	Cut and beaten
Jane Read	Glanville Street	5 May 1790	Threatened?
Servant to Mr Vickery	Cheapside	6 May 1790	Arm scratched
Jane Hooper	Vigo Lane	Early May 1790	Clothes cut
Miss Aride	Jermyn Street	Early May 1790	Wounded
Servant to Mr Pettit	Fleet Street	10 May 1790	Clothes cut
Unnamed lady	Bank	11 May 1790	Clothes cut
Mary Fisher	Charing Cross	Mid-May 1790	Knocked down
Mrs Smyth	King Street	15 May 1790	Face injured
Unnamed woman	Johnson's Court	Mid-May 1790	Threatened
Unnamed woman	Pall Mall	18 May 1790	Cut several times
Two women	Edgware Road	Late May 1790	Wounded
Lady Wallace	Green Park	27 May 1790	Frightened?
Unnamed woman	Westminster	10 June 1790	Threatened with nosegay

List of
ILLUSTRATIONS

6. The first poster of the St Pancras Monster patrol, from Miss Banks' Monster scrapbook in the British Library. (Reproduced by permission.)

7. *The Monster Cutting a Lady*, a print by Isaac Cruikshanks published on 1 May 1790. The face and figure of the Monster was reconstructed from the evidence of several wounded ladies, and they afterwards approved of the drawing, thinking it a good likeness. Note the diabolical spikes on his knees; this was after the ferocious assault on Mrs Payne. Also note the door marked 'Angersteein' and the Monster reward poster pasted on the wall. (Reproduced by permission of the British Museum.)

8. *The Monster disappointed of his Afternoon Luncheon, or Porridge Potts preferable to Cork Rumps*; a bawdy cartoon published at the height of the Monster-mania. (From the author's collection.)

9. *Copper Bottoms to Prevent being Cut*, another print by Isaac Cruikshanks, issued at the same time as *The Monster Cutting a Lady*. A lady wearing only a chemise and a hat is standing before the kneeling brazier, who is hammering together the back seams of a short copper petticoat. A placard on the wall reads: 'Ladies Bottoms covered on the most Reasonable Terms and kept in repair by the year by Anti:Monster'. In the shop window are three copper petticoats of increasing size, intended, in turn, for young ladies of fifteen, for ladies of thirty, and for very fat ladies. (Reproduced by permission of the British Museum.)

10. *Old Maids Dreaming of the Monster*. An anonymous satirical print that ridiculed the London Monster's propensity to attack fashionable, beautiful young women. Two old maids dream of the Monster, since if he attacks them, this will be ample proof that they are still young and attractive. The Monster suddenly appears in the guise of a grotesque, three-headed ogre, with the Devil seated on the middle head. One of the old maids hastily tries to get out of bed, but steps in the chamber-pot by mistake. (From the author's collection.)

11. *Glaucus and Scylla, or The Monster in Full Cry*, a satirical print by Isaac Cruikshanks published on 18 May 1790. The immensely fat Miss Jeffries, one of the Queen's ladies-in-waiting, is pursued by George Hanger, one of the cronies of the Prince of Wales. He is depicted with a tail and clawed, deformed legs, and aims to prick her with a long spike attached to the

end of his bludgeon. A man lying on the ground tries to pull him back by the tail, and William Pitt races up to the right, armed with a warming pan, to save her honour from this monstrous assailant. (From the author's collection.)

> *A little Dagger with a Tube, was fill'd*
> *With Juice of Plants, which such a Liquor yield*
> *That when to Womans velvet flesh apply'd*
> *It makes no Entrance if a Maid is try'd.*

18. A late eighteenth-century interior of the Old Bailey. (Reproduced courtesy of the Wellcome Institute Library, London.)

19. *Representation of the Monster*, a satirical print by W. Dent that is a good indicator of the amount of prejudice against Rhynwick Williams. This satirical print by Dent depicts Rhynwick Williams on trial (right) and prowling about in one of his disguises (left), with the grand scene of him cutting the Misses Porter in the middle. It is clearly published in the interval between the two trials, while the Twelve Judges' opinion was awaited. Its anti-Monster author boldly agitates that Rhynwick Williams should be hanged, and not transported, since the latter punishment would give him an opportunity to exercise his cruelties on the females of another country. (From the author's collection.)

20. A drawing of the Monster attacking the Misses Porter on the (non-existent?) steps of the Bagnio, with doggerel verses underneath. This was a cheap print issued just after the first trial to cash in on the great ballyhoo about the Monster. (Reproduced by permission of the British Museum.)

21. Prime Minister William Pitt is depicted as the Monster in the satirical print *Spanish Rupture: The Monster – The Guardian*. Pitt dashes his diabolical nosegay into Britannia's face with gusto, and stabs her in the hip with his rapier. The rival politician Charles James Fox stands looking on aghast, calling out that had she trusted to him for protection, he would have her on such a BOTTOM that none would have dared to insult her. Pitt had been unjustly accused of truckling to Spain over the Nootka Sound affair, and this was but one of the several caricatures lampooning him. (Reproduced by permission of the British Museum.)

22. Rhynwick Williams cutting a lady, a print issued just after the first trial. (Reproduced by permission of the Guildhall Library, Corporation of London.)

23. *Essay in Duelling*, a satirical print by Collings, issued on 10 July 1789. Colonel Lennox, brandishing a pair of murderous-looking pistols, shoots Theophilus Swift in the stomach with one of them and shoots a curl off the Duke of York's head with the other. The startled Duke exclaims 'There goes the best part of my poor head!' The Prince of Wales stands far right, armed with blunderbusses, rapiers and pistols, saying 'Never mind your head I am your *corps de reserve!*' George Hanger, in the attitude of a pugilist,

says 'Blast my eyes, I'll tip him Ward's damper in no time at all!' (Reproduced by permission of the British Museum.)

24. A letter from Rhynwick Williams, the most injured man living. (From the archives of the Public Record Office, Kew (HO 47/17). Reproduced by permission.)

25. *Le danger d'être femme ou la suite des piqûres*, a satirical print published at the height of the Piqueur craze in Paris 1819. (Reproduced courtesy of M. Jean-Loup Charmet's picture library, Paris.)

26. A map of the London Monster's hunting grounds, with Rhynwick Williams' former dwellings in Duke's Court (A), his mother's house in Jermyn Street (B), the George public house where Rhynwick Williams lived (C) and Pero's Bagnio at No.63 St James's Street (D) marked. The nearby Monster assaults have also been plotted.

27. A contemporary map of London, with all possible Monster assaults plotted.

PICTURES IN THE TEXT

Page 49. Mr Angerstein's first Monster poster, dated 29 April 1790. (Reproduced by permission of the British Library.)

Page 58. Mr Angerstein's second Monster poster, issued on 7 May 1790. (Reproduced by permission of the British Library.)

Page 91. Rhynwick Williams, as portrayed in the *New Lady's Magazine*, July 1790. This portrait bears little likeness with the more reliable portraits of Williams – see illustrations on pages 109 and 111. (Reproduced by permission of the British Library.)

Page 109. Rhynwick Williams in the dock at the Old Bailey, a drawing purported to be by James Gillray, yet 'not by Gillray' according to a note at the Department of Prints and Drawings at the British Museum. (Reproduced courtesy of the Wellcome Institute Library, London.)

Page 111. A drawing of Rhynwick Williams at the dock in the Old Bailey, by Nixon. (Reproduced by permission of the British Museum.)

Page 178. Newgate Gaol in 1790, at the time Rhynwick Williams was a prisoner there. A print by F. Bourjot. (Reproduced by permission of the Guildhall Library, Corporation of London.)

Page 202. The 'Brooklyn Monster' claims another victim. A drawing from an unknown newspaper showing a maniac cutting the lower leg of one of the several women he assaulted. (Reproduced courtesy of the Wellcome Institute Library, London.)

INDEX